A Colorni-Hirschman International Institute 5

"The Philosophical Illness"
and Other Writings

Eugenio Colorni

"The Philosophical Illness" and Other Writings

Edited by Luca Meldolesi
Translated by Michael Gilmartin

Bordighera Press

Library of Congress Control Number: 2021937643

Printed in the United States.

Published by
BORDIGHERA PRESS
John D. Calandra Italian American Institute
25 W. 43rd Street, 17th Floor
New York, NY 10036

A Colorni-Hirschman International Institute 4
ISBN 978–1–59954–187–7

Table of Contents

NOTE

Some of the text titles marked by an asterisk recur in Part One (as "Background Articles") or Part Two (as "Variety") of the "Project for a Journal of Scientific Methodology" (Ch. 8). It is likely that when Eugenio writes at the end of the paper that "the following are the drafts of some of the articles from the first and second parts" (and then in his correspondence with Ludovico Geymonat when he speaks of "summaries") he is referring primarily to extracts and/or summaries of these essays and fragments. Furthermore, it is clear from a letter of 10 September 1942 from Virginia Scarfiotti Geymonat to Colorni (written for her husband Ludovico for safety reasons) that "On the Concept of Love," "On the Oedipus Complex," "On the Idols of Physics," and "The Need for Unity," should also have been included in the "Project" (cf. Quaranta 2011, p. 128). Note, finally, that "Philosophy and Science" includes "Universal Constants and Units of Measurement" and "Concerning the Principle of Identity," so that these are not published here separately. The title of the first of these excerpts in any case shows up in Part One of the "Project."

Editor's Note

Aside from his extraordinary "curation" of Leibniz's *Monadology*, it is well known that Eugenio Colorni published only one book (and that in his youth), *The Aesthetics of Benedetto Croce: A Critical Study*. In the case of his articles and essays, those with political themes (often excellent) were published abroad or underground (including his important introduction to the *Ventotene Manifesto*). A different fate awaited his autobiographical or philosophical texts. Some of these, it appears, were finished and ready for publication — such as "The Philosophical Illness" and "Apologue on Four Ways of Philosophizing"; others, while completed (or nearly) — such as some on Leibniz and "Philosophical Criticism and Theoretical Physics" — were conceived as chapters of books under construction that never appeared; still others were incomplete or just fragments. Some of them were meant to be part of the projected "Journal of Scientific Methodology," as short articles or explanatory notes.

This collection, on the other hand, is meant to conclude the first part of a small Colornian series addressed to a literate but interdisciplinary public, edited by "A Colorni-Hirschman International Institute" and published by joint agreement both in Italian by the publisher Florindo Rubbettino and in English by Bordighera Press in New York.

With this in mind, I have proceeded as follows. I have made use of the two anthologies of philosophical and autobiographical texts edited by Norberto Bobbio (1975) and Geri Cerchiai (2009) and the "didactic" edition I published in 1998. I have excluded (not least for reasons of space) Colorni's youthful works and those on Leibniz. My preference has been to follow as nearly as possible the order in which the main texts were written,[1] and I have revived

---

[1] The most absolute respect for the chronology of the life and work of Eugenio Colorni represents, in my opinion, an elementary decision from a philological point of view, and one that is in no way irrelevant or redundant. Especially for someone who maintains, as I do, that in the case of Colorni, politics and philosophy cannot be separated by a Great Wall. The ensemble of materials we have at our disposal (correspondence, political writings, dialogues, autobiographical and theoretical writings, federalist and socialist experiences) must be considered in unison in its development if we are to understand its author's rea-

Bobbio's "Fragments" section and kept its sequence (although with two exclusions suggested by Cerchiai: Colorni 2009, p. 175, n.13). Lastly, I have integrated the writings collected here with four of Colorni's five methodology texts that Cerchiai (2016) discovered in the papers of the Somenzi Fund: "General Relativity," "On the Axiomatics of the Laws of Mechanics," "Geometry and Experience" and "Program." The fifth of these ("Commodus to Ritroso") and two other fragments ("Ritroso to Commodus" and "Fight, but Listen!" which I found in the archives of the Department of Physics of the Sapienza University of Rome) are actually related to the Ventotene dialogue "On Psychologism in Economics," and have recently been published in Colorni-Spinelli 2020 (cf. Ibid., p. 53, n. 106 and pp. 166–76).

Luca Meldolesi

---

soning in the different phases of his experience — including the decisive turning points that mark it and the various projects that were cultivated and replaced as different aspects of his work alternated in predominance (without any being lost from sight). In fact, it is this patient reconstruction that makes it possible to gradually reveal Eugenio's (mobile and thorough) way of moving forward along multiple paths and variants, gradually choosing the methods of work (and expression) most congenial to his current theoretical and practical situation. In this way, even a hard-working autodidact (in philosophy and the natural sciences) can enter into Eugenio Colorni's ingenious process of "saying and doing" and thus gradually absorb his extraordinary lesson.

Introduction

"The answer [Eugenio Colorni's, to a question of Ursula Hirschmann's on the existence of "concentric circles" in explanations of reality][1] is this: that the philosophical illness is more difficult to eradicate than you think, and that it lurks in the most unimaginable places and people [...]. All these concentric explanations are in fact "philosophies." Each coherent in itself, each "true" from a certain point of view, each "beautiful," "satisfying," "habitable"; sometimes "exciting." Because philosophies are indeed made to be "satisfying," "calming," to explain coherently. No wonder, then, if they turn out to be satisfying, calming and coherent. Now just take each of these concentric circles and ask yourself — what good are they beyond giving me all this satisfaction? And then you will see all this beautiful concentricity and coherence fall apart, and each of the circles will prove no longer to be a self-contained whole, but something detached and fragmentary. The utility of the dialectic is in interpreting some spiritual things and some historical phenomena, and that's all — it's not good for anything else. Analytic psychology is useful in treating certain nervous disorders, and helping us understand certain mental processes even in healthy people, and that's all — it's not good for anything else. Kant helps physics deal with time and space and causality his way. And he's not good for anything else. You ask me if it also makes me nervous to see how easily our minds think in analogies — which we then take to be facts. Does it make me nervous?! I've been nervous for twelve years,[2] and only now have I begun to sort this out.

I like the fact that you have also felt this pull toward "coherence," and then you immediately get suspicious. The pull is of course philosophy. People who are passive and just "let themselves live" may be immune to it. But anyone who wants to construct, think about and control their own actions seldom escapes the net. The difficult thing, the exciting thing, is precisely this

---

[1] Ventotene, 7 giugno 1939; now in Colorni 2019a, pp. 123–24.
[2] That is, since 1927, when he began to work on Benedetto Croce's *The Essence of Aesthetics*.

being able to build and control, while resisting all the magnets that continually pull you towards some "coherence" or other.)[3]

"This Colorni, who was he?" A question (involuntarily paraphrasing Alessandro Manzoni) that one of Albert Hirschman's many friends might have asked. Because Hirschman, in his travels, often spoke of his brother-in-law and of the influence Colorni had in shaping his thinking. But the editing of Colorni's texts,[4] and (above all) their unavailability in English have long prevented many from satisfying this legitimate curiosity.

The brief series of Eugenio's writings, published at Soveria Mannelli by Rubbettino Editore and in New York by Bordighera Press is designed precisely to meet this need from a number of points of view — political, intellectual, personal, etc. And the present volume, focusing on some of the philosophical writings from Colorni's early maturity, aims to enrich and complete (within certain limits) the picture that it has been possible, little by little, to piece together.

To this end (and to an even greater extent than in the preceding books) I have thought it important to avoid the typical "lapse" into the sort of intellectual partitioning of the works backed for professional reasons by so many, but which in my view has up to now blocked an effective and accessible reading of Colorni's extraordinary output.

I have thus chosen as an epigraph the above passage from Eugenio's Ventotene letters to his wife Ursula because[5] it sets out in a nutshell a very delicate aspect of his work (as well as of Hirschman's, and ours), one that we might call "the art of violating the rituals and limits" of his own discipline and of the relations between the various disciplines (*trespassing*).

On the one hand, it suggests following the best of one's own creative impulses because the different things we know, even most remotely, can boost one another through unexpected, instinctive,

---

[3]"I'm feeling fine and happy," Colorni writes to Ursula Hirschmann the afternoon of 6 April 1939 (now in Colorni 2019a, p. 116) "but a little disheveled. I'm letting myself do whatever I want to do in the moment. One moment I study physics, then geometry, then I read a novel, then Nietzsche, then I write a page, then I stretch out and think of you."

[4]Long the disciplinary preserve of philosophers, historians, and professional political scientists.

[5]Along with the one cited in n. 3.

even mysterious twists and turns.

On the other, however, it warns that possible analogies between different phenomena cannot be substituted for facts. To actually understand something (rather than explain, soothe, or accommodate) requires focusing attention on the phenomenon to be understood, delimiting the field of observation (precisely, perhaps in a novel way) and keeping its limits in sight, letting oneself be struck by reality, isolating the theoretical-practical experiences to be examined, concretely grasping what is actually being sought, and questioning, finally, the specific utility of the results achieved in order to put to good use the positive aspects and to fight (neutralize or at least soften) the negative ones.

Basically, it is a relentless battle against falsehood, against rampant intellectual hypocrisy and the "hold" it has on us ourselves, and also against our own illusory tendencies, which are often spontaneous.

Albert Hirschman would later add that sometimes the tangle of motivations behind any investigation is better left to the workings of the subconscious, and the same goes for the many pathways, which do in fact exist, between different cognitive experiences. But elsewhere he deviated from this prescription,[6] and in general he left more than one opening for processes of re-composition between different types of knowledge.[7]

Absolutely right, — Eugenio Colorni[8] would undoubtedly add — but without falling into the web of the philosophical illness, without surrendering to the lure of some notion of coherence, or of a system or conception of the world, of a *Weltanschauung*.

What surrounds us is always there to be discovered, to be conquered — and the main purpose of the pages that follow is therefore to contribute to a better understanding of how this "shifting imbalance"[9] among the various aspects of the issue arose and developed, and how Eugenio Colorni gradually made use of it, connecting vastly different fields and obtaining remarkably useful re-

---

[6]Consider the preface to the German edition (1974) of *Exit*, 1970.
[7]It is no accident that this is the main inspiration for *Essays in Trespassing*, 1981.
[8]Whom Albert always considered present.
[9]On the idea of optimal imbalance, cf. Meldolesi 1994a.

sults (in both thought and action).

Putting it another way, I felt the need to get ahead of the curve, to construct a "pre-emptive counterweight" (to the current intellectual partitioning of the work) that would make it possible to frame the texts that follow (as far as possible) in a well-defined, "truthful" horizon. Consequently, my "ruminations" led me in the end to favor an interpretive biographical sketch of the path that (first and foremost) led Eugenio to become Eugenio in the mid-thirties of the last century.[10] That is to say, the extraordinary intellectual and political personality indelibly engraved in the memory of anyone who had the good fortune to know him.[11]

I

1. Eugenio Colorni was born in Milan on 22 April 1909 into a well-to-do Jewish family. His father Alberto, originally from Mantova, was a liberal businessman, a dealer in agricultural machinery (which he sold primarily in England), who had built a rather affluent style of life for his family.[12] But in 1920 he died suddenly of

---

[10]It is a "sketch" put together by an economist (with popularizing intent, but not without some anxiety) aimed at the non-specialist reader (of philosophy). To my philosopher friends lying in wait (and "everyone else") I would ask them to consider for a moment, as an analogy, what Colorni wrote about Leibniz (1935, p vi), for whom "philosophy proper was only one aspect of a larger whole: like a fragment within the big picture. For us [students of philosophy], this fragment has become the center: we draw from it concepts and ideas that are actually living, methods which, expressed in terms of current problems, could yield new and very interesting results. But in studying this philosophy we must not forget that it was conceived as part of a totality, which must be taken into account, at least in the background. And concerning this harmonious and comprehensive whole that Leibniz envisioned but never was able to realize — this universal panorama — we can have no better or clearer idea of it than by recounting his life."

[11]Cf. below, Appendix A to the present introduction, and Colorni 1998, pp. 163–98. With the caveat (however elementary) to take into account the era and the temporal succession of philosophical contributions along with contemporary writings on other subjects (literary, political, personal, etc). At the same time — as Colorni himself wrote in the Preface to Leibniz's *Monadology* (1935, p. iii) — "having to choose a method of exposition I have preferred to let the author speak as much as possible, and have included for each subject selected passages from his works, limiting my own contribution to the order and succession of the problems, and to brief comments interspersed between the texts."

[12]"The Colornis moved in the upper circles of Milanese society, were clothed by the best tailors, and had season tickets at La Scala. Starting in 1916 they lived at via Guido d'Arez-

influenza, contracted during a business trip to Germany.

Colorni's mother, Clara Pontecorvo, a woman of character and principle, from a family of Pisan entrepreneurs (in the textile sector), at this point dedicated herself fully to the education of her two children (Silvia and Eugenio) and to administering the considerable inheritance left to her by her husband. Thus, though belonging to the Jewish upper middle class that had spontaneously emerged in the liberation of the Risorgimento, Eugenio, at the age of just eleven years old, found himself facing considerable hardships in his life — a life made even more difficult (unconsciously) by his mother's austere behavior.[13]

As we know, Colorni presented an image of himself in early adolescence as lazy, introverted, awkward, self-deprecating, and miserable.[14] It is likely, however, that even then he was already nursing a certain duplicity of response[15] which, as it matured, would later become a distinctive personal characteristic — the ability to extricate himself (often in unexpected ways) from difficult situations.

Initially, in a Milan troubled by a certain social and political uneasiness,[16] family and school were (inevitably) his points of reference. But a third one was superimposed on these — his three

---

zo 8, in the residential "Magenta zone," where the head of the family had acquired a stately five story house" (Gerbi 1999, p. 7 — much of the biographical information that follows comes from the first two chapters of this book).

[13]"In the home, Clara reduced unnecessary expenses and instilled in her children a degree of sobriety in keeping with her own behavior, which was more austere than that of her husband. The children thus grew up in a severe atmosphere, to which their mother's imposed return to Jewish tradition contributed" (Gerbi 1999, p. 7).

[14]Cf. below, ch. 4. The autobiographical picture presented in "The Philosophical Illness" may seem introductory, "to be read first"; but in reality, it is best understood if saved for last, after Eugenio's intellectual trajectory has been followed (and explored). It is only then, in fact, that this famous text reveals itself — in the sense that the subsequent experiences enumerated here (the clash with [Mimmo] Emilio, the interest in literature, the approach to Ennio [Enzo], Zionist leader of the family, Croce's *The Essence of Aesthetics*, ideological infatuation, etc.) take on their true position and function in Pierino-Eugenio's intellectual adventure, even beyond the clash/meeting with Umberto Saba.

[15]If nothing else, "Don Cavillo" ["Mr. Quibble"], the nickname he was given at school, indicates a certain convoluted quality (touchiness, pettiness) in his reasoning. Nevertheless — compared to the standard reasoning of his peers — it also suggests his need for a more subtle sort of discourse, well-prepared in reading and adequately articulated.

[16]In fact, in the Milan of long socialist tradition, beneath the blanket of enforced silence, renunciation and isolation, the members of opposition smoldered both within the factories and outside them.

cousins, Enrico, Enzo and Emilio. Here it is worth referring briefly to the page of "The Philosophical Illness" dedicated to them.

"He [Eugenio] spends the summers [at Forte dei Marmi] with certain cousins, all older than himself. They are at once the scandal and the pride of the family. They do not — and would not ever — apologize, even under torture. They say some things that make him shudder, but which after all, on reflection, are not entirely wrong — for example that to follow their ideals they would be ready to trample on any duty to the family. They are full of ideals, of things that excite them. Every summer there is something new. They read many books, many newspapers. It is impossible to beat them in a debate. They crush you with their limpid, linear, unassailable arguments" and so on.[17]

2. On one hand, then, there was the sense of dissatisfaction (and impotence) that came with daily life in Milan; on the other, the busy (and demanding) world of his Roman cousins (and his mother). Eugenio began trying to find his way between the two, without losing sight of either.[18] In high school (the classical "Alessandro Manzoni" school in Milan) we find him somewhat revitalized. He begins to assume a Socratic role. "He likes to be a confessor," he would later write about himself. "He has a naïve confidence in his qualities as a psychologist. [. . .] His sincerity sometimes borders on impudence."

Even within the limits of his age and the conditions in which he lives, he begins to have an established attitude of his own. Like

---

[17]"The three brothers," wrote another of Eugenio's cousins, Enzo Tagliacozzo (1980, p. 51), "would all three violently barge in, especially Enrico and Emilio, subjecting you to a third degree interrogation and making no secret of their superiority. And for anyone subjected to this process of 'indoctrination' (which I also knew well), it is hardly surprising that in the face of their pretensions, a younger, less mature, and more doubtful individual such as Eugenio should develop an inferiority complex as he painfully tried to respond to his cousins pressures and develop his own personality, humanly finer and richer than that of his over-achieving cousins."

[18]To understand the importance Eugenio attributed to his cousins' influence on his development it is sufficient to read what he wrote in memory of Enrico Sereni. "A Master: if by that word we mean one who knows how to give profound meaning to every aspect of life. [. . .] How many of us, inferior to him and indebted to him for all our spiritual development, felt almost embarrassed to see him put himself on our level, treat us as equals!" (Colorni 1931b). Colorni also dedicated *The Aesthetics of Benedetto Croce; A Critical Study* (1932) to Enrico Sereni.

many of his peers, he encounters along the way Benedetto Croce's *The Essence of Aesthetics*, which interests him for its artistry and philosophy, but also, no doubt, because of its famous author's role as an opponent of the regime.[19]

Ab initio, then, was art,[20] aesthetics, the passion for understanding artistic data — for the development of a type of philosophical speculation that respects art in its complex articulations. "The moment one becomes aware of the peculiar characteristics of the act of aesthetic intuition," he later wrote,[21] "the question of its meaning also arises implicitly. The problem facing aesthetics is not only 'what does art look like?' but also 'what does art mean? What place does it have in the world of the mind?' [. . .]. Croce himself stated [. . .] that the science of art or aesthetics is alive only in its infinite individuations — as the science not of one but of all 'the infinite problems that have arisen and will arise' in the course of its history. And each problem should provide an aspect, an essential side, a fundamental and eternal point of view regarding this totality that is art — whose function and meaning, its position, should flow from all the work of collection and should coincide with the conclusion of it."

More generally, I see Eugenio, the high school and then university student, as a very perceptive young man, attracted by numerous stimuli from a vast Italian and European cultural horizon, which he absorbs and reworks spontaneously on his own. From poetry to literature to the visual arts to music, from an interest in exploring the psyche and the cosmos to an admiration for the everyday liberal and pacifist presence of Benedetto Croce, the list goes on. All are aspects which, in the era of art deco and the Bauhaus, morph into a passion for philosophy and politics; but in so doing they do not fade into the background. Rather, they serve as qualifiers, these

---

[19]"The 'Italian family' was the name Benedetto Croce gave to a group of trusted friends that the Neapolitan senator met in Rome, Florence, Turin and Milan when he left Palazzo Filomarino to go on working holidays in his beloved Piedmont. It was the period in which Croce's firm opposition to the regime inspired and guided intellectuals of the most varied political tendencies" (Gerbi 1999, p. 38).

[20]Music and painting, certainly. But literature above all, and aesthetics in general — as he himself makes clear (cf. below, chap. 4) and as a number of later youthful writings suggest (Colorni 1928, 1930, 1931, 1931a, 1931c, 1931e, 1932).

[21]Colorni 1932, p. 15.

passions, bringing with them a distinctive self-ironic and irreverent "mix," a taste that is at once humanist, decorative and rationalist, in the key of an (anti-fascist) insurgency.

3. Eugenio got to be good at arguing his positions. His final exam results were the best in the school. At university he initially enrolled in the law school, perhaps because — as it was said — "it opens all the doors" (including the eventual administration, one might assume, of the family fortune). But the following year he moved to Literature and Philosophy, happily entering into the "rebel" (anti-regime) atmosphere driven by two very different professors who nevertheless got along well with each other: Giuseppe Antonio Borgese, who taught aesthetics, and Piero Martinetti, professor of general philosophy.[22]

A Palermo native, "Borgese was a strong speaker and possessed the art of the agile turn of phrase that strikes the imagination. He spoke as if excited by his thoughts, seemingly seeking them out and pursuing them with his dark eyes raised somewhat languidly aloft, and often strolling in front of the lectern."[23] A brilliant extrovert and authoritative contributor to the *Corriere della*

---

[22]Borgese, a brilliant character, had taught the history of German literature in Rome before being invited to the State University in Milan — where in the second half of the 1920s he published a series of essays on aesthetics (or poetics as he puts it) that he later collected under the title *Poetics of Unity. Five Essays. Aesthetic Precursors* (1934). Borgese, as Enzo Tagliacozzo wrote (1980, now in Colorni 1998, pp. 193–94), "was one of the few professors who did not mind stopping to talk after class with his students, continuing the conversations on the street or at his own home. He was known as an anti-fascist, and his most dedicated students, including Eugenio, repeatedly got into fights with fascist students. Another determining influence for his students was the austere Piero Martinetti, who explained Kant at eight o'clock in the morning. Martinetti introduced students to the rigor of Kantian ethics, while the brilliant G.A., more easygoing, discussed aesthetics and comparative literature." Martinetti also had problems with Fascist 'squadrism.' He obtained a gun permit and warned the rector that he would shoot if he had to. (Gerbi 1999, pp. 29 ff. and 49–50).

[23]Piovene 1963. In Borgese, wrote Libero Lenti (1983, p. 37), "youthful boldness had given way to authoritative arrogance. He faced his listeners without notes and kept them riveted, breathless, for an entire hour." In "Figuration and Trasfiguration" — an essay that Martinetti liked, written for the National Congress of Philosophy in Milan in 1926 — Borgese wrote, among other things (1934, p. 134) that "the new era, it appears, will hold on to the capital conquest of recent Italian aesthetic thought — that is, the affirmed autonomy and non-transience of art, and the distinction of its means and ends from those of other activities of the mind" — a judgment that the student Eugenio perhaps shared..

Sera, he was drawn to the cultural circle Il Convegno,[24] which Colorni, from a certain point on, took part in as well.

Martinetti, on the other hand, from Ivrea in Piedmont, was austere, stoical, anything but worldly. Colorni appreciated his "extraordinary clarity whether he was speaking about Kant or Spinoza or other authors he liked, such as the 'heretic' Schopenhauer. A page or two of notes and three quarters of an hour of concentrated empathy with his audience, seduced as they were by those eyes deep in their sockets, by that forehead towering over his bony face."[25] It was Martinetti who "encouraged [Eugenio] to explore Kant in depth."[26] Kant, he taught,[27] "said: do not make yourself anyone's servant! [. . .] Only those who feel in themselves the need for this moral dignity, this unyielding pride, are men in the true sense of the word: the rest are the flock, born to serve." Colorni, Tagliacozzo wrote,[28] "loved Spinoza, following an initial infatuation with Italian idealism. And in those years who was there who didn't read Croce and Gentile, but especially Croce? [. . .] Eugenio knew Hegel, but he was never a Hegelian. He studied Marx, but he was never a Marxist."

4. A glance at the weighty philosophical tomes Eugenio studied reveals that they must have kept him busy for more than a few afternoons. Significant in this regard, it seems to me, is the *History of Modern Philosophy. An Exposition of the History of Philosophy from the End of the Renaissance to the Present Day,* by Harald Höffding of the University of Copenhagen, re-translated from German by Martinetti and then checked against the original text (2 vols. over 900 pp., 1st ed. 1926). In a brief opening note, "the translator" (Martinetti) maintains that "the breadth of information, the pleasant arrangement of the subject matter, and the clarity of the exposition make it

---

[24]"The 'stroke of genius' of Ferreri" [founder of the circle], wrote Antonello Gerbi, "had been to enlist certain of the Milanese upper middle class to serve the purposes of an original and enthusiastic cultural circle that moved in various directions. The reigning regime inadvertently lent an aura of resistance to these gatherings of men of letters, in the midst of so many well-meaning, socially indifferent, budding rebels."

[25]Gerbi 1999, p. 46.

[26]Tagliacozzo 1980, now in Colorni 1998, pp. 193–94.

[27]Cit. in Gerbi 1999, p. 49.

[28]Tagliacozzo 1980, now in Colorni 1998, pp. 194–95.

one of the best works of its kind — suitable both for those who wish to orient themselves easily in the history of the ideas of the modern age and for those who wish to make it the starting point for deeper and more detailed studies. The Italian reader will be particularly interested in the scope given to the philosophy of the Renaissance, the true golden century of Italian philosophy, which alone occupies a third of the first volume." Thus, as regards the four main themes dealt with in this work — "the problem of knowledge (the logical problem)," "the problem of existence (the cosmological problem)," "the problem of valuation (the ethical-religious problem)" and "the problem of consciousness (the psychological problem)" — we can imagine how interested Eugenio was in what Nicolò Machiavelli, Giordano Bruno, Tommaso Campanella,[29] Galileo Galilei etc. had to say. And how he then conscientiously studied the development of philosophical thought in Europe: *The Grand Systems* (of Descartes, Hobbes, Spinosa, Leibniz), *The English Philosophy of Experience* (of Locke, Newton, Berkeley, Hume), *The French Enlightenment* (of Voltaire, Montesquieu, Diderot, Rousseau). And again in the second volume: *The Philosophy of the German Enlightenment, Emanuel Kant and Critical Philosophy, The Philosophy of Romanticism, Positivism, and Philosophy in Germany 1859–1880.*[30]

5. Then, of course, there were the original texts of the main philosophers and Martinetti's lessons and books, above all his *Introduction to Metaphysics* (2 vols. 1903, reprinted 1929) and *Liberty* (1928). The professor was actually proposing to the students an ingenious arrangement of philosophical thought and its history, based on the inseparability of the subject from the object of knowledge (which led to the rejection of the thesis sustained by the idealists that the subject takes precedence over the object) and also on the need to continue undeterred along the path of philo-

---

[29]Cf. E. Colorni, "Utilità e moralità nella filosofia di Tommaso Campanella," [Utility and Morality in the Philosophy of Tommaso Campanella] 1931d.

[30]With the exception of positivism, the second volume is thus the preserve of philosophy in the German language. But it is interesting to note that within it, Kant takes pride of place with 85 pages, while Hegel is covered briefly (15 pages) in the chapter on the philosophy of romanticism.

sophical construction starting from experience.[31]

In the review he wrote when *Introduction to Metaphysics* was reprinted (1932a), Eugenio wrote that Martinetti "undoubtedly represents, in our philosophical climate, one of the most outstanding personalities and deepest minds. [. . .] Concerning all the classical authors, and also many others who are less well-known and whom he himself has popularized in Italy, Martinetti has direct and deep ideas. But he considers them from a point of view that differs from what we are used to. He, too, maintains[32] that in each individual there is something alive and something dead, but what is new and original is the part that he takes to be alive — and his argumentation is so tight that it convinces one to agree, if not on the final results, at least on the essential nature of certain points."[33]

This is essentially a different perspective. "M[artinetti]'s book," Colorni continued, "is presented as a vast historical exemplification of a particular doctrinal scheme. [. . .] A completely ideal model of the history of philosophy, in which the succession of time no longer has any importance, in which philosophy and the history of philosophy are truly the same, since every doctrine becomes a moment of the ideal dialectic of the spirit. For M., building a system means making it emerge from the clash of systems that have preceded it. And these are organized into the various essential forms in which the human mind manifests itself; eternal modes

---

[31]"Even in the field of philosophy," Sandro Gerbi in any case writes (1999, pp. 46–47), "Martinetti was an inconvenient character. [. . .] There was something esoteric about his thinking, inspired by a "transcendent idealism" of Kantian origin, with mystical connotations and strong influences from Indian philosophy. Be that as it may, [. . .] Martinetti did have some fixed points. He had a very vivid sense of evil, which for him was something real, to be fought relentlessly. His anti-fascism was a moral attitude, but since morality and religion converged in him, his political position reflected a religious vision."

[32]Along with — is the implication — Benedetto Croce and his followers.

[33]"In such a way," the passage continues, "that although the book does not offer a 'new philosophy' it introduces readers into a new environment and opens their eyes to many aspects of the truth; in a word, it enriches. And the ones who need this most of all are young people, who are led by the pressure exerted by highly celebrated doctrines to have difficulty seeing outside the schemes such doctrines provide. They find it hard to free themselves from this subjugation and go outside these doctrines to find the weapons and sustenance they need to resolve issues that they know they cannot eliminate." Reading Martinetti's book, Colorni thus finds grounds for liberation from the schemes of the most celebrated doctrines. But, as we shall now see, this happens "from within" the philosophical mainstream.

of thought that always recur, so that ancient and modern philosophers are united in sharing one of them [. . .].[34] In this way, history is truly reduced to the system [. . .]; and each thinker appears as a piece with a well-determined place in the great game that is gradually evolving — in overcoming obstacles without leaving a residue, and in philosophical progress."

At this point in the review, a series of critical observations[35] and clarifications naturally emerge, but do not in any case undermine the basic logic of Martinetti's construction. Indeed, for a while Colorni considered it interesting and useful — enough so that he could conclude: "we repeat — the value of M. should be sought in the theoretical foundations of his speculations; in his criticism of idealism and in the concept of pure and objective experience that he seems to point to as a way out of the difficulties modern thought finds itself embroiled in. This is where the work needs to be put in. And above all, the maestro in the methodology of the work should also be M.; for the discipline to resist speaking except of things that are known in depth; for that spirit of untiring research that keeps one from immediately embracing a system or a terminology just to be able to see everything through the prism of it, but inspires real participation in each thought and almost a virginity of spirit in looking at it. So that the system, if one has the stamina to build it, arises as a result and synthesis of a broader and more secure spiritual experience."[36]

---

[34]"Nothing helps [. . .]," wrote Martinetti concluding his introduction to *Liberty* (1928, p. 8), "as much as recalling and examining the great systems of the past if our aim is to see problems in their true light, consider them in all their aspects, discover their difficulties, and avoid useless repetition — at least to the extent that this is possible with these eternal questions [. . .]. A philosophy cut off from philosophical tradition will always be puerile and useless, full of vanity and illusions. Because another advantage — and not the least of them — in delving into the past is this: that it makes one more modest [. . .], less accessible to personal feelings and more instead to the serene satisfaction of continuing to pursue an immortal work in silence and with humble toil." It certainly cannot be said that Martinetti had any doubts about such immortality!

[35]First among these is "the gnoseological vision [which] is transformed into a religious vision."

[36]Ibid., p. 57. Reading this passage you almost have the impression that Eugenio is alluding to a work program of his own — from "this is where the work needs to be put in" to "almost a virginity of spirit in looking at it [each thought]" (a precursor to his "innocent courage," which Albert Hirschman would call "naïvety.") It is also clear, reading between the lines of this review, that Colorni was actually recognizing that his teacher had freed him from the

6. In other words, in spite of the amount of intellectual effort required, Colorni undoubtedly placed himself, mentally, in the framework of philosophical thought proposed by Martinetti — while maintaining, within certain limits, his own independence of judgment.[37] "At that time Eugenio was strictly the philosopher and rigorous moralist. At our university he was the great hope for philosophical studies. But in addition he had a gift, that of being irresistibly likable. As he always remained, he was stern and boyish at the same time. Even though he wasn't an eloquent man, he had an influence on those who approached him that was often decisive. It was as if his philosophical rigidity was infused with natural emotional exuberance, his need for contact, his vitality."[38]

"It seems Eugenio was a member of the 'Student Groups for Freedom,'" writes Sandro Gerbi,[39] "an association formed following the Matteotti murder by Lelio Basso and Rodolfo Morandi." He undoubtedly moved in "Justice & Liberty" as well as socialist circles.[40] Under the pseudonym Carlo Rosemberg, he published his first article — "Roberto Ardigò" — in the Gobettian inspired journal *Pietre*, which was later suppressed by the Fascist authorities but edited at the time by Lelio Basso.[41] For both professional and conspiratorial reasons

---

psychological subservience to Hegel that was so common among the many intellectuals in thrall to classical German philosophy (and the Marxists). On the other hand, it also contains several important reference points that would recur in Colorni's reasoning once it was freed from the requirements of the system.

[37]"As a university student," wrote Enzo Tagliacozzo (1980, now in Colorni 1998, p. 194) "Eugenio saw his way forward as that of the philosopher and university philosophy professor, and he was conscientiously preparing for this. He would say that he couldn't solve any of his everyday problems unless he posed them in philosophical terms and that, in a nutshell, 'he couldn't live without doing philosophy.' The pre-eminence of knowledge over will that he reaffirmed as long as he lived was something he was already claiming when he was still a student" (Cf., on this subject, "Di alcune relazioni tra conoscenza e volontà" [Concerning some relations between knowledge and will] – 1932c, now in Colorni 2009). But it is an interactive relationship in which an act of will is sometimes indispensable in opening the way to knowledge (cf. Cerchiai 2018, p. 21 n. 31).

[38]Piovene 1944; now in Gerbi 1999, p. 296.

[39]Gerbi 1999, p. 41.

[40]More the former than the latter, according to Lucio Luzzatto: "Eugenio spoke to me more than once of this contrast between his early education in philosophy and his later political [socialist] orientation," Luzzatto wrote in 1973 to Ursula Hirschmann (cit. in Gerbi 1999, p. 43, n. 23).

[41]Also, around the time of his graduation (1930–31), he wrote reviews of a series of texts (by Ascoli, Debenedetti, Tilgher, Praz, Cardarelli, Calogero, and Petrini), mostly on aesthet-

he kept his intellectual and political activities as separate as possible.[42] He already knew French and English quite well (along with some Hebrew)[43] — German would come later. He had an open-minded attitude toward foreign countries.

"He preferred the great Russian writers," according to Guido Piovene[44] — Dostoevsky, Tolstoy, Gogol, Chekhov, etc. — while Italian authors didn't interest him much. Perhaps with the exception of Pirandello, but Svevo, Saba or Montale had not yet achieved exemplary status. He detested D'Annunzio; for Croce, on the other hand, he had greater respect, except when trying to demolish him in academic exercises (these were in any case the tastes of Borgese [who had in the past been a "pupil" of Croce's])."[45]

7. Thus Colorni found the opportunity to return to his thoughts on the aesthetics of Don Benedetto.[46] What would become his only

---

ics, which put him into circulation in the country's literary and philosophical circles — cf., for example, the reviews of books by Cardarelli and Praz now in Colorni 1998, pp. 32–42.

[42]"I remember," declared Franco Formiggini Pasotelli (who was very close to Eugenio around 1930: cf. Gerbi 1999, p. 42), "that one day I organized a small exchange of views at the home of my cousin, Remy Assayas, [. . .] between Colorni and the future philosophy professor Enzo Paci, who at the time belonged to the "J&L" movement. A very heated debate ensued, in which Eugenio unleashed his entire theoretical arsenal, putting Paci in some difficulty."

[43]On Eugenio's (significant, but temporary) interest in Judaism (and Zionism) — following (mostly) in the footsteps of his mother and cousin Enzo [Ennio] Sereni — see "The Philosophical Illness" below; and Cerchiai 2018, pp. 32ff.

[44]Piovene 1963.

[45]Gerbi 1999, p. 45. "It certainly did not escape Eugenio," wrote Alceo Riosa (2011, p. 272), "that in the conviction expressed by the professor [Borgese] that 'the discoveries, meditations, and doubts of Croce are what is most important today regarding the history of literary taste and research' there was a desire to keep alive a constructive debate on Croce's ideas." "In denying every form of arbitrary, disordered life," Borgese had in fact said of himself (1928, p. 22; cited in Riosa 2011, p. 272 n. 25), "I have made a long-standing effort to fit into contemporary culture and I do not deny this effort; I think that being aware of what has already been done in philosophy, in the tradition of Croce, is indispensable for every serious scholar [. . .]. Our position, therefore, should be one of respect and recognition towards the Crocean method, and acceptance of his indisputable discoveries."

[46]"During the course of my studies," Colorni wrote at the time in a CV (Gerbi 1999, p. 52), "I have dealt especially with philosophical and aesthetic questions and, under the direction of Prof. G.A. Borgese, I have drafted works on the aesthetics of Roberto Ardigò and Italian positivism, Bergsonian aesthetics, and the aesthetics of Benedetto Croce." During Borgese's course Eugenio also had to prepare a conference on Croce. Borgese (1930, p. 146) characterized as "Very useful, concerning Croce, Colorni's exercise and the discussion that followed." In addition, Colorni prepared a text for Borgese on "How to interpret the contrast between the two phases in the aesthetic ideas of Flaubert, and their exemplifi-

monograph — *The Aesthetics of Benedetto Croce. A Critical Study* — began to take shape.[47]

For our purposes,[48] it is worth noting (first and foremost) that in this study Eugenio shows high esteem for "the great work of Croce."[49] He considered it important to immerse himself in this "precious" material, painstakingly collected — a step which represents the starting point of his own elaboration. Colorni also asserted in his preface that "to speak of an author is always, in a way, to speak of oneself. All the more so in the case of Croce, who has provided the entire Italian world with a base of concepts and considerations that is now part of the substratum of the culture and which, whether accepted or rejected, it is impossible not to take into account and use.[50]

Not least because at the time Eugenio had already developed his characteristic mental position that (as he wrote in a review in 1930[51]) "a clearer understanding of the problems that in traditional doctrines still remain unsolved" would require incorporating the "fundamental data into one's own attempt at a system" instead of limiting oneself "to the acceptance or partial correction of a set way of thinking."

This clarifies Colorni's intentions when he writes, again in his preface:[52] "this booklet is meant neither as a defense nor a refuta-

---

cation in his work" (Riosa 2011, p. 275).

[47]"In the home of a classmate of yours [Eugenio Colorni] nobly versed in philosophical studies," Borgese recalled (1931, p. 119) during an academic lecture [. . .], "a theoretical and aesthetic discussion took place which later gave rise to some manuscripts, one by Colorni, who discusses what seem to him to be my most important theses, and others either embracing these or opposing them from points of view very close to those of idealism."

[48]Here I have drawn briefly from Bobbio 1975, pp. XVI ff. and Cerchiai 2018, ch. 2.

[49]Colorni 1932, p. 86.

[50] Colorni 1932, p. vii. "What is written about him [Croce]," the passage continues, "turns out more often than not to be an examination of conscience arising from the need to come to grips with something that represents an integral part of our own personality and to establish how much of it ought to be maintained and strengthened as an indispensable element for any further advancement." As we can see, in this *ouverture* Colorni is already perfectly aware of the essential subject-object fusion his analysis is based on and of the subjective purpose it implies.

[51]Colorni (1930), Review of "La giustizia" (Justice) by Max Ascoli. As we shall see, it is precisely this aspect of the systemic question that would be "overwhelmed" by Eugenio's radical revision of his own previous theoretical awareness.

[52]Colorni 1932, p. vii.

tion, but rather an inquiry that seeks to grasp and distinguish the living elements in Crocean thinking and remove the part of it that is superstructure; an attempt to create work opportunities that resonate with its spirit, even without accepting any of its formulations or its systematic organization" in a Hegelian vein.

The idea was essentially to liberate the Crocean elaboration from its dialectical construction which, in Colorni's view, did not spring from the data but had been imposed on it.[53] "Rejecting this," Colorni in fact adds, "does not mean admitting the possibility in general that there can be isolated data without their own system, but only affirming that Croce's system is extraneous to its most vital data and derives from other requirements of thought that have been improperly superimposed.[54]

So Eugenio had learned to "philosophize" (Gennaro Sasso) and to appreciate art and aesthetics from a different point of view. The search for a system that would fit the collected data was the need underlying the *Critical Study*. This was a goal that revealed the influence of Martinetti on Eugenio's text (both in the sense that subject and object are originally inseparable so that the latter cannot derive from the former, and in the sense that only reflection on "pure and objective" experience[55] allows one to continue to move forward), but which in the monograph . . . was not successfully achieved.

---

[53]Croce, of course, did not like the idea. Perhaps naïvely, Colorni, then 23, sent the manuscript of his monograph accompanied by a letter in which he explained that "the work more than anything sprang from a need for clarification, or from my increasingly felt need to acquire a clear awareness of how much we owe to your teaching and how much in it constitutes a premise for moving forward." But Croce replied: "You perhaps thought you could apply to me the same procedure I applied to Hegel, when I accepted most of his doctrine but rejected his system-building. But I was careful not to consider as empirical or psychological what I got from Hegel — I considered it rather as his true system, oppressed and truncated in its development by the traditional and scholastic arrangement he retained." (Letters of 25 February and 3 March 1932 are now in Croce 1955, vol. II, pp. 31–32). Also see Cerchiai 2018, pp. 52–53.

[54]"What lies beneath the exterior organization," continues Colorni (1932, pp. vii–viii), "is in Croceanism the true system, not yet clearly formulated, but agile and rich in possibilities. Looking for such richness beneath a largely dissatisfying scaffolding is the task of whoever experiences this idea as a part of their own life. And to follow its possibilities for continuity and development even beyond the form it has given to itself seems to us the greatest tribute that can be paid to a philosophy." And what is more — this illuminating passage also has a lot to say, in my view, about the way of working that Eugenio would develop later.

[55]Colorni 1932a, now in Colorni 2009, p. 57.

8. This was probably one of the reasons Eugenio changed his perspective and became deeply involved in the history of philosophical thought. Already in October 1930 he had graduated under Martinetti, discussing a thesis on *The Development and Meaning of Leibnizian Individualism*. He passed the state exam to teach philosophy in the middle schools (considering it a first step toward the university career he intended to pursue).[56] In 1931, immediately after graduation, he went on a study trip to Berlin. In 1932–33 he was lecturer in Italian at the University of Marburg, at the same time carrying on with his Leibniz studies at the Staatsbibliothek in Berlin. He won an advanced degree in 1933 with a Master's thesis on *The Youthful Philosophy of Leibniz*.[57]

In choosing Leibniz, Eugenio was perhaps attracted by the image of the "sage" who reflects on the individual and the "other," and on reality across the board, without boundaries. He was attracted by Leibniz's rational objectivism, extending in every direction, and by his immanentist belief in an underlying universal harmony — also as an antidote to the prevailing idealism.[58]

---

[56]The record of the proceedings of the meeting of the Royal Lombard Institute of Sciences and Letters of Milan of December 17, 1931 for the award of a scholarship — a competition to which Eugenio had submitted three of his writings on aesthetics, some reviews and his degree thesis — states that Colorni "shows lively interest in philosophical problems, with a sharp and subtle intelligence that is not satisfied with the usual solutions [. . .] and a penetrating critical spirit that strives to highlight the weaknesses and contradictions of the doctrines studied." (Cit. in Cerchiai 2009, p. xix.)

[57]It was in any case a subject that was in fashion. "Italian idealism," Norberto Bobbio wrote (1975, p. xxi), "had never run across Leibniz; it had only brushed past him along the way, as the great contemporary and antagonist of Vico. But around 1930, for a little under ten years, partly thanks to the Catholics' reacting to their ostracism by the idealists, and partly in an attempt from the idealist side to find precursors more or less everywhere, especially before Kant, there was a real flowering of Leibniz studies. It was unusual and was never repeated."

[58]"If we wanted to define what [Leibniz] considered the main purpose of his lifetime of thinking and his specific cultural mission," Colorni wrote later (1935, p. xxii), "we probably ought to look at the striving toward unification, conciliation and harmony among the sciences that pervades his whole life, from beginning to end. His highest ambition was to give humanity a simple and comprehensive way of embracing all aspects of life and solving all its problems. The man who went into every science with the utmost respect for what is peculiar and irreducible in it, who knew how to appropriate the specific character of any method, nevertheless set the general method as the ideal of his life. It is a method that applies to everyone, that is applicable to any discipline — a way of thinking that makes him almost a link between the universalism of the Renaissance and the rationalism of the Enlightenment."

As often happens, there was a complex of circumstances that favored such a development. The legacy of Renaissance philosophy that "passed instead to Germany (with Leibniz and Schelling)."[59] The interest in an *emendatio intellectus* (Norberto Bobbio), an improvement in understanding, which perhaps with a leap into the past would free him from current philosophical conditioning and allow him to think with a fresh mind.[60] The attraction of a way of thinking like Leibniz's, divided up into a thousand streams but striving to reconcile the "mechanical" philosophical systems of Descartes, Hobbes and Spinoza that had followed the rise of Leonardo, Kepler, and Galileo's "new science" with "ideas from the most opposite sides of the spiritual world."[61] There was Martinetti's teaching, which suggested an in-depth commitment in such a direction, and the advice on the subject he gave to some of his students — such as Gadda,[62] Barié,[63] and Colorni. The theme itself — the life and work of Gottfried Wilhelm Leibniz — was well-suited to a specialization that would allow entry into a philosophical-professional network inspired by Leibniz that was present in Italy and abroad, and into his desired career.

---

[59]Deleuze 1996, p. 96.

[60]There is in my view an analogy in this regard with Albert Hirschman's *The Passions and the Interests* (1977), which allowed Hirschman to distance himself explicitly from the logic of economics.

[61]"And in this work," Höffding maintains (1926, reprinted 1943, pp. 270–71), " he produced a richness of thought that is perhaps unique in the history of philosophy. In almost every intellectual field he appears as a creator or precursor, and although he worked on the most disparate subjects, his concepts nevertheless possess an intimate harmony and a common type."

[62]In February 1926 Martinetti wrote to Carlo Emilio Gadda: "Dedicate your limited free time to two things: German and exploring your author, Leibniz. In view of your background and considerations of time, I think this is for you the shortest and safest way forward. If in three or four years you could come out with a good exposition on Leibniz (don't worry about competitors on this subject!) your path at the university (in the history of philosophy) would be open." (Gadda 2007, p. 63; cit. in Vigorelli 2011, p. 255). Obviously, in Italian schools philological work was particularly prized — the careful reconstruction of someone's thinking — perhaps more than the originality of one's own.

[63]On Giovanni Emanuele Barié, on *La spiritualità dell'essere e Leibniz* [*The Spirituality of Being and Leibniz*] (1933), and on Eugenio's critical review of the book, cf. Geri Cerchiai's note in Colorni 2009, pp. 47–49.

II

9. But for Colorni the early thirties were also crucial years from a personal and political point of view. In 1931 the Fascist oath was imposed on university professors. Borgese went into self-exile in the United States; Martinetti refused the oath, left teaching and would later be investigated. In one fell swoop, Eugenio's "philosophical home" was left unprotected and his own university prospects were inevitably compromised.[64]

So . . . what to do? In Oct 1931 Colorni took part in the conference on Hegel in Berlin,[65] where Giovanni Gentile commissioned him to edit Leibniz's *Monadology,* to be published by Sansoni.[66] Soon after, he met Ursula and Otto Albert Hirschmann.[67] He stood by helplessly as Hitler came to power. He helped Ursula and Albert in some small efforts to oppose to this dramatic turn of events. In contrast to snobbish skepticism about the "staying power" of Nazism (then prevalent in Berlin high society), he was well aware of the collective tragedy that was by then looming. He convinced Albert to flee and saved his life.

The early thirties were thus a period of upheaval for Colorni that

---

[64]"How could we forget," wrote Enzo Tagliacozzo (1980, now in Colorni 1998, p. 195), "that antifascist intransigence barred Colorni from a university career, since from 1932, in order to participate in public competitions, not only for university positions but also at the middle school level, a Fascist Party membership card was required? Colorni started teaching high school without a membership card because he entered before 1932, and he resisted the pressure that was put on him to join."

[65]With the intention of meeting the leadership of the Young German Social Democrats on the side. In Berlin, before sending him his manuscript, Colorni also saw Benedetto Croce. Such was Eugenio's conspiratorial caution at the time that Croce thought he was not involved in politics.

[66]Colorni 1935. "Colorni harbored a disgust for Gentile which later, over the years, turned almost into contempt, and this went beyond politics — Colorni considered his ideas a monstrous falsehood, something like an enormous disease" (Piovene 1944, now in Gerbi 1999, p. 296). Evidently, the regime's main philosopher had come across Colorni's work on Leibniz and wanted to make use of it in the "Scholastic series of philosophy texts" he was editing. At the same time, Eugenio had good reason to accept the offer to get his work some exposure. But also because such a connection might serve as a useful cover for his own political work (as happened, for example, when he took part in a conference in Paris on Descartes, probably prompted by Gentile, which gave him the opportunity to meet directly with the leaders of the Socialist Party).

[67]As known, Otto Albert Hirschmann changed his name when he emigrated to the United States in 1940 (and enlisted in the American armed forces) to Albert O. Hirschman.

brought a profound change of perspective. He tried to adapt to the new situation. Understandably, he completed what he was working on (first, *The Aesthetics of Benedetto Croce. A Critical Study,* then the editing of Leibniz's *Monadology*[68]). Then, after a brief period at the "Severino Grattoni" High School in Voghera, he reorganized his own life in Trieste, where he took the position of professor of philosophy and pedagogy at the "Giosuè Carducci" female Teacher's College.

This undoubtedly strengthened the official image of himself that Colorni now intended to present (for conspiratorial reasons as well) — of a professor of philosophy fully absorbed in his educational and scholarly work.[69] At the same time, however, he had

---

[68]The "curation" of the *Monadology* that Eugenio delivered to the publisher in June 1934 is a philological masterpiece of erudition. The little book opens with an ample "Bio-bibliographical note." This is followed by Colorni's 125 page expository anthology of Leibniz's system, divided into "Truth and Factual Reason," "Individual Substance," "Force and Motion," "The Monad," "Perfection and Imperfection of the Monad," "Matter, Soul, and Preordained Harmony;" which finally gives way to the 23 page "Monadology." Not least through this work Eugenio becomes a full fledged expert on Leibniz in the Italian philosophical environment. "Leibniz and Descartes," he later wrote to Ursula (letter of 1 June 1939, now in Colorni 2019, pp. 70–72) "were people who really did have something to say in the field of science [. . .]. Only they preferred, for reasons of convenience, to express these things in the language then in use, a theological-systematic language. Therefore, to understand them it is necessary to "translate" from that systematic language to ours. Once this is done, the theses and demonstrations that appear to be senseless games take on an important meaning." "The methodological pluralism opposing the idealistic method of reducing the multiple to unity," wrote Quarta 1977 (quoted by Cerchiai in Colorni 2009, p. 174 n. 9), "is the most theoretically valid result of Colorni's approach to Leibniz's work."

[69]It is known that Colorni tried for some time to mold himself in the "tradition" of Leibniz (cf. the preceding note). He wrote a number of essays and planned to conclude his work with the publication of a monograph on Leibniz (announced by a Paris publisher); but "he was shipwrecked in this multi-year quest, eventually becoming annoyed by it." (Tagliacozzo 1980, now in Colorni 1998, p. 195). Browsing through selected passages from his own letters (Colorni 2019, pp. 55 and 58; 2019a, p. 107) one can appreciate the significance Colorni attributed to "this interminable Leibniz of mine" — how he had long felt the need to bind himself "perhaps a little artificially to a job or study that does not give one hundred percent satisfaction," but also "how many, how very many [. . .] futile and mediocre daydreams there are in eight years of working on the philosophy of Leibniz." "These are jobs," Eugenio explained in a letter to Ursula dated 28 November 1938 (2019, pp. 57–58), "which, in order to do them, you have to live somewhat separate from the world, in a clique of people who, by university convention and to give themselves the illusion of being profound, etc., attach importance to these things. There are some people who live their whole lives in enclosures of this kind — the literati, the professors, almost everyone. But then you happen to be standing in front of someone from the real world and you read in their eyes the question, 'well, what's the point of it all?'"

by then arrived at some radical conclusions[70] that soon resulted in a great intellectual and practical transformation in his life.

10. Pressed by events, Eugenio had to up his game and transform his status as a recently graduated researcher into that of a teacher (and politician) — deploying his precocious maturity with volcanic energy. If he had been able to look back on himself as a university student, he almost wouldn't have recognized himself. In fact, what he had experienced up to that moment became (mysteriously, magically) a simple apprenticeship for what he was about to experience, in thought and action — a kind of training, a largely unconscious intellectual exercise that suddenly found its genuine expression, its practical value. Certainly it could be argued that Colorni had already been on the right track, the one he now decided to embark upon with such determination. It could be argued that, in the end, his search for a system adequate to Crocean aesthetics had not been successful, that not even the Leibnizian labyrinth was leading him into port. And more generally, therefore, that doubts regarding philosophical systems must already have arisen in his mind.[71]

But to me it seems undeniable that it was the concrete historical conditions he lived through that prompted him (a latter-day Atlas) to transform his somewhat Hamlet-like doubts into the solid foothold for an extraordinary theoretical-political revolution.

It is true, on the other hand, that nothing we have documented (or implied) up to now — concerning Eugenio's family background, his religious, social and cultural conditioning, his scholastic, cultural and professional choices, his openness to learning foreign languages (and to traveling beyond the Alps), and even the process of his gradual anti-fascist politicization — is so strange. It

---

[70]Leibniz, he said, never imagined the role that the subject inevitable has in the cognitive process, superimposing personal desires on reality. Cf., for example, E. Colorni, "Libero arbitrio e grazia nel pensiero di Leibniz" [Free Will and Grace in the *Philosophy of Leibniz*] (1937 or 1938, now in Colorni 2009, p. 168).

[71]"Besides," as Piovene wrote about Colorni in 1944 (now in Gerbi 1999, p. 296), "even his own thinking predicted a decisive orientation against philosophy. He was against systems, and said that every system is nothing more than a collection of construction material."

is not surprising that a young man who is initially discouraged and suffering is then able, by degrees, to "take off." It is not so remarkable that, having been trained under the wing of a good institute of philosophy and influenced by the "insurgency," he would later use what he had learned for other purposes. Nor (given the times) is his militant turn so surprising — the reorganization of his life that took place in the early thirties, when the regime decided to intimidate and progressively suffocate — in parallel with the workers and public employees — the country's anti-fascist intelligentsia.

Instead, what literally astounds the observer is *the very high quality of his reaction*: the ability, the ingenuity, the incomparable drive, the surge, the edge[72] that he brought to his own life and which gradually emerged when he returned from Germany and moved to Trieste (in 1933–34). Eugenio discovered and set in motion numerous creative projects, both small and large, of a personal, intellectual and political nature that rapidly placed him "on another planet" with respect to his peers, even those whose careers were most similar to his own.

11. The amazement that all this sparks in us even today is the key element that in fact needs to be put (Colornially!) under the microscope. How was it possible, at such a dramatic turning point in history, for a young man of integrity and ability (who up to that moment had been committed primarily to learning to "philosophize") to suddenly write about politics in such a penetrating, perceptive, clear, and convincing way? How did he discover he could do it? How did he manage to get on the right track right away while carefully minimizing the inevitable mistakes? And at the same time, how was he able,[73] back in his Trieste days, both on a theoretical and autobiographical level, to devise the program of work that he would be able gradually to carry out during his years of confinement?

---

[72]"One of my ambitions as a writer," Piovene declared in 1945 in an issue of *Mercurio* dedicated to the Roman Resistance (cit. in Gerbi 1999, p. 239), "is to be able to somehow express that small part of him [Eugenio Colorni] that I was able to take in, given that his intellectual spark, his sheer impact, have unfortunately been lost along with his persona."

[73]To see this, one need only glance at the index of the present volume.

These are key questions that need to be asked looking in both directions — not only from Eugenio's youth to his maturity,[74] but also in reverse, which is anything but straightforward. There is probably a gnawing issue hiding behind Colorni's autobiographical writings. In all likelihood, I would suggest, in order to understand it it would be worthwhile to reread them à la Hirschman — that is to say, to relieve them a little of the psychoanalytic self-inquiry (which, as we know, "the Eugenio," as the Milanese would call him, was very fond of). Probably, to understand how things really were we would need to carefully re-evaluate Colorni's daily experiences in high school, at university, and as a graduate researcher as they appear in the fragments provided by those who knew him.[75] And we would then have to speculate and conjecture with a "possibilist" eye pointing to ways out and proposed solutions.

During his intellectual apprenticeship Eugenio was barely involved in politics, but he had long been a participant observer (and sometimes an actual participant) — generally lining up on the correct side. He had become aware of the many weaknesses, many contradictions (let's call them) in anti-fascism. So that when the moment arrived when he *felt he had to commit himself directly* (and that he could actually do so), he put what he had *already* understood to good use — he verified it and used it as the basis for new acquisitions.

In this, Colorni's "German" year was no doubt crucial — a year in which he had overcome many insecurities and seen that despite his somewhat hypochondriac tendencies, he was actually able to "move" quickly and effectively — much better than the young Ger-

---

[74]"We have not come to politics naturally," wrote Carlo Levi in 1933, "but almost reluctantly, because of the obligations of the times we live in." "Therefore," commented Sandro Gerbi (1999, p. 41) in reference to this passage, "no ivory tower, but a serious and total commitment, which developed in Colorni starting in his high school years thanks to a set of favorable circumstances that included his natural temperament, his solid cultural background, his entourage of anti-fascist relatives and friends, the trauma of the Matteotti murder, and later the influence of professors like Martinetti and Borgese." It a prime example of what Albert Hirschman called a "constellation of circumstances" that gradually pushed Eugenio in the direction of politics — which then, under the "obligations of the times," became "militant." All this is no doubt true. But is it enough to explain how things actually went? I have my doubts.

[75]Cf. below, Appendix A and Colorni 1998, II.

man social-democrats, who were at the time completely unprepared for the sudden (and ruthless) unfolding of historical events that they were experiencing on a daily basis.

It was as if two roads in Eugenio's life — philosophical and political — had suddenly switched places in terms of power. For reasons that were both professional and subversive, the two strands had evolved in parallel (and perhaps tortuously), side by side, observing each other in turn. Now the political one took precedence, but only in the heart of the protagonist, in the minutia of his daily life — while outside, in professional (and social) officialdom, none of this could ever appear.

As a result, however, the scientific side of his personality reacted by opening up to new knowledge (in psychology and natural science) and devising a program of work and study that would later develop in extraordinary ways.

It might at first appear that starting in the mid-thirties of the last century, one of the two great passions of Eugenio's life — the political and the theoretical — took over in turn from each other, one phase at a time. But a closer look reveals that this is not the case — that in the Triestine period he laid the groundwork for the theorizing that he would later develop while in confinement; that there, keeping his distance from most of the other detainees was consistent with the political debate in his own federalist circle and with the incredible daily battle he fought with the authorities[76] to get himself transferred to the mainland; and that the frenetic activity of the Roman Resistance did not prevent him — right to the end, as Guido Piovene has testified[77] — from obtaining scientific results that in the end (unfortunately) slipped through his fingers.

It must be understood then that during Eugenio's early adulthood it was precisely the interaction between his theoretical and practical passions that led him to acquire a remarkably fluid and mobile epistemological attitude and intellectual working style — nourished by doubts, reversals of point of view, inductive learning, resistance to any sort of systemic logic, etc. — in the daily search

---

[76]Colorni 2019a, p. 54–63.
[77]Piovene 1944; now in Gerbi 1999, p. 297.

for what he was looking for. It was a style that allowed him again and again to tackle this or that aspect of the issues he cared about, allowed him to identify openings and opportunities that could then be transformed into concrete and intellectual acquisitions, and allowed these latter to feed back and fortify his own adventure — in both what he wrote and what he did.

12. As Albert Hirschman would later argue in reference to development economics,[78] it was, in my opinion, this "turning point" between the two great phases of Eugenio's life that unleashed in successive waves his extraordinary energy and creative capacity on different levels — precisely because this "pivot" contained great energetic potential that had until that moment been unexpressed.

As regards political developments, his thoroughly trained critical-philosophical mind now fizzed and sparked as it grappled with a host of problems[79]: the Abyssinian war, political work in the context of fascism, spontaneity as a form of organization, teaching in Fascist middle schools, the creation of border posts, etc. — yielding a set of key articles that inaugurated the truly historical discovery of a mental inclination that Albert Hirschman would later give the name "possibilism" (concerning exit routes and proposals).

On a cultural level, Colorni's long dissatisfaction with literary and philosophical "convention" exploded into a merciless and radical critique. Eugenio was clearly aware of the responsibility of contemporary culture towards the collective political tragedy that now loomed following Hitler's accession to power.[80] This brought even greater force to his corrosive (and definitive) critique of the ubiquitous tendencies prevailing in philosophy and elsewhere (including the "concentric circles" critique I have chosen as an epigraph to this paper). It was no longer a question of seeking (or postulating) the system best suited to containing or organizing duly collected concrete facts, of taking one's place in Martinetti's inter-

---

[78]Hirschman 1958, 1961, and 1984.
[79]Colorni 1935a, 1936, 1937, 1937a, 1937b; now in Colorni 2019 ch. 1, 2 and 3; 2019a ch. 2 and 6.
[80]He prefigures, in fact, the rejection of the allure (and seductiveness) of German high culture that Wolf Lepenies (2006) would discuss later.

pretation of the history of philosophy as the research, creation and successive transcending of philosophical systems, or of looking for "the needle in the haystack" in the endless correspondence of Leibniz (which had long represented for Eugenio an oasis of serenity and intellectual compensation).

What was necessary instead was to leave to their fate the "satisfying" (calming, consistent, consoling) explanations that systems of every imaginable variety endlessly offer people — as a need of the human mind. Because this is vital to opening the doors to a valid cultural reconstruction that can only (and perhaps exclusively) come about through the acquisition of specific, carefully verified knowledge, through the study and systematic assimilation of disciplines that are sometimes overlooked (but often ignored), and also through further discoveries that need to be pursued with renewed energy.

Finally, at a practical level, Colorni sought a "moving imbalance"[81] between politics, research, work, and his personal and everyday life. And, with a circle of anti-fascist friends and acquaintances (evidently formed out of a widespread and growing impatience with the regime), he was so successful in this "acrobatic sport"[82] that he set in motion out of nowhere a small "high tide" in Trieste — thanks to an attitude that was "admirable as a way of conceiving political activity and of linking public and private life" which, as we now know, received (at the time as well as in retrospect) the unconditional appreciation of Albert Hirschman.[83]

13. So it was that out of this *Sturm und Drang* another person emerged. Eugenio's practical aim was to develop a double life —

---

[81]Cf. above, n. 9.

[82]"He was a dynamic man with a great zest for life," wrote Guido Piovene in 1945 (*Mercurio*, quoted in Gerbi 1999, p. 238), " — for this reason risk was for him not only a duty, but also a pleasure, almost an acrobatic sport."

[83]Hirschman 1987; now in Hirschman 1995, cap. 9. "The one who breathed new life into our [anti-fascist] group," wrote Bruno Pincherle (Rebeschini 2004, p. 89), "was Eugenio Colorni [. . .]. He was younger than the rest of us, more enthusiastic and better prepared as well, and above all more full of life. [. . .] It was thanks to him (and his brother-in-law Albert Hirschman) that new documents arrived from France, and above all a lot of propaganda material from the war in Spain (sent, moreover, in a suitcase with a false bottom that caused much anxiety); it was thanks to him that we returned to our debates, analyzing the situation in Italy and examining our relationship with the exiles."

official and unofficial.

On one side he launched into a professional and personal life that was above reproach but also extremely visible. He showed himself to be highly dedicated to study and to teaching. He married a beautiful woman (Ursula Hirschmann)[84] who enjoyed keeping up with him, and they moved in élite social circles. He enjoyed a rather enviable standard of living (subsidized by his mother), including a nice house, vacations, a box at the opera, tennis, etc. On the other hand, it was at this point that Eugenio gave full vent to his surprising political and intellectual iconoclasm.

Somewhat disenchanted with the Justice & Liberty movement, he became a socialist.[85] As such, he committed himself totally to semi-underground politics, examining, correcting and reworking many traditional ideas from the Workers' Movement, building his own unprecedented theoretical-practical "passion for the possible," wisely bringing together and orienting numerous anti-fascist intellectuals, and finally, drawing up his own program of intellectual work at a scientific level that appears (ex post) truly "Promethean," because it aims to overcome the cognitive limitations of high culture that have actually favored the (often unconscious) affirmation of Nazi-fascist dictatorships.[86]

14. It was thus an ingenious quest for an original but practicable direction in his life, a deliberate duplicity which, however, could not go unnoticed as time went on. Colorni suspected this.[87] Yet he decided to persist in his behavior — for moral and political

---

[84]"I fell in love," wrote Ursula (Hirschmann 1993, p. 146), "with his cheerful and irreverent way of attacking all the taboos and bringing into politics the full freedom of his cultural background. In this way, his political commitment did not diminish, but rather became stronger, losing its dogmatic security, but gaining immensely in vitality and imaginative possibility."

[85]This choice is generally considered to have been dictated by a social-political need for contact with anti-fascist workers. But we cannot exclude the possibility that his intellectual association with the J&L circles had also disappointed Eugenio — enough that he preferred to go it alone: the *chevalier seul.*

[86]It is from this, in fact, that the Ventotene dialogues (with Altiero Spinelli and others) emerged, along with the well-known "Project for a Journal of Scientific Methodology" (cf. below, chap. 8).

[87]Cf. his letters to Joseph (alias Giuseppe Faravelli) of August 1937 (now in Colorni 2019a, pp.79–97 passim).

reasons, on one hand, but also (probably) because there were no acceptable alternatives, and perhaps because (at first unconsciously but then with increasing awareness) he began with notable intelligence to exploit to his advantage the dark areas and inconsistencies of the Fascist apparatus of repression.

The truth is, as documents from the Central State Archive now show, starting from the beginning of 1936 the police were kept up to date on professor Colorni's political activities by two "spies," one from Trieste and the other from Paris — hired infiltrators. But it is also true that the police couldn't (then nor thereafter) prove the validity of their information to the judicial authorities without compromising the identity of their informers. And this allowed Eugenio to argue for years that he was being unjustly persecuted — even to some of the heavyweights of the regime.[88]

Looking at the different aspects of the story, we are left *breathless* in the face of Eugenio's numerous, unforeseeable, possibilist discoveries, prompted first and foremost by the need to oppose the regime (and also to "sell his skin at a high price"), discoveries that recur throughout his now adult and conscious experience in a wide variety of fields — practical, theoretical and personal.

It is this "qualitative leap" that comes to the forefront and dazzles the eye. A change of gear that had evidently been building behind the scenes in the previous years, which Eugenio himself would try to understand better introspectively,[89] and which would guide his choices, not only personal and political, but intellectual as well — on the one hand his interest in psychology and psychoanalysis, and on the other his accelerated learning of mathemat-

---

[88]Cf. Colorni 2019a, p. 54–63. "I knew him [. . .] at Ventotene," wrote Police Commissioner Marcello Guida of Colorni in a memorial of 19 March 1945 (cit. in Gerbi 1999, pp. 225–26), "where, even though we were on opposite sides, a tacit understanding developed between us, quite apart from other considerations. Colorni was an absolutely scrupulous person who never, for any reason, would have allowed himself to be contaminated by people who were not honest. When we met again in September 1943, he accepted my friendship and offered me his. We understood each other unreservedly [. . .]. Thus began a feverish period of secret activity for me, the details of which I omit for obvious reasons."

[89]Probably illuminating an examination of his childhood and education with a less than benevolent light — cf. below, Eugenio's autobiographical writings and the letter to Ursula of Dec. 28, 1938 (now in Colorni 2019a, pp. 108–09).

ics, geometry and natural sciences (physics above all) as a decisive contribution to understanding the methodology of science.

One cannot but note with a certain amazement just "how far," often beyond the point of understanding, *he dared to cast his penetrating gaze,* on both the cultural and the practical side — so as to leave no stone unturned, it might be added.

15. Thus, by degrees, the actual dimension of Eugenio Colorni's greatness reveals itself (indeed, in exploring it one never ceases to learn and discover more) — a revitalizing spring, whichever of the three final key periods of his life we focus on: Trieste (1933–38), jail and exile (1938–43), and the federalist and Roman Resistance period of 1943–44.

Understanding this trajectory requires not only that many aspects of the question be brought together, but that at the same time they be developmentally analyzed in detail, even given the impermanence and incompleteness of the situations that brought them out. This makes it clear that (toward the middle of the 1930s) Eugenio's plans actually began to work, that he began to find his footing on a political and intellectual level (at the same time), and that along with his circle he enjoyed a miniature up-swing that multiplied his own and others' efforts, and that this was halted by the authorities when Eugenio was arrested in the summer of 1938.[90]

---

[90]At the news of Colorni's arrest, his principal, Giovanni Quarantotti, jumped in and hastened to write to the Superintendent of Studies (in a confidential letter dated September 14, 1938) that yes, he knew that "Professor Colorni is of Jewish race and does not possess a membership card of the P. N.F. [National Fascist Party]. However," he added, "out of respect for the truth, I must frankly declare that in the three years that he has been in my employ, Professor Colorni has never offered me the slightest reason for complaint either in his political or moral conduct. "Only afterwards," wrote Diana De Rosa, 2004, pp. 125–28, "when in the following months the press took charge of the case painting the professor in dark colors as a dangerous character at the center of a Jewish anti-fascist plot against the State and organizer of clandestine anti-fascist centers, did Quarantotti realize the serious position in which Colorni found himself, and he opened an inquiry whereby, in defending Colorni, he also defended himself from possible or probable accusations of lack of vigilance. He informed the superintendent of the results of the inquiry [in a letter of 24 October 1938, in which he declared]: 'All twenty-three tenured teachers in service at this institute [. . .] have unanimously and jointly declared to me that on no occasion and in no public and attested conversation did Professor Colorni ever show feelings or intentions contrary to Fascist directives and doctrines [only one, Dr. Giovanni Buggeri, had affirmed that in con-

Closely assisted by Ursula, Colorni faced prison and confinement with great courage, trying to maintain his commitment to
making as much intellectual progress as possible. Moreover, while
confined to Ventotene, he unleashed a tireless campaign for the
reunification of his family and for his transfer to the mainland.

For a while, initially, he achieved good results intellectually. But
then he began to suffer serious bouts of depression. At the same time,
as we have seen, he engaged in dialogues and political debates[91] with
Altiero, Ernesto and Ursula that led finally to the *Ventotene Manifesto*.

Ursula gave him her support for a long time. But then she began (at first unconsciously, then in her heart) to lose touch with
Eugenio's Herculean efforts as he gritted his teeth and tried to proceed with his extraordinary (but for many observers abstruse) in-

---

versations with him Colorni had revealed himself to be 'anti-Fascist']. [. . .] In the autumn
of 1933,' the principal continued, 'when Colorni was assigned one of the teaching positions
in philosophy and pedagogy at this institute, it amazed me that he had been able to obtain
this tenured position without being a member of the P.N.F. I called him to my office and
explained to him how useful and expedient it was for him to apply for a membership card.
He very calmly replied that he had never belonged and did not wish to belong to any political party, since he was totally dedicated to his studies, and that in any case it was too late to
apply for a membership card without running the risk of being labeled an opportunist.' On
the other hand," De Rosa continued, "as witness to Quarantotti's extremely positive assess-
ment of Eugenio Colorni there are reports on his record for the school year 1933–34 and
1934–35 [written for Eugenio's period of provisional employment]. The first of these states
that 'Dr. Eugenio Colorni [. . .] is now completing his second year of non-tenured service. I
can only say that I am fully satisfied with the didactic and pedagogical activity he has carried out in this Institute during the current school year. Dr. Colorni is a very serious young
man, very studious and very intelligent. He has very distinguished manners, a calm and
balanced temperament and a firm character. He leads a very disciplined life and divides all
his time between school and home, though he is not completely estranged from social life
and the city environment. He loves school and teaches with great skill, warmth and confidence. He truly animates his students, knowing how to constantly stimulate their attention
and interest with nothing more than the fervor of an eloquent and precise presentation. He
asks questions with courtesy and patience and maintains good and constant discipline without effort. In judging his pupils he is always temperate, prudent and even-handed. With his
urbane manners, with the seriousness of his conduct and with the exemplary fulfillment of
all his scholastic duties he also exercises a remarkable educational effect on his students.'"
The praise goes on and on. Conclusion: even in light of the truly extraordinary essay "The
Function of the Teacher in Fascist Schools" (1937a; now 2019, ch. 3), one cannot help but
admire Eugenio's incredible composure.

[91]"I don't care about being cited or publicly remembered." Colorni wrote in his "Last
Wishes" of 3 May 1943 (now in Colorni 2019a, p. 150). "The only thing dear to me is the
thought that I will continue for a while to be a part of my friends' conversations — those
conversations which were perhaps the purest joy of my life."

tellectual work. This is reflected in the letters that Colorni wrote to his wife, which were initially full of ideas and bursting with energy, then much less responsive, and finally poetic, almost literary.

Even while enduring great hardships, then, Eugenio resisted "retreat," while Ursula (who could no longer truly understand him) drew further and further away. Their separation was painful. And yet in the end Colorni found the strength to get himself moving again in search of a new leap forward. This was the beginning of the road that finally led him to a second high tide in the making, the Roman period of federalism and resistance[92] — the first chapter in the people' s epic from which the Republic would spring.

III

16. Having nearly arrived at the key juncture of his life, Colorni[93] wrote in opening the "Bio-bibliographical Note" at the beginning of his editing of the *Monadology*, that "the rhythm of Leibniz's biography resonates far beyond the evolution of his concepts [. . .]. In the work as a whole the philosophical writings are not predominant, nor are they organic and systematic. They give the impression of having been written without a prearranged plan, almost in his spare time. And it was not only as a philosopher that he was known in his time; his fame as a mathematician and scholar at least equaled his reputation as a metaphysician. But precisely for this reason his biography is a necessary element for understanding his philosophy. [. . .] Its own fragmentary nature takes on a particular flavor from its connection with such a vast and heterogeneous world of studies and activities; every thought, every formulation is linked, even before its connection with other philosophical thoughts and formulations, with a concrete situation, a particular encounter, a precise and determined set of empirical circumstances. [. . .] Every piece of Leibniz's philosophical writing, it can be said, is occasional. His biography gives us the overall set of occasions that gave birth to his various ideas, the actual

---

[92]Cf. Colorni 2021.
[93]Colorni 1935, p. v.

historical and cultural soil from which the body of thought arose."

There is one thing the reader will already have understood — in the face of Colorni's extraordinary lessons, which take in many areas of life at the same time, I would appreciate it if, firstly out of respect, each specialized field would "lower its weapons," and also if (even though reasoning by analogy, and of course *mutatis mutandis*) social scientists of different disciplines — and I hope many will be involved — would keep in mind the caveats that Eugenio wanted to make plain with regard to Leibniz's work.

The fact is, the particular "chemical reaction" by which a simple middle school teacher of philosophy and pedagogy like Colorni achieved a leading role in both thought and action on the Italian and international scene certainly stemmed from his social position and education. It came out of the cultural intimacy he had reached with the work of Borgese, Martinetti, Croce, Kant, and Leibniz, from his personal and political experiences as a young man, from the tragic era he was living through, and so on. But it has not yet been truly understood.

17. Because in my opinion it is essential to reflect further on the surprise, indeed the amazement,[94] provoked by the existence

---

[94]Looking back, I wonder if his naïvely ingenuousness toward Croce (cf. above, n. 53) didn't already contain, in a nutshell, Eugenio's "possibilism of amazement." I was reminded of what Borgese wrote from New Ghiffa in October 1933 (Borgese 1934, pp. 20 and 22): "Croce tried for a long time to put the new wine of new ideas into the old wine skin of his system. In the end, the old wine skin of his system gave way." And again: "*The Essence of Aesthetics* [. . .] is an exquisite little book. It may be that even after much time has passed, we will gladly re-read it when we want to find a concise and representative document of late Romanticism — almost with the same pleasure we get when we re-read Horace and Boileau in order to understand and enjoy the neoclassical mentality in our own way." Once he had joined, with his *Critical Study*, the trend toward liberation from Hegelism orchestrated by Borgese and Martinetti, Eugenio's naïvety towards Croce was not simply what Albert Hirschman speaks of as a starting point (i.e. it's good to be naïve if you want to learn not to be naïve). In my view it takes on a different meaning. The fact of a young philosopher seeking dialogue with the great Croce already has in itself a disarming, non-confrontational flavor — it puts the old philosopher on the defensive (while it corresponds in a certain sense, as an attitude, to what Borgese would write with the plural *maiestatis*: "To Croce, then, with whom we were not adversaries, and whom it was wrong to treat as an adversary and even more wrong those who tried to collaborate in good faith on a common body of thought, we readily acknowledge the '*circonstances atténuantes*.'" 1934, pp. 21–22). At the same time, in analyzing *The Essence of Aesthetics*, Eugenio had

of a great Italian who lived his entire adult life under Fascism, learned to fight his own theoretical-practical battle with acumen and ingenuity, obtaining results that — indirectly through Albert Hirschman — have already significantly influenced the international intellectual and social world, and who now, with the translation of his texts, can do so directly, becoming a source of inspiration for the present and for the future. Understanding Eugenio is an essential part of learning (and teaching) a *modus operandi* which, through observation, doubt and discovery widens the field of the possible little by little and reveals the existence of a range of alternatives and possible choices that had previously been unknown — that we didn't even suspect could exist.[95]

And because — as I have learned from experience — we can make further progress in this direction only by putting ourselves in his shoes and identifying ourselves with Colorni through empathy. We can even do this through a series of "possibilist" exercises that might include: reconstructing in detail the concrete situations Colorni was in at certain given moments as a way of better understanding the choices he made; drawing from a set of his decisions (intellectual and/or practical) some logical thread connecting them; considering how he would have acted in the face of a different situation (his own and/or someone else's); using one or more of

---

already found the key by which he could "blow up" the entire edifice of the philosophy of his time; even if (probably) he did not fully realize it. It is this, in fact, that is so astonishing. Even though he was in step with his professors, at the same time he was not. A question found in a specific area of philosophical reflection (aesthetics), which at first sight seemed minor, would instead turn out to be decisive. Therefore, Eugenio learned very early on to fully exploit duplicity and intellectual ambiguity, which he then transferred (or had already transferred) to political plotting, and vice versa.

[95]Cf. Colorni 2019a. This statement, however, poses the problem of achieving a better understanding of the nature of his "possibilism." Partly for reasons of character, Albert Hirschman's was above all a "possibilism of words" — of a successful (stateless) intellectual: cautious, measured, worked out with patience and circumspection. Eugenio's, on the other hand, was a "possibilism of words and deeds" that opened up unexpected theoretical-practical vistas; a possibilism that could suddenly leave even the most sympathetic observer off-balance and perhaps even stunned — especially if the intention was to transpose Colorni's teaching from one era to another. My advice, then, is always to start with Hirschman (as we do, for example, at "A Colorni-Hirschman International Institute" in our International Conferences on Albert Hirschman's Legacy — 2018, 2019, 2020); but without ever ruling out drawing from Colorni. Because Albert and Eugenio were expressions, in different ways, of an extraordinary genius.

his stratagems for dealing with new realities; taking an interest in Einstein's way of working; referring to Albert Hirschman, who of Eugenio's entourage was the only one who really understood him (and followed — in part — his teaching).

In essence, it is a matter of patiently connecting Colorni with other subjects and with the objects both he and they are related to, of understanding the uneven advances of our "actor" on different fronts, and interpreting, in this context, the sometimes feeble signals coming in from different directions, and so on.[96] All this seems necessary for anyone who intends to examine (even briefly, as I will try to do now) the results of Eugenio's intellectual efforts in the nearly five years he spent in prison (in Trieste and Varese) and confinement (at Ventotene and Melfi).

18. He is known to have moved in a number of different directions at the same time. I will list them briefly by theme and outcome, but with the proviso that, as can be seen from his correspondence (for example, see n. 3 above), he often proceeded in reverse, jumping from one thing to another to distract himself, to enliven one research topic with another, and finally to "try out" an idea in one field that had perhaps popped up elsewhere.

For this purpose I will use the different existing sources — the collections of Eugenio's autobiographical, philosophical and political writings, the Ventotene dialogues, the letters to Ursula — almost like spinning a wheel, in an attempt to integrate his (more or

---

[96]Still, nobody's perfect. Even as a young man — as Guido Piovene has testified (1975: cf. Appendix A below) — Colorni had brilliant intuitions; but "his ideas would die out if he put them down on paper." And in effect even later on, his peculiar mix of philosophical culture and intellectual and political iconoclasm sometimes made his texts "difficult." Furthermore, as Eugenio wrote paradoxically to Ursula on 8 June 1939 (Colorni 2019, p. 124), "I can never manage to make a routine study of all the subjects of physics and mathematics, and I am always coming up with new ideas. I really need a period of sterility, to complete my preparation." Then again, as Hirschman told me at the end of the nineties, "Eugenio had too many ideas" — in the sense (perhaps) that he could not carry them out, bring them to completion. Finally, it is more than just regret to argue (in my opinion) that perhaps Colorni would have gotten away with it, if he had made himself understood a bit better and taken a few more precautions. This can be inferred from the reactions to his passing of the people closest to him — such as Luisa Villani, Ursula Hirschmann, Albert Hirschman, Altiero Spinelli and Ernesto Rossi (see Appendix A below). Reassuring moral: everyone must find the boldest (possibilist) step possible, but they must also tailor it to fit the case.

less) finished texts with various scattered insights and clues. The purpose, as I mentioned at the outset, is to "give an idea" (impressionistic as it is) of how, through multiple processes (sometimes systematic, while in other cases deliberately "disordered") and by thoroughly committing himself, Colorni managed to progress.

In brief: a) Aesthetics, and literary criticism in particular, were a field long favored by Eugenio. It makes sense that this would have a leading role during his imprisonment and internment, and as a subject in his dialogues with Ursula. In many of his letters to her Colorni in fact communicates his impressions of what he has been reading, from the great writers he often praises (Dante, Shakespeare, Goethe) to famous ones he severely criticizes, down to many minor texts he found in the small libraries of the system of repression. The result was a vigilant and unforgiving attitude towards any sort of self-satisfaction, any subordinating adaptation to the current state of affairs, and a critical attitude towards the submissive use of language — to the point of maintaining that writers should write for themselves, not for the cultural marketplace.[97] b) Politics is inevitably an undercurrent in much of the material examined, which often had to "pass" police censorship. We know in any case that Eugenio's democratic-federalist position was already present in the Trieste period, so that his participation in the discussions on European unity with Altiero Spinelli, Ernesto Rossi and Ursula Hirschmann at Ventotene undoubtedly rested on preexisting convictions. In addition, these debates, along with the "dialogues,"[98] represented one of the key moments in his life, because they probably opened unprecedented horizons at a general level (both political and intellectual) and because they allowed him to put his long-term thinking to good use, both for himself and for the small Ventotene circle.

---

[97]"First of all," wrote Alberto Cavaglion (2011, p. 96) "Colorni's sensitivity and skills as a literary critic should be re-evaluated [. . .]. On this point, Sasso's insight is quite enlightening, where he speculates that in the last period of his life Colorni would have been careful to give expression, 'in addition to his scientific side, to the literary vein that was in him; that with more determination he could have entered the world of fiction, which he had frequented since his youth.' Such a literary vein would warrant a specific study of its own."
[98]Colorni and Spinelli 2020; cf. above, n. 91.

It is notable, however, that beginning with the two letters to Altiero of May-June 1943,[99] Colorni began explicitly to develop a point of view of his own. He criticized Altiero's ideological drive and "fever for action," and argued for a (possibilist) focus on the actual way events developed, the careful testing of hypotheses, the need to concretely reiterate the European and world federalist perspective (under the new conditions that the course of the war was shaping), the possibility of influencing the political choices of the victorious great powers, and the construction of economic, social and political "magnets." Out of this rib, Eugenio would later develop his own universalist and socialist federalism.

c) How? Among the topics at Ventotene, one that began to come to the fore was the theme of love[100] — in interpersonal relationships, in treating others as they would like to be treated, in political action. We have seen that in his Melfi will this theme was singled out to his children as the most important experience in life. It would later come to its full development in the incredible, exciting episode of Eugenio the federalist and socialist, partisan of the Roman Resistance.

19. Even with all this in mind, however, we still need to examine the central core of Colorni's thinking in his confinement, which concerned philosophy, the sciences of the mind and the natural sciences (physics, biology, mathematics, geometry), and which led him (only seemingly paradoxically) to plan a journal of scientific methodology,[101] shortly before he went underground.[102]

---

[99]Now in Colorni 2019a, chaps. 3 and 4, Part III.

[100]Cf. Colorni 2019, ch. 2, Part II.

[101]"The project of the journal," — cf. below, ch. 8 — "whose publication was the subject of fruitless negotiations with the publisher Einaudi, was extensively discussed in all its particulars (structure, orientation, publishing house, collaborators, etc..) with Ludovico Geymonat, during the year of confinement in Melfi (1942) — the editorship was meant to have been entrusted to Antonio Banfi; the release was scheduled for the end of 1943" (Bobbio 1975, p. xxxiii; Quaranta 2011; Cerchiai 2009, pp. 173–75).

[102]In his "Last Wishes" of 2 May 1943 (now in Colorni 2019a, p. 150), Eugenio wrote: "I leave my manuscripts and scientific typescripts to Ludovico Geymonat. If he has the will and patience to use my puerile and incomplete notes to trace the main line of my research, and either make use of it as his own or transmit it to others, one of my most vivid desires will have been fulfilled." Why, then, do we still today not have a complete and intelligently annotat-

From Melfi, Eugenio wrote to Ursula on 10 May 1942 (and repeated, word for word, in the *Addendum to the Program* attached to the letter written for reasons of prudence by Ursula to Geymonat on Eugenio's behalf on September 17, 1942)[103]: "First of all I want to say that I conceive of the journal as having a very definite orientation — that is, a precisely set program and concrete arguments to be developed and advocated. What this orientation will be is difficult to set out in a few words, but it is very clear in my mind, and I'm sure that it fits completely with the concepts I recently read about in the article "Scientific Culture," published in *Philosophical Studies*. Briefly, the idea is to start from a "conventionalist" or "adequatist" conception of science, but rather than limiting it to the philosophical interpretation of scientific facts the way the Vienna School or even Gonseth does, to apply it instead to the basic concepts underlying the edifice of science and show how a rigorous clarification of the hypotheses implicit in the adoption of such concepts can effectively transform and further clarify many scientific formulations, and perhaps resolve some of the knottiest problems modern science faces. A radical challenge, then, to any "realist" or "finalist" position, and also to the facile and equivocal idealist interpretations of the "uncertainty principle" etc. An explicit recognition, rather, of the Kantian origins of such a viewpoint." A glance at the titles (and the number!) of the texts marked by an asterisk in the table of contents of the present volume, and then at the correspondence with Ludovico Geymonat[104] shows that Colorni intended to bring together in the journal numerous ideas about scientific methodol-

---

ed edition of the "manuscripts and scientific typescripts" of Eugenio Colorni? Why doesn't some young historian of science and philosophy try their hand at such a worthwhile task?

[103]Cf. Quaranta 2011, p. 130 and Colorni 2019, pp. 78–81.

[104]Quaranta 2011, pp. 126–30 and Colorni 2019, pp. 78–81.

ogy[105] taken from his work while in exile.[106]

This, moreover, is the chapter in Eugenio's story that more than any other has attracted the attention of specialists. In my opinion, however, it can only really be "probed" at a cognitive level within the framework of his experience and his cumulative decisions. Therefore, in order to avoid any philosophical esotericism, I would proceed by degrees, by successive steps. The confined Colorni was interested in Nietzsche — the only philosopher he was still able to read. He realized that the *pars destruens* of his reasoning was already present in this philosopher's work. But the *pars construens* was missing. That is to say — the contentious iconoclasm of Nietzsche was an end in itself; it did not point to a desired result. Our thoughts therefore turn to the many political, social, psychological, literary, cultural, etc. writings of Eugenio's examined thus far. To his senior partnership with Albert Hirschman in Trieste, to his disputation with Ernesto Rossi on economics, and to his long intellectual and political confrontation with Altiero Spinelli.

It is, in essence, a broad theoretical-practical construction in the making which, when observed carefully, suggests that it is pos-

---

[105]In fact, in his letter to Ursula of 10 May 1942, Colorni wrote (among other things) "I wouldn't favor starting to bring out anything on "*Philosophical Studies*." We need to keep what we have in reserve, so that we're not short of material when the time comes for the magazine [bi-monthly] to come out." Moreover, in the letter to Geymonat (through Ursula) of 17 September 1942 Eugenio insists on the key point that it must be "a journal of scientific methodology" and not a journal of simple epistemology. On the other hand, adds Ursula (for Eugenio), "Eugenio was in full agreement with Ludovico's evaluation of his abstracts. [. . .] He pointed to them as an indication of the direction in which he thinks the magazine should carry out its task" (Colorni 2019, p. 80; Quaranta 2011, p. 129).

[106]"All this," Geri Cerchiai has suggested (2009, p. 174), "would have found its own conceptual foundations in 'Philosophical Criticism and Theoretical Physics' and 'Philosophy and Science' [chaps. 5 and 7 of the present collection]. This program was meant to develop beyond the boundaries of a specific field and to embrace [. . .] the most varied areas of knowledge, and each field of science was meant to take advantage of the results progressively achieved in the others." "What we have to do now," Colorni argued in "Philosophy and Science" (cf. ch. 7 below), "is bring together these scattered elements and identify their common thread, proceeding systematically where up to now we have proceeded almost at random" and set in motion a real campaign against finalism and anthropomorphism. Not least for the reasons mentioned above (in ns. 96 and 102) Eugenio left behind a mass of writings, sketches, and notes, sometimes repetitive, some of which are collected here, which (to continue reasoning by analogy with what Colorni did in 1935 for Leibniz) would benefit from a careful project of "anthological exposition" — that is, of comparison, selection of salient passages, and thematic arrangement, in the context of a well thought-out review.

sible to build an even broader theoretical-practical horizon.

And philosophy? In philosophy, he argued, there was always a suspicion that beneath rational and empirical knowledge there was another deeper and more intimate kind of knowledge. Now, thanks to the new psychology, there was a criterion — the solution to an interior tangle — for recognizing whether this kind of knowledge had actually been attained. Observation of this type, which Eugenio compared to the discovery of electricity (partly to argue that we need to carefully determine its different fields of application), must be added to those that went before.

It is a point of view that allows the author to "turn to what man does" (Rossi-Landi), to draw on the history of scientific discoveries and devote himself to a critique of the metaphysical-finalist substrate of research.

For some time Eugenio had been interested in psychology and psychoanalysis. Already in Trieste, he had become increasingly passionate about this subject, and even about the idea of applying to himself what he was learning about it. This led to autobiographical insights that were later transformed at Ventotene into the essay that gives its title to this collection — "The Philosophical Illness," an introspective study designed to clarify how he had contracted the illness and how he finally managed to free himself from it (with the help of the poet Umberto Saba).

In his letters[107] he specifies that psychological studies are more important for healthy people than for those who are ill, that confessing one's own motivations in itself produces a cathartic effect, that it is possible to explore and keep under control parts of one's own unconscious, that the most profound type of knowledge is the type that passes through you and makes you blush (because it disproves preexisting ideas, which you are suddenly ashamed of), that psychologically an earnest commitment hides the fear of not being clean or the desire to know how your "toy" works, that by freeing yourself from psychological burdens you recover valuable energy that can be applied to other ends.

---

[107]Colorni 2019 and 2019a passim.

20. There is also, in Eugenio's letters to Ursula a curious sort of "Cliff's notes" for philosophy, constructed "on the fly" to help her with her exam.[108] In keeping with his style, Colorni aims to define specific contributions for each author, carefully avoiding systemic generalizations.

It is clear, however, that the beloved philosopher is Immanuel Kant and that Eugenio's ambition is to become a sort of "rebellious son" of Kant's (cf. below, chaps. 3 and 6: "Program" and "Apologue on Four Ways of Philosophizing"). Kant cast into doubt the canonical categories of space, time, substance, causality and number, showing that their nature is not objective — they are products of the mind, human projections on the surrounding world. But he was not able to recognize that such categories are simply tools and do not represent anything real — they do not constitute the necessary essence of our being.

In addition, Colorni argues, if Reality, Truth, the Universal etc. (absolute concepts written in capitals) cannot be known in themselves, it doesn't make any sense to continue talking about them as if this were possible.[109] It would be better to shift our attention to the ways or techniques by which man relates to things. This because, by adroitly and systematically taking charge of such methods in the most wide-ranging fields of application humanity can actually make progress.

"Philosophy today, rather than constructing pretty palaces out of paper-mâché [. . .]," Eugenio explains,[110] "should first of all examine the keys we already have — that is, the research criteria, the hermeneutic methods we have for grappling with reality and making it useful to us. By now it is abundantly clear that such criteria radically transform reality by forcing choices that let us see only

---

[108]Letter of 1 June 1939, now in Colorni 2019, pp. 70–72.

[109]"If regularity and harmony are not actual attributes of reality," Eugenio wrote, for example (cf. below, ch. 6), "but conditions that we impose on it, then you might argue that recognizing this will bring down the edifice of science and leave nothing in its place but brute randomness. What actually happens is the opposite. Once the origin of laws is understood, [. . .] we are inside the internal mechanism by which this regularity is projected into the world; [. . .] we hold in our hands the threads of the tangle from which this illusion originated and we control them."

[110]Cf. below, ch. 3.

what they are able to grasp. What we call reality is obviously conditioned not only by our senses, but by the entire set of forms, categories, and associative and interpretative criteria [. . .]. What we call reality is therefore neither subject nor object, but something that man, with his criteria and his categories, has played a big part in building — something that we, for ease of study momentarily regard as a fact standing in front of us, aware that in doing so we are placing before us something that we ourselves participate in."

21. This was the origin of Colorni's passion for the natural sciences, physics in particular and the theory of relativity.[111] From the examples of Descartes and Leibniz, wise philosophers who had no hesitation in offering their contribution to geometry and mathematics, and his study as an autodidact of the natural sciences, to which he dedicated an important part of his energy,[112] Eugenio reached radical conclusions about philosophy[113] and searched for an attitude of mind consonant with the cognitive needs of the present, not least

---

[111]On Colorni the specialist in the methodology and philosophy of science, see the by-now classic essay by Mario Quaranta. "The scholars who have studied Colorni's thinking," he wrote (p. 122), agree in recognizing the novelty of his methodological framework, such as the fact that his premature death interrupted a program of undoubted modernity (the critique of the idols of anthropology, the value of the method of Kant, the use of psychology in dissolving cognitive and moral absolutes, the value of the a priori in scientific knowledge, the distinction between scientific rationality and philosophy, between knowing and doing)."

[112]Mario Quaranta wrote (2011, p. 122) that Colorni "is the only Italian philosopher from the 1930s that I know of who moved from initially studying aesthetics (Croce, Ardigò, Bergson) and history of philosophy (Leibniz) to research on the theory of relativity [. . .]. He studied the theory of relativity seriously, delving into the study of mathematics; he corresponded with Nobel Laureate Louis De Broglie, with Giorgio De Santillana and others, to whom he made his work known."

[113]Guido Piovene wrote (1944; now in Gerbi 1999, p. 296): "I saw him again [perhaps in March 1939] "during a brief holiday from confinement that had been allowed to him for the birth of his daughter. He had begun his studies of mathematics and physics. He told me he hated philosophy and couldn't bear even to hear it discussed — he considered all of it the symptom of an illness. It was an extreme position that left me upset." It was "a position of rejection bordering on aversion" that came from studying Louis De Broglie's books on physics (cf. his letter to Ursula of 4 January 1939; now in Colorni 2019, p. 109–10) and perhaps the two texts by Bernhard Bavink (1944 and 1947), which he then translated. "Moreover, "commented Mario Quaranta (2011, p. 123), this anti-philosophical radicalism is the central theme of his masterpiece, the 'Dialogues of Commodus'" (now in Colorni and Spinelli 2020).

in order to proceed further along the road of discovery.[114]

An adequate exposition of the cognitive process advocated by Eugenio Colorni is obviously beyond the scope of this brief introduction.[115] Still less do I intend to deprive the reader of the pleasure of "getting a sense" of the different gnoseological aspects of the question and of the arguments by which, page after page, we feel Eugenio's enormous conscious effort to emerge from the "straitjacket" of the philosophical tradition. At the same time, I do think it is necessary to intuitively propose a small, oversimplified anticipation of these theses,[116] because it will help bring into even

---

[114]This marked the birth of Colorni the pioneer in the philosophy of science (Rossi-Landi 1953, Somenzi 1968): the origin was "free philosophizing" that allowed the transfer to a new field of research what had been learned in the original field (and vice versa). "Colorni's thought," wrote Alberto Santacroce (1975, p. 94) reviewing the collection edited by Norberto Bobbio, "is not only anti-fascist but above all anti-totalitarian in the widest and most positive sense of the term. In fact, it is in the rejection of forced rationalizations and optimistic syntheses that we can find the quality that made the young philosopher a natural and precocious opponent of any dogmatic prevarication." Therefore, according to Altiero Spinelli (1989, p. 179), he was a radical critic of a particular way of thinking which he called "forced" and considered "false."

[115]Norberto Bobbio (1975) and Geri Cerchiai (2009 and 2018) have done their own reconstructions of Eugenio's philosophical itinerary. Colorni, on the other hand, inevitably uses a language adapted to the philosophical culture of his time, so that to a non-specialist intellectual of today a number of his pages seem somewhat "indigestible." If, as I have always wished (and by analogy what Colorni tried to do for Leibniz), one were to allow access to his extraordinary theoretical output to a wider audience, a careful work of translation of Eugenio's endpoint (however temporary) would be necessary — a translation perhaps produced by the collaboration of scholars of different backgrounds (humanistic, natural scientific, and social). In other words, it seems to me that my aspiration to a full-fledged "Colorni for everyone" (Meldolesi 1998) has yet to be achieved.

[116]We are very well aware, Eugenio would have said, speaking colloquially (and accessibly) to the young Roman anti-fascists (federalist and/or socialist) in the last year of his life, that our perceptive capacities could be less than they are (as in the unfortunate case of the blind) or greater (as those of the scholars of the Academy of the Lynx are supposed to be — since the lynx, the mythical animal referred to, would have seen better and farther than women and men). We perceive colors and sounds only because we have eyes and ears. But it doesn't even cross our mind that these things and the world around us (as we know them) would not exist without us. That the mental constructions we associate with that world are not independent of us. That reality, in and of itself, does not exist. . . . Conclusion: if instead we think about all this, we realize that these simple observations conceal great cognitive and transformative potential. This is because, generation after generation, human desires and beliefs have constructed an intellectual environment and narrative that may turn out to be wrong. Because the error in any one of its aspects can be identified and corrected — so as to free unexpected human energies, make powerful discoveries, and generate another and less peculiar environment (and narrative), which in turn can be challenged on one point or another; and so on. It is only a gateway, as limited and partial as you want it to be; yet it was

sharper focus the problem I have been trying to evoke.

For Colorni, "knowing" a specific object means knowing how to master it through processes of dismantling and reconstruction. The object is not separable from the subject. This latter creates around them an interpretation of the surrounding world that in any case includes the "deeds and misdeeds" that they encounter, one by one, in daily experience.

This representation is therefore defined by a series of concepts belonging to the subject. If we say that time passes, we are obviously referring to the passage of hours announced by our cuckoo clock. If we say that the size of an apartment is a certain number of square meters, it is because it has been accurately measured. In both cases we have the idea of an exact quantity that can easily be checked.[117] Einstein and his theory of relativity — space and time actually being "curved" by the gravitational force of celestial bodies — never enters our minds.

For Eugenio, on the other hand, Einstein demonstrated the Kantian thesis of the attribution to humans — that is, the anthropomorphism — of concepts such as these (along with causality, substance, number, etc.). Hence the need for a close dialogue between literary-philosophical and mathematical-scientific knowledge that would allow the continued pursuit of such a promising path.

Because, as Colorni explains, whenever humanity manages to identify the anthropomorphic aspect of part of its representation of reality and truly masters it, it derives great benefit thereby. This is where the reasoning, often implicit, behind so many discoveries came from. This is what gave rise to his need — omnipresent in the last years of his life — to be always on the alert for anthropomorphism (and also automorphism). This was the source of the advice to restrain our senses (put them in a state of watchful waiting) in

---

enough to intrigue the young Roman anti-fascists and make them think.

[117]In the same way that before Copernicus, Galileo and Kepler it was believed (following Ptolemy) that the world was flat and the sun went around it. These are ideas that are still with us as expressions — for example, when Pope Francis claimed to "come from the end of the earth," or when meteorologists talk of sunrise and sunset, of the sun going up or down. . . . Not to mention the Aristotelian-Christian vision of the late Middle Ages that has led us even now to speak of being "in seventh heaven," or use expressions like "prime mover," "celestial vault," "empyrean," etc.

order to try to grasp as much as possible how things actually are. And to engage in a struggle with oneself to get rid of points of view, conceptions, ways of seeing, etc. which, initially acquired to account for some aspect of what surrounds us, have instead become a serious impediment to understanding it.

Eugenio thus believed that human beings, starting with those who are most enterprising, by wisely and intelligently setting in motion diverse yet interactive forms of knowledge, would be able to usher in an era of accelerated invention and technological progress — with important consequences for their concrete living conditions, and their own future prospects (and vice versa).

It is a point of view in a certain sense similar to Carlo Cattaneo's "civilizing," which also appears in Colorni's political theses and which today seems incredibly topical. Indeed, it takes but a moment's reflection to intuit its meaning in the conflict-ridden world we live in today. The great resurgence of nationalistic rivalries, though dangerously present in various parts of the world, has not yet degenerated into open conflicts. Thus far, autocratic impulses (reactionary, dictatorial, communist and fundamentalist) have not succeeded in overpowering liberal democracies with market economies. The re-establishment of hierarchies underway in many areas and dimensions of life is finding various stumbling blocks in its path. Economic, military, civil, and religious oppression, though widespread, is seemingly hampered by important counter-trends.

Which is to say that negative impulses, reminiscent of humanity's violent past, coexist today with contrary tendencies — from research in every field to open innovation, from concern for the environment to the liberation of individual and social energies, from the processes of development to those of justice and democratization that now touch all of humanity, from the enormous connectivity and reduction of distances to the immense growth of the desire to gain knowledge and to know each other, area by area, country by country, etc.

If we jump back in memory to the conditions of the war and the postwar period we can get an idea of the great changes that have taken place and bring into focus the Colornian problem facing us today — that of implementing a series of possibilist imbalances that might even be staggering (small and large, local and general), which at a technological, cultural, political and social level would reverse negative tendencies, encourage actors of all kinds in the drive (spontaneous and cultivated) toward civilizing humanity, create hope and purpose, facilitate progress, attract the interest of others (the famous magnet effect), and in this way begin to master and gradually tame the dangerous trends we are currently witnessing.

To open the way to the future.

IV

22. Colorni's is a story of thought and action which, after a pioneering volume of many of his *Writings* edited by Norberto Bobbio (1975)[118] followed by a long period of amnesia,[119] began finally to be told, with the re-publication of many of Colorni's philosophical and autobiographical texts by Geri Cerchiai (2009) along with the three 2009 conferences, organized under the auspices of the Presidency of the Republic, that marked the centenary of Colorni's birth.[120]

And yet, because of its extraordinary theoretical and practical importance, it still calls for a substantial cultural commitment, at both the national and international levels.

It was in this way that studying Colorni's life and work from different angles (biographical-epistolary, political, cultural, philosophical, etc.) in the end gave me the idea of launching a small series of books of Colorni's texts both in Italian and in English.[121] On both the Italian and American sides, what now remains is to

---

[118]Unlike what happened in the period right after the war thanks to Ludovico Geymonat, Vittorio Somenzi, Giuseppe Vaccarino and the magazines Aretusa, Analysis, and Sigma (cf. Cerchiai 2018, Appendix), the (still partial) collection of Colorni's writings then became the object of a protracted project initiated by Ferruccio Rossi-Landi — so that much later (1975, p. xxxi n. 12) Norberto Bobbio could state that Rossi-Landi had published in 1952 "the only (to my knowledge) critical and interpretive essay on Colorni's thought," which he had to take into account in his well-known introduction to *Writings*.

[119]Interrupted only by the volumes of Solari 1980 and Colorni 1998.

[120]AA.VV. 2010, 2011a and 2011b.

[121]I refer here (on one hand) to Colorni 2016, 2017, 2018 and Colorni and Spinelli 2018 published at Soveria Mannelli by Rubbettino editore, and (on the other) to Colorni 2019a, 2019b, 2020, 2021 published in New York by Bordighera Press.

conclude the discussion (temporarily, of course) by focusing on Eugenio's original theoretical-philosophical work; or rather on the part of it that is not included in the *Ventotene Dialogues*.[122] More than as an end in itself (as philosophers say), my intention has been to reconsider it, this work, in close association with the many aspects of the question that have been mentioned so far.

The present volume thus contains in essence some of the principal autobiographical and philosophical texts written mainly (but not only) in the period of Colorni's imprisonment and confinement, when his aim was a direct confrontation with some of the frontiers of knowledge of his time — through scattered notes of autobiography and psychology, through the methodology of the natural sciences and the battle against anthropomorphism and teleology, and through seemingly minor forays into economics, politics, and the social sciences in general that would in fact pave the way for the work of Albert Hirschman.

But in the light of what I have written up to now, a note of caution must be added. Disciplines, by their nature, tend to "break things up" according to pre-drawn lines that are strictly observed. Here again, many critics have thought it possible to study a scientific facet (of aesthetics, philosophy, psychology, mathematics, physics, economics, etc.) that belongs to their own discipline, independently of the political (and socio-historical) dimension, or vice versa — not understanding that, even in a polarizing way (as seen above), the one is linked to the other, one feeds off the other. In essence, they have at times unwittingly fallen into an anthropomorphic procedure that transfers the researcher's limitations onto the object studied (instead of making an effort to personally bridge such limitations, especially the practical ones). The choice has been to work as if this problem didn't exist. With all due respect for the contribution of each, I disagree. And I hope that my own work may be useful to those who wish to reverse this trend, perhaps "cutting" their work with a mix of disciplines, and with original, or at least unusual, rationales and boundaries.

To conclude.

---

[122]Cf. Colorni and Spinelli 2020.

a) His great breakthrough in thought and action in the early thirties potentially freed Eugenio of the philosophical illness (in the sense that from then on he would be able to gradually get rid of it) — that is, it freed him from subjection to the gilded world of ideas, from the constraints within which his professional philosopher's reasoning had inevitably been forced to evolve.

But it obviously did not uproot him from the Italian and European culture he had grown up in as an intellectual. On the contrary, it seems reasonable to suggest that in his great quest (as Ursula Hirschmann put it) he had set in motion a mental process of profound review and reconsideration that his brief life did not allow him to finish.

This is an attitude that emerges repeatedly in his letters — expressed mainly through his impatience with his Profession (with a capital p). And yet, if I am not mistaken, it did not touch his wide-ranging cultural curiosity, even those aspects of it that remained from his youth. Perhaps because he did not feel any need that it should. Because in his surprising innovations he made use (more or less consciously) of a friendly "cultural breeding ground" that was European and international, even as it was Italian and federalist.

b) Indeed, his polemic against nationalism is decisive in this regard. Unlike its powerful neighbors, Italy did not have behind it (and does not have to this day) a consolidated national philosophical tradition. Not least through imitation, our country tried to put together such a culture during the post-Risorgimento and Fascist periods — through the work of Bertrando Spaventa and Giovanni Gentile. But this was precisely the approach that Eugenio abhorred, even as he invoked, often *incidentally,* the best of Italian philosophical culture both present and the past.

c) I learned in this regard (Esposito) that this latter culture had ended up overflowing, through a sort of cultural federalism before its time, into Leibniz himself. This helps explain Eugenio's youthful choice, encouraged by a constellation of circumstances (the influence of German philosophy, Martinetti's proposed solution, and professional opportunity, of course, but also the logical development of his own research).

Which goes to show that even while surrounded by nationalist philosophies, his intellectual leanings pushed him in an entirely different direction — that of federalist harmonization among different realities. This is already one root of his originality.

d) All this gives us a glimpse of Eugenio's universalist message. And the sense of our own cultural efforts, which cannot be allowed to spring only from a position above the fray — where we just pick the best flowers of Western cultures. Our enterprise needs to take root "somewhere" not least so that we can reinterpret in our own way the work of Hirschman (who, let us not forget, habitually used 4 or 5 languages at the same time).

Colorni bequeathed to us not only a great personal contribution[123] that arose in the North (in Milan and Trieste with contacts in Germany and France) and later matured in the hothouse of the culture and socio-political problems of the Center and South (at Ventotene and in Melfi and Rome). He didn't just offer us a general federalist-democratic political perspective that relied on civilizing magnets.[124] He also gave us the possibility, setting out from a peripheral location[125] (Italy and Southern Italy), to reshape (for ourselves and for everyone) his and Albert Hirschman's ideas starting from the best of the "Bel Paese's" culture from different periods,[126]

---

[123] Without which the small movement we belong to would not even have come into existence.

[124] Meldolesi 2019a and 2021.

[125] Eugenio wrote, for example, in May 1943 (now in Colorni 2019a, p. 159): "Europe today is not an undifferentiated mass such that a unifying center could be indiscriminately created just anywhere. These centers exist in well-defined places, visible to all. We need their backing if we do not want to fall once again into nationalistic particularism or empty utopianism. In the Europe of today, Italy has a strange, peripheral position, which can nevertheless be decisive for unification." Am I wrong in thinking that, in addition to Europe, this democratic federalist angle is useful today for different regions and continents, and for the whole world?

[126] German and Italian culture (and more generally, German and Anglo-Saxon on one side and Latin on the other) have deep and ancient roots (and have not evolved on the same plane for a long time). Their meeting/clash in certain subjectively and objectively favorable conditions can be particularly fertile — in the sense that each subject starts spontaneously from what it has (or can have) but then moves, in successive bursts, towards what it lacks. In a general sense, for Eugenio and Albert, who moved in reverse directions (as in, on the one hand, bringing a certain order to problems, "breaking out" of the old shell and developing free thinking in various directions, and on the other, the creative use of this point of view and its progressive refinement) this is how things actually went. And what is more, the turning point in Trieste — when the relationship really took off on different levels and both were "on top of the world" — remained unforgettable in both their memories (Meldolesi 2010).

That said, it is nevertheless clear that we are looking at two very different bodies of work. The one, Albert's, is very well-structured and complete, while the other, Eugenio's, is marked to put into play concrete experiences that are out of the ordinary, and to promote both of these steps world-wide, so as to encourage others to do the same in a planetary phase that seems to be in dire need of it — intellectually, practically and morally.

Luca Meldolesi

A Colorni-Hirschman International Institute — Roma[127]

APPENDIX A: TESTIMONIAL EXCERPTS

Colorni was convinced, without being drawn into Freud's circle, that philosophy must be traceable to psychology — for this reason he enjoyed conversing with everyone he came across, especially with artist-psychologists, who seemed to him more useful than professional philosophers [. . .]. Our conversations and reading were sustenance during the nightmare of underground life. The official in hiding, the American or English prisoner, the incriminated journalist, the partisan — all took turns at the same table as if in some strange tavern. The dinner companion of the previous evening often had been arrested, sometimes killed. The reading was interrupted by the voice of Radio London. But this very fact gave our conversations an intensity, almost a nervous charge. Opinions were sharper, as between people who want to talk in depth, in a few hours, without wasting time.

— Guido Piovene, *Portrait of Eugenio Colorni,* 7 June 1944

---

by destiny and fragmented — very different depending on the circumstances and subjects it is addressing (so much so that the critics have long been able to proceed in two different directions — philosophical on one hand and historical-political on the other). It makes sense, in my opinion, to identify the internal connections within each, and to look at one through the eyes of the other, in a certain sense to re-position one with respect to the other (and vice versa). But any attempt to synthesize or actually go beyond this would be truly unforgivable. On the contrary, the purpose of our Institute is to show the multiplicity and richness of their cultural and cognitive interaction, to encourage the free inspiration that can be drawn from them to move in different directions, and to suggest, in the end, further horizons inspired by observation, doubt and discovery — and therefore by the possible.

[127]For discussion and comments, I thank Mario Quaranta, Vinni Marino, Adriano Scaletta, Max Leone, and of course Nicoletta Stame.

Any outsider who witnessed the heated discussions at our [Socialist] Youth Federation meetings would have noticed that one name was repeatedly on everyone's lips. Whatever the topic, that name cropped up, sometimes as a question, sometimes as a request for advice, sometimes as a confirmation of being on the right track. [. . .] The name was Angelo. And in truth Angelo is still with us. The papers might have reported in the obituary columns on the heroic death of Prof. Eugenio Colorni. Words may have been written and spoken extolling his exceptional character as a man, a philosopher, and a scientist. Ceremonies may have taken place in his honor, streets and scholarships named after him. All Italians can count him among their great departed. But Angelo is ours.

There came a day when Eugenio Colorni put aside his already famous name. It was the day when he sprang into action — the 'day of courage' as he himself called it. Free of all ties to the past, ready for whatever the torrid time that was about to begin would bring, he became Angelo and appeared among us. So simple, so spontaneous and total was this gesture of his that many of us didn't know until the last who this man was, radiating strength and goodwill, who 'captured' us so instantly and almost magically, and without imposing himself or taking command, swept us along in his wake and toward his idea.

He went into action after September 8, committing himself to the task of military organization in the different zones. In one rendezvous after the other he made contact with all those who felt the struggle was a necessity. Even in organizational work, he found a way to initiate people into political life, helping them clarify their ideas and put them in order. Without any premeditated plan, young people who wanted to contribute to the resumption of Italian political activity both through practical action and intellectual energy tended more and more to gravitate towards him. The natural consequence was that these individual interviews turned into actual lessons, which Angelo organized with some of his better-prepared comrades, and which he firmly wanted to continue — until the rush of events forced everyone to more immediate duties. This well-trained group of young people laid the basis of our

Youth Federation, and Angelo, who had become editor of *Avanti!*, continued to be their spiritual and political guide. In this feverish activity Angelo did not spare himself. When we think back to the many and not always necessary risks he exposed himself to on a daily basis, we are overcome with remorse for not having stopped him from giving all of himself with the impulsiveness that comes only from great courage.

> — Luisa Villani, *The Socialist Revolution* 1, 14 June 1944

I've just now read in the Roman newspapers that the Nazi-Fascists, a few days before leaving the capital, even gunned down Eugenio Colorni. Now is not the time for commemorations, but it is impossible for someone like me, whose life has for twenty years been in many ways intertwined with his, not to say something. They killed him in the breach, while he was on his way to an underground meeting to recruit patriots in the "Matteotti Brigade." He died without saying a word, so as not to betray his comrades. In him Italy has lost a young man of exceptional worth. We, his friends, have lost an irreplaceable brother. And there is still something else to say. And that is that Eugenio went consciously to his martyrdom, simply carrying out his duty.

> — Paolo Treves, *Radio Londra,* 22 June 1944

"It is pointless to describe to you what I feel — it is a great pain and a great loss." "I can think of nothing else. I have the feeling that the wound this has caused me will only grow. It is only now that I realize what a fount of hope Eugenio still represented for me — what an example, what an idol I had."

"I lacked the imagination I should have used to help him, to prevent him from exposing himself, and at least to find a way to see him again."

> — Albert Hirschman *Letters* to his wife Sarah,
> 22 and 25 June 1944.

"I am completely broken by the news of Eugenio's death."
"A large part of any interest life held for me is now lost. I now

see how much faith I had in him."

— Albert Hirschman, *Diary*, 23 June 1944
(Excerpts quoted in Adelman 2013, p. 231).

In the last months I happened to meet [in Rome] Eugenio Colorni, who had been the greatest friend of my youth. He had just emerged from years of jail and persecution. By day he was always on the move — he often came by my place in the evening and at night. [. . .] We passed many hours talking and reading manuscripts to each other. I could not penetrate the field of physics and mathematics, which was where perhaps the most remarkable part of his speculation was focused — we met in the field of psychology, where his conversation was truly illuminating. Colorni was a true revolutionary, and this was the source of the fascination he exerted on those who approached him — but at the same time he had a balanced mind, thanks in part to his physical energy. [. . .] His law was intellectual courage, beginning with the continual, uninterrupted destruction of ourselves, and of any law under which our hope for peace and quiet seeks refuge. His acumen was implacable in pointing out in mental attitudes the vestiges of selfishness and habit. He said that great scientific discoveries came through the destruction of an anthropomorphic and egotistical law that we impose on the universe to make it similar to ourselves — and that the same thing happens in the field of morality. In the hours spent by his side I felt all the falsehoods, the settled truths, going up in smoke within me — I became nothing, just an active brain. But this destruction of his had a vital quality — it had the effect of a tonic. Instead of tearing you down it brought strength and optimism.

— Guido Piovene, *Non furon tetri*, 1945

Eugenio was born in Milan into a family of that literate and patriotic bourgeoisie that from Daniele Manin to Rosselli had a tradition all its own. Mazzini, who knew them well, once wrote that such Jews constitute an Italian province in themselves, without a territory. The climate of these families, which Eugenio grew up in, is in some ways Protestant. There is almost no remaining trace of the old religion or of observance. What remains is a moral rigor, something

spare and upright, that makes the sons of these people so similar, in their virtues and limitations, to certain men of the Risorgimento.
— Paolo Milano, *Italia libera*, New York, 1 July 1944

Like all original spirits, he had in him at the same time a child-like innocence and the intransigence of a destroyer of idols.
— Giuseppe Saragat, *Avanti!*, 29 May 1945

He was ready to let himself be permeated by a thought and to experience it by inhabiting it, with empathy, so that he could take hold of it. And then sometimes he would turn it around and transform it "into something rich and strong," in Shakespeare's words. If I think of a disconcerting and miraculous intelligence, capable of absorbing even superstition, astrology or magic and transforming them into an original treasure, I think of Eugenio Colorni.
— Guido Morpurgo-Tagliabue, *Ricordo di Colorni*, 1945

Still today, of the large group of students who followed me during my teaching years, I wish to remember and present to the memory of all only one: Eugenio Colorni.
— Giuseppe Antonio Borgese, *Problemi di estetica e storia della critica*, for academic year 1951–52

I will tell you about Eugenio — more than about myself — because I know he loved storytelling, and he surely would have done it himself if he hadn't happened to die. I would venture that I can talk about him better than others because he and I had one thing in common that we held onto right to the end, even though everything else, our life together — with all our continuous searching and not finding — ended badly. Eugenio would have smiled, for example, at the hagiographic mystification in the way anti-fascism and the resistance are now spoken of. With all his smiling contempt for heroism, with all his breathless and unhappy but not entirely useless searching, he freed himself from pomposity, and from any hint of double-talk. He left his comfortable home with its antique chests of drawers for a cold rented room; his bourgeois fiancée for a liaison with who-knows-who; his assured career for an adventure of the spirit; he said he was anti-fascist and he was; he talked about revolution and he conspired for it; he laughed in the face of death and he died a hero. Most of all, his story deserves to be written to remind us that the most moving quality of the hero is always innocence.

> — Ursula Hirschmann, *Rievocazione Incompiuta* [Unfinished Commemoration], mimeograph, Rome 1963, from the Italian

Thanks to his mother's hospitality, his university classmates often met at the Colorni residence to talk politics. Eugenio "tended to bring together those who displayed an instinctive aversion to fascism without clear reasons. He let them talk, and little by little changed their repugnance into motivated opinions. Not pushing too hard, speaking as equal to equal, recommending readings [. . .]. The discussion would have the tone of an intellectual and almost academic joint research project, with no one dominating anyone else." Eugenio "already had brilliant insights." But "his ideas would fade away if he put them on paper. They came to life when he spoke. He possessed the ability to guide others in expressing complex ideas so that they were free of inconsistencies and defenses, and exposing their plain and inevitable extreme logical consequences. But perhaps this would not have been possible without a more fluid element that served as a carrier — an intimacy [. . .] a confidence that brought everyone to accept painful conclusions and demolitions. The emotion flowed fervidly, without limit or mercy, toward courageous thinking and clarity of mutual understanding. None of the meetings were gloomy or even too serious, and tension was often dispelled in laughter."

> — Guido Piovene, *Le furie,* 1975

Anyone who knew him as I did [. . .] at Ventotene might easily have concluded that Colorni was an intellectual absolutely incapable of practical action. He was continually in spiritual crisis. Every day he wanted to re-examine every problem over again, for the fear that his thinking would crystallize into well-defined categories, that it would settle into some comfortable system. It could be said that he loved the search for truth more than truth itself. For this reason he often assumed a contradictory position in political discussions, even if this led him to contradict both of the opposing positions at the same time. He made true friends this way, he was well-liked by everyone for his goodness and selflessness, but he didn't join any of the groups formed by the internees by membership in political parties. Shortly before he left Ventotene, Eugenio told the socialists that he had worked underground as a socialist and still considered himself one of theirs. [. . .]. After his transfer to Melfi he was able to maintain clandestine postal contact with the federalist friends he had left behind at Ventotene until mid-May of 1943, when he escaped from Melfi and resumed his outlaw life in Rome [. . .]. After that Colorni showed that he was a different man from the one we had known.

— Ernesto Rossi, *Eugenio Colorni,* 1975

He had the purest heart. One night during the underground struggle he confessed to me that for him the problem of physical fear was acute — although this did not stop him from doing his duty to the fullest. One day on the Colle Oppio [in Rome] I handed over a package of dynamite to him. I told him what it was and what he was risking. It was perfectly clear that he was afraid. He took the package without a moment's hesitation and walked away. I watched him and realized that with each step he was fighting and overcoming his fear. He carried out the action perfectly. If there is a gold medal of the Resistance that was earned the hard way, it is his.

— Sandro Pertini, *Eugenio Colorni,* 1978

An accurate perception of the nature of Colorni's itinerary [. . .] is impossible without an effort to see the way his journey also reflects his spirit in dealing with other things as well and, more generally, with life — a spirit constantly affected by strong moral tensions, which thus held him to a rigorous standard; a spirit that was reflective, problematical, investigative and introspective, and at the same time directed toward a coherent personal commitment to action; an anti-dogmatic spirit, iconoclastic and anti-conformist in every way, but not from a proud desire to be contradictory so much as out of a love of truth, an urgent need to get to the bottom of everything, to explore new pathways "in search of the new" — a spirit irreducibly devoted to the idea of freedom not only because it is necessarily driven by a conceptual construction but, above all, by a natural inclination to respect the way others feel and think.

— Leo Solari, Eugenio Colorni, 1980

In the summer of 1927 I was invited to spend a whole month at the villa at Forte dei Marmi, and for me it was an unforgettable month of beach life, tennis, readings and interminable discussions late into the night for two 19-year-olds who had common interests in politics (Zionism and anti-fascism) and philosophy (Croceanism, at the time), and more generally in aesthetic tastes. The generous hospitality of the Colorni family put guests completely at their ease. The "Forte," not yet disfigured by building speculation, appeared marvelous to me on summer mornings with its long wooden pier jutting out into the blue sea, with the profile of the Apuan Alps silhouetted in the background, and an immense white beach dotted with a few scattered cabins. In one of them, with his family, towered the bulk of the philosopher Gentile, whom the Colorni family and Eugenio, a student of philosophy, knew but did not associate with.

— Enzo Tagliacozzo, L'uomo Colorni, 1980

Stirred by a demon that was somewhere between Socratic and Mephistophelian, he was keen to uncover the unconscious deep motivations behind every type of behavior in himself and everyone he knew, especially his friends — to bring these into the light of day, to proceed to demystify and most likely modify behavior that until then had been accepted as normal, to demolish the satisfied and uncritical acceptance of one's self, one's beliefs and values, one's own rules of life. In doing this he was not motivated by skepticism, but by the desire that he himself and others should as much as possible abandon certainties that were rooted in the mysteriously shifting sands of our unconscious, and aim to reach others founded on the rock of conscious awareness.

— Altiero Spinelli, Eugenio Colorni, 1984

What fascinated me [about Eugenio and his friends] was the fact that a mental orientation free of ideological commitments was intimately bound to a commitment to an extremely dangerous form of political activity. But it was precisely in this spirit of experimental curiosity that Colorni and his friends faced the philosophical, psychological and social questions that spurred them into action in situations in which freedom of thought was under attack or in which the injustice was obvious and the stupidity intolerable.

— Albert Hirschman, I, 'Detective' of the Fascist Economy,
Laurea Honoris Causa in Political Science,
University of Torino, 12 November 1987

APPENDIX B: A COLORNIAN DECALOGUE *À RETENIR*

1. What we have is an intellectual style, a construction of ideas based on an "essential appraisal" between past and present, between the humanities (above all philosophy) and the natural sciences (especially physics); one that should be extended, in my opinion, to the social sciences and, more generally, to every area of life.

2. Its starting point is a "conventionalist" conception of knowledge based on the five senses and on the forms, categories and associative and interpretative criteria that we use (in science and consciousness, without realizing it), "without which it is not possible for us to attempt or pursue anything."

3. In particular, under the pressure of historical circumstances Colorni identified his point of view by maneuvering between his initial subject, philosophy (Kant, positivism, idealism, irrationalism) and those that followed: physics, mathematics, geometry, psychology and psychoanalysis.

4. He argued for abandoning the use of capital letters as a way of progressively dethroning the anthropomorphic "idols" of con-

temporary views of the world (Space, Time, Causality, Number, Reality, Truth, etc.) in order to gradually achieve new, specific cognitive acquisitions. Knowing for Eugenio is taking possession of a certain phenomenon (human, natural, social, etc.) — it means knowing how to break it down and reassemble it so it can be used for one's own ends.

5. Women and men can never get outside themselves, even in the process of cognition. But the refutation of some aspects of their own theory of knowledge allows them to simultaneously acquire new ways of seeing and therefore new types of mastership. For this reason, it is necessary to question past knowledge relentlessly in the light of the developmental processes we experience and our own observations concerning our surroundings. That is to say — in addition to books, it is essential to learn from experience.

6. To successfully intercept stimuli that arrive from the external world it is useful to deploy our senses in a receptive position, reducing as much as possible our anthropomorphic projection onto the observed phenomenon. Furthermore, we need to actually welcome messages that challenge what we have acquired previously. Indeed, we ourselves have to develop an acute sensitivity that will allow us to glimpse the openings through which this process of new understanding can manifest itself.

7. The aim is therefore to arrive, case by case, at an awareness (short and long term) that places the subject in a relationship that corresponds as closely as possible to "how things actually are." Discoveries, innovations, and individual and collective changes concern every aspect of human life. For each event, positive or negative, the outcome depends on circumstances, intuition, imagination, learning in other fields, and the ability to find an access point, along with mobility and the capacity of the person or persons involved to pull things together.

8. As this transformative process becomes better understood and more conscious, it can become commonplace, routine. But it can also

suggest new stimuli both near and far, even very far removed from the usual ones. It can engage and infect other subjects through love (as in "do unto others what others would like"). It can spread, suddenly setting in motion unexpected economic, political, and social processes. It can inject into our societies, all at the same time, freedom, development, democracy, federalism, fraternity, social justice, peace, respect for the environment, art, beauty etc. It can promote a process of "becoming civilized," a "magnet effect" that attracts the attention of peoples and promotes the evolution of humanity.

9. Conscious awareness (with discovery, innovation and change as its consequences) can therefore exert a powerful individual and collective force capable of keeping at bay (and gradually taming) the aggressive tendencies that have long bloodied humanity's violent past — up to the appalling nationalist tragedy of the Second World War (and beyond).

10. On scales both small and large, the art of the possible (possibilism) involves the acceleration of these positive processes through continuous efforts to widen the spectrum of opportunities and choices, as well as through initiatives (intentional and/or casual) involving "optimal imbalance" that can play a cutting-edge role in providentially correcting existing negative trends.

APPENDIX C: "NEVER AGAIN!"
THREE CONVERGING INTELLECTUAL PATHWAYS

Without doubt, Eugenio Colorni, Albert Hirschman and myself are "sons" of the Second World War. Eugenio was born in 1909, Albert in 1915. I myself was born in 1939 — thirty years after Eugenio and twenty-four after Albert. (In the spring of 1944, at the age of four and a half, I was seriously burned in a fire at Montepulciano di Siena, still in the Nazi-Fascist zone. I was saved by my father who, returning from liberated Rome with American penicillin in his pocket, had passed through the front lines at night by bicycle, at the risk of his life. I had very extensive burns that the doctors thought would never heal, and they wanted to perform a skin transplant from other parts of my body. But my mother refused, saying I had suffered too much already. She invented a method of treatment herself that consisted of tightening a bandage over my knees every half hour and slowly forcing them down, which saved me from the wheelchair. In time the enormous wounds began to close. Yet even now — more than 75 years later — there is a small point on my right calf where they sometimes reopen, a concrete reminder of where I come from . . .).

As we have seen, Eugenio Colorni's interest in literature and aesthetics began while he was still in high school. At university, after some brief initial confusion he entered the field — in philosophy. He had two important teachers guiding him: the extrovert Giuseppe Antonio Borgese and the austere Piero Martinetti. He was attracted by Martinetti's philosophical framework (with the exception of his quasi-religious conclusions, which didn't convince him). Under Martinetti's guidance, he embarked on an in-depth study of the history of philosophy (then considered the pinnacle of learning), and then entered the mainstream of modern philosophy — metaphysics — as heir (possibly inverted) to a tradition that had arisen during the Renaissance and spread throughout Europe. This was the product of a perennially evolving effort to construct successive philosophical systems, and was the preserve of an international community of more or less enlightened "sages" that Colorni wished to belong to.

Navigating between Borgese and Martinetti (who got along despite their differences), Eugenio applied this way of looking at things to *The Essence of Aesthetics* of Benedetto Croce (who, understandably, was not pleased). In addition, on the advice of Martinetti, he undertook to explore the work of Gottfried Wilhelm Leibniz. The fact is, he learned a lot. But even though he was working in an environment that was opposed to Fascism and its nationalist style of philosophy, he was living a dream (and a hope) that reality would dramatically repudiate shortly thereafter.

In practical terms, he had to face the fact that this way of thinking was in the end covering (more or less knowingly) for the atrocities of European nationalism. In this way he became a scathing critic of philosophical systems and therefore of the philosophical illness. Eugenio's "Never again!" took the form of an accelerated hermeneutic work of reconstruction of thought that ranged in all directions — including, as we know, mathematics, physics, psychology, etc.

Passing from one European country to another, Albert Hirschman, got what was at the least an uneven education in economics, with influences from political Marxism, the German historical school, the business and economics mix at a Parisian *grand école*, the statistical-economic-social appeal *á la* Simiand, etc. It was only during the year he spent at the London School of Economics that he learned what the mainstream of the discipline was actually about.

Initially, in Trieste and Paris, Hirschman worked in statistics and economic journalism (anti-fascist) before entering the profession. His economic and political ideas began to germinate in discussions with Eugenio (who, not surprisingly, he remembered as "a constant critic, questioner, stimulator. That is [. . .] *homme d'áction* and *penseur critique* at the same time"). In *National Power* (written in 1941–1942) he successfully sought to reshape on his own (and our) behalf one of the cornerstones of economics — the Marshallian benefits from trade, a key part of the "pure theory of international trade." But after the war, during the intense apprenticeship of the Marshall Plan, Albert was able to launch a whole new field of activity — the art of renewing and complicating economics. From then on, the few times his work got a boost from traditional political economy, it was generally from the mainstream — as in the appendices to *Exit*, in *Shifting Involvements*, or in "Against Parsimony." This does not alter, however, the fact that he prized the contribution of Keynes in some of his essays, and even theorized a kind of micro-Marxism.

Hirschman was basically stateless, a person without a country, devoted to working *for a better world* from a universalist and federalist perspective. His "Never again!" was rooted in the Holocaust and the annihilation of his schoolmates, and he tenaciously (though gently and quietly) argued for the ineluctable political and civic responsibility of the true intellectual (and, perhaps — he hinted — of every human being).

My problem, if I may, in the midst of all this wisdom, is that my background is not in the philosophical and/or economic mainstream. Being younger, I am a child of critical economics (Keynesian/classical Marxist, from Piero Sraffa and Joan Robinson). Therefore, as I explain in *Eppur si può! Saggi ed istruzioni possibiliste* [*But you can! Possibilist essays and lessons*], 2020, it took the experience of the great social movements of the sixties and seventies to persuade me to try again, to start afresh, to embark on a real struggle with myself (to the point of stepping outside the box of my previous theoretical consciousness), and to arrive, finally, at the Colorni-Hirschman perspective.

I have reexamined this modus operandi at length in both thought and action. In its current version (among ourselves — teachers, ex-students, colleagues, friends), it makes free use (and often halfway between the two authors) of what we believe most corresponds to our philosophical, economic and political needs — in Italy and throughout the world. This means the daily use of trespassing and "possibilism," which sometimes "overflows" from thinking into action and vice versa, and which spreads from one location to another, whether near or far. It is a "Never again!" that encourages us to fight totalitarianism and the absolutism of those who stubbornly refuse to learn from experience, a "Never again!" which, from the "tears of the past" (always with us, together with Eugenio and Albert), questions the present and the future on a daily basis, and in the course of its work derives theoretical-operational consequences from them that need constant and careful verification. Does all this represent a breakthrough in the continuum? Does it open the way to innovation by other pioneers? Perhaps . . . but let's not "count our chickens!"

1. Beginning of an Autobiography

It is not my intention in writing these pages to make my business known to the public. I am not famous, and if I were, I hope I would find better things to do than feed my own vanity and the curiosity of others. I write because I take great pleasure in describing and telling, and because I sometimes think of things that I then enjoy seeing set out in front of me.

It would be dishonest to say that I write "for myself." Anyone who can think feels an irresistible desire to communicate their thoughts to others. This desire is why I write. My friends are no longer enough. I need to imagine that the whole world can hear me. This is what paper is for.

Another person wouldn't ask the question: why do I write? I ask it because writing is not my profession. My profession is philosophy. I have never asked myself why I am a philosopher. That is my essence, my personality itself, my mission in life. But writing down the things that have happened to me and the thoughts I've had — this is something extra that isn't included in the picture, the mission. It is a luxury. It is letting yourself live life.

And who's to say this won't turn out better for me than the other thing? And that it won't be these pages written for fun that bring me recognition, rather than philosophy?

It has happened to a lot of people. For myself, though, I would be very sorry, because being able to see clearly in the field of philosophy is the greatest hope of my life. People want success in the arena of their main occupation; they feel no respect for glory that doesn't fit with their normal activities. Napoleon probably would have been bored by the satisfactions felt by Kant or Goethe, and vice versa. Myself, I couldn't care less about becoming famous as a statesman or a novelist, an inventor or a poet. What I want is to become famous as a philosopher.

Nevertheless, this "voluptuously" writing gives me a great advantage over professional writers, who are bound to respect order and development. When they think of something or see something, they have to make it fit into the "economy of the work." They can rarely just serve up their thinking the way it comes to them. They have to fit it into a framework that, like it or not, always imposes itself on a work of art, be it a novel, poem, essay, short story or article. A character cannot simply be presented as seen, observed, thought of — he or she has to change names, merge with another character, serve as an ingredient; a feeling has to pervade the lines.

I know about aesthetics, so don't come telling me that this is what art is, this transformation of experience through contemplation, etc. etc. I know this better than you. I only mean that for me, this transformation, this development, would be intolerable. It is precisely this that is presumed to be the mark of absolute seriousness, lifetime commitment, a sense of building something. But it is precisely this that would deny me all the joy of the superfluous. I realize now that it is just not possible to make art as an amateur.

This is why what I write will surely never be art — if anything, it will be "humanity." I got this idea reading Voltaire and Diderot. They wrote non-essentially indeed; they weren't building anything. They took risks. Reading them, you don't get an artistic feeling — you get the sheer delight of participating directly in a conversation. They were men who knew how to photograph the human personality directly and immediately in their writings.

I saw that for them writing must have been an enormous pleasure, so free and without worries. So I wanted to try it for myself.

I said before that I don't write to tell others my business. But I do write my business, what I have experienced and thought. And I will spare myself the intention to tell all — to be sincere, as they say, to the point of cruelty. I would be willing to do so, I should say, but I'm not such a fool as to think I could.

I know that it is customary to view as false any autobiography that leaves things out. I can hear the criticism already: "Everything is important, even the most insignificant things." My answer is, no. For you things are important (and with good reason) that are unimportant to others. But that doesn't mean that for you there aren't also unimportant things, and they might be the very things that others focus all their attention on. Just let me do it. I will tell you the things that to me, as the person I am, seem important. Don't worry: if necessary I will even manage to overcome my modesty. But let me be the one who chooses. And if you don't like it? Don't read it.

Not leaving anything out is a requirement in the era of the great psychological discovery that has revealed unsuspected riches in regions of the mind that were barely looked at previously. Now a fever to dig everywhere has broken out, for fear that gold mines will be distractedly trampled underfoot. But what goes unnoticed is that when you think you are digging everywhere, you are actually always digging in the same field, the one that is now exposed. "Everywhere" is for us always and only what we are able to pay attention to, what is already a priori important to us. Enlarging this "everywhere," finding a new and previously unrecognized field, making something important that was hitherto ignored, this is the job for the genius, the creator.

Every new perspective in art or culture is a matter of revealing to mankind something that hadn't been noticed before, and involves overcoming human efforts not to notice. Suddenly something is brought into the daylight either that people had been doing or thinking without noticing it, or that they considered private, intimate and personal. Humanity blushes at first — then recognizes itself, realizes it is in good company and, freed of modesty, enjoys the moment. Enjoys breaking the ice. Then, ice broken and modesty overcome, it lingers with delight on the theme, which becomes a style. And lingers not in a spirit of imitation, but because it cannot do otherwise. A new tool has been put in its hands that needs to be used. A new field that has to be thoroughly tilled. Nobody before romanticism would have had the courage to cry or howl in public. Or before *verismo*, to write "shit." Nobody before Freud would have constructed a novel based on their own idiosyncrasies. Apart from those ahead of their time, of course. But don't hold someone up as a model of honesty who uses tools someone else has put into their hands.

Honesty is only applicable to the person who made the leap first, and to whoever makes the next one. It is such people as this who make real discoveries and create new things. They alone can claim to have told all. And even their "all" is relative.

Every new thing that is said (really new) is just one step forward along the road of honesty. So anyone who says: "I want to be genuine, I want to tell all" might as well be saying: "I want to discover a new world, I want to be a great man." Telling all means saying something deeper, more intimate, more hidden, more difficult and dangerous to say than anything imagined before.

Everyone recognizes the limits of their intelligence. But everyone believes they can be honest. And they do not know that honesty is the most difficult thing in the world and is never completely attainable — that being honest means being brilliant and courageous at the same time, always being on guard against yourself, standing against every set phrase or fixed idea, devising new ways of doing research on yourself, sniffing out new ways in. It means never tiring, not relaxing for an instant, monitoring, investigating with the patience of a scientist and the imagination of an inventor and an artist. Anyone can do an inventory of what is before their eyes. And that can sometimes be interesting, instructive, stimulating. Before pointing to it as honest I would ask for something more.

This idea of honesty is a fixation of mine. I shall return to it often.

2. Justification

[Trieste, July 1937]

The author would have preferred to put a pseudonym at the top of this page. He is embarrassed to sign it with his own name.[1]

The author's profession is philosophy — and there is nothing he hates more than continually taking the pulse of his time, seeing brilliant prospects, and analyzing "contemporary anxiety." He considers philosophy a science, not a simple search for a "point of view." A concrete science that can achieve positive results, discoveries that constitute a gain for mankind. A science with an infinite variety of methods, each extremely difficult to learn, requiring a violent struggle against oneself. He despises those who think philosophy means having a formula for interpreting the world. He knows that the real works of philosophy are not those whose readers have the joy of seeing thoughts and feelings expressed that they themselves have experienced in a confused way. They are rather those in which things are said that the reader has never believed and usually rebels against. Preferable to the philosopher whom the public loves because they feel "understood" is the one the public hates because they don't understand and it makes them angry.

This is the only way the author would like to do philosophy — to invent, to discover previously unknown explanations. Not to express what is currently in the air.

But he knows that such a task requires circumspection, relentlessly hard work, and very long silences. He knows that a philosopher cannot claim to have said anything until late maturity.

It is precisely for this reason that he has felt the need to write these articles. In the hope that they will make his scientific work easier and make the silences less solemn.

A philosopher's work needs to be even more precise than a physicist's or biologist's; it requires monitoring and testing that can be extended to the most far-flung fields. The philosopher must un-

---

[1] Why did he, then? There are two ways of giving in to one's modesty: hiding and showing off.

derstand from the inside both polar opposites and heterogeneous worlds. This is the torture of it — seeing this vast world pass beneath his eyes, actually joining it, and yet not being able to speak. It is true that every science requires what is known as development of the material. But here, the material is the philosopher's own life, the set of problems he suffers with every day as a human being. The silence is all the more painful.

He is constantly afraid that he will arrive too late — not for others, but for himself. That in the course of his investigating and verifying, the material will crumble away in his hands. He is forced to work constantly on himself to keep alive the thing that he is examining and describing, and this task requires him to be hot and cold at the same time.

Many give up and decide to let the wave of life take them, with the theoretical justification that this letting go is exactly what philosophy is meant to be. But in reality they have given up philosophy to become "interpreters of their times."

The aim of the present writings is to save the author from this danger. They are meant to serve as a reference point for questions and problems and attitudes that he hopes one day to be able to thrash out in depth, to allow his thinking about them to crystallize calmly, without anxiety or impatience.

These writings are not in any sense meant to be philosophy. They are not meant to be searched for answers or theories. If these things should turn up, they ought not to be considered as such, but only as an incentive to thinking in a certain direction. The author has tried to guard against the temptation to pursue arguments too far, or let himself be led to solutions. He has also chosen the most ephemeral literary form: the letter, the fragment, the article.

For this reason he is not troubled by accusations of inconsistency. A coherent system is not what he is looking for here. What he has written represents his temporary conviction, and precisely because it is temporary, its purpose is not to be accepted or debated. It is useful only to the author himself.

And anyone who might want to ask him why he has published these pointless things should know that there are some people who write not to benefit or please the public, nor to improve it or to broaden its knowledge, but rather because they need to communicate their

3. Program

Let us suppose that man lives in a palace whose doors are all locked. He doesn't have the keys. That is — he has a set, but he doesn't know if they fit the locks, or which key fits which lock. He tries them, tries them again, makes new keys and tries them — in the continual hope of one day being able to occupy the whole palace. The scientist is a person who has managed to open one of the doors. One key, thanks to his skill or good luck, turns in the lock. He opens the door and finds a room filled with treasures. He uses them and makes them available to others, who thank and admire him. From then on that room is accessible to everyone. In his excitement, the scientist wants to open all the doors. The key he has found becomes a dangerous instrument in his hands. He wants to use it everywhere. The result is, he breaks the locks, and it's going to be an enormous job fixing them and then finding or making new keys that will fit them. (Metaphor aside, medicine was plagued for centuries by its obsession with the mechanistic method, which had worked wonders in the field of physics. It was thought that everything could be worked out based on anatomy and ratios and tissue modifications. In most cases this got them exactly nowhere).

And what about the philosopher? What does he do? He hasn't had the luck or skill to open a door, but he is nevertheless in the grip of the same obsession to open one, either with the scientist's key or with one that he has made himself. His obsession is perhaps less dangerous than the scientist's, but it is more intense. For the scientist it is secondary, an added complication. He has already expended his greatest efforts in finding the key. Trying to use it elsewhere is often only a roughly sketched idea. But the philosopher, on the other hand, is consumed by this need. He is clever enough to realize that running from one door to another with the same key only leads to damage and disorder. He wants to satisfy his need in a systematic way that doesn't leave any loose ends. He is obsessed with the idea that all the rooms in the palace can be opened and lived in, from drawing rooms to closets. What can he do to achieve this? He constructs a palace for his own personal use, as similar as possible to the real one, in which all the locks can be opened with just one key, or with the various keys he has at his disposal. And he shuts himself in and seems to be at peace. But the palace is made of paper-mâché, not real brick and mortar. In a short time it collapses, it falls apart. The rooms are identical to those of the other palace, but they are empty. Being able to open them has yielded no riches, no power. It sometimes happens that during the work of construction the philosopher comes across a new key that other people can use in various locks. In this case people admire and study him for this invention, whether it arrived by luck or design, which in his mind was meant to be nothing more than a detail of the great palace. And the great palace itself disappears. After a century nobody believes in it any more — nobody can live in it. It is seen as a beautiful ruin, the interesting documentation of an era, appreciated for a certain stimulus it provided indirectly, in its general shape, to humanity's struggles and strivings. The historians, the explainers, start taking it apart to see whether, since it is no longer of any use as a whole, something of value might not be found among the building materials. And they begin distinguishing between "what is living and what is dead" and manipulating the system for their own ends. The result of this is that the thinkers (and often the poets as well) are as a rule valued by posterity for reasons they never would have imagined and have nothing to do with their basic intentions. What they had thought was their true contribution to culture and civilization is regarded as useless. The expenditure of energy is enormous. We see the most intelligent human beings direct all their efforts toward achieving goals that are later completely lost, and we are forced to work hard to scrape together any remnant of their labors.

In science things seem to function a bit better. At least we are in the real palace, where the rooms are full of riches, and in the case where the key did open the door the capacities of humanity were infinitely increased. But if the door won't open? From the Greeks to the Renaissance, for two thousand years, people busied themselves building keys of all kinds and magnificent paper-mâché palaces. But there was not one door in the palace that yielded to their efforts. Starting with Galileo and Bacon, some of the doors seemed to give a little. The one concerning physical mechanisms actually opened wide. But so many are still closed! For them what will be the right key? Do we already have it in our hands or do we have to make it? And how do we get away from the continual temptation to try the key that worked once in all the doors and risk ruining everything? Philosophy today, rather than constructing pretty palaces out of paper-mâché, ought to set itself the task of facing these problems and trying to bring a certain order to them with a view of avoiding wasted effort and achieving results that are as concrete as possible. It should first of all examine the keys we already have — that is, our research criteria, the hermeneutic methods we have for grappling with reality and making it useful to us. By now it is abundantly clear that such criteria radically transform reality by making choices for us that let us see only what they are able to grasp.

What we call reality is obviously conditioned not only by our senses, but by the entire set of forms, categories, and associative and interpretive criteria without which it is impossible for us to perceive or attempt anything. Criteria that we can study, take apart and modify — without ever being able to get away from the field of activity of the subject, which constitutes reality itself. In our present state of knowledge we do not possess any means of eliminating the subjective aspect from our notion of reality. Indeed, we have strong indications that the notion of an objective reality independent of us is a figment of our mind due to our fundamental need to set up something in opposition to ourselves, to have something to push against, to polarize the content of our consciousness into passive and active parts. (See Fichte, Internal Transcendence). What we call reality is therefore neither subject nor object, but something that human beings, with their criteria and categories, have played a big part in building — something that we, for ease of study, momentarily regard as a fact standing in front of us, aware that in doing so we are placing before us something that we ourselves participate in.

Now this thing — this "something" — people will strive to manipulate it to their own ends, to penetrate its structure, to predict what it will become and to build on the basis of such predictions. Depending on whether the objective or subjective character of this work is emphasized, they will see it either as "penetrating the laws of nature" or as "extracting a certain number of elements from nature and adjusting them to be used for human ends" — either "yielding to nature" or "doing violence to it." And they are called positivists or pragmatists. But this distinction concerns the metaphysical meaning of such human activity, not its conformation, its procedures, its purpose — which is what we are interested in investigating here if we want useful results. A scientist does not pose the problem of whether his or her work is practical or theoretical. Scientists never seriously ask if what is driving their research is "the need to know" as an end in itself rather than the hope that people can derive some use from their discoveries. They follow their own aptitudes into fields that are closer to pure or applied research. But in their minds, research and its application make up a single whole that is sometimes split up only for convenience of study and the need to divide up the work. Discovery is seen as the natural, self-evident precondition of invention; invention as the consequence of discovery. The positivism-pragmatism antithesis makes no sense to a scientist and doesn't change his or her behavior in the slightest.

Scientists work in other words on what they have in front of them, things whose constituent elements are "forms" or "categories" that come from the scientist's own mind, that frame reality and make it comprehensible and graspable. Some of these forms and categories are considered as belonging to reality itself — as existing absolutely outside the scientist.

What are they? They are those that the scientist feels necessarily tied to and cannot possibly do without — whose absence would make it absolutely impossible to see and think. Kant listed some of them: space, time, causality, number, etc. He of course recognized that these are imposed on things by the human mind, but by giving them a necessary and a priori character, he warned of the impossibility of escaping from them. Most people in fact don't care where they come from and in simply accepting that we can't do without them, undoubtedly attribute them to reality.

But Kant's observation put everyone on edge, and the curiosity to see beyond the "Veil of Maya" of mental categories became more and more intense. Scientific philosophical thinking can be said to have gone in two opposite directions on this issue, depending on whether Kant's warning was observed or not.

(1) Among those who heeded the warning:

(a) The scientists went on considering the categories as real and working in a world built with these categories as a base, sometimes contenting themselves with keeping in the background the shadow of some Unknowable (Spencer, the positivists), or taking cognizance of the relative nature of their efforts, limiting the task of science to the construction of simple and manageable hypotheses (Poincaré, the pragmatists). Following this path they continued to achieve a notable number of successes, following on with the investigations and the exploitation of nature that began with Galileo and Newton and consisted of the systematic use of the categories that Kant later listed. But for some time now there has been an impression that the field is about to dry up and that nothing much remains in this direction except specific discoveries of limited importance.

(b) The philosophers, on the other hand, intolerant of any sort of dualism or relativism, and concerned with consolidating the unity of reality, opted to eliminate the temptation of the "thing in itself" by denying its very existence; and to attribute absolute reality to thought in its universal makeup. In this way they satisfied both the Kantian requirement not to go outside the laws of reason and the typically philosophical need to resolve the problem of reality without leaving loose ends, regardless of whether or not this system might lead to any appreciable result other than the satisfaction of their need for completeness.

(2) Those, on the other hand, who "disobeyed" appear at first glance to hold Kant's warning in contempt and to disregard the limits he set — but in reality they are much more his children than those who obeyed. The limits — that barrier — stimulated them to get beyond it. It showed them which way to go. We'll begin this time with the philosophers.

(a) The philosophers want to taste the forbidden fruit. But by now they know they can never get to it with the categories whose limits Kant so clearly indicated. They abandon forever the illusions of metaphysics and teleology — that is, attempts to confirm absolute reality using the instruments of reason — and they continually seek some other tool that will allow them to reach their goal. Will, faith, intuition, inspiration — in a word, the irrational is what they rely on. To it they attribute all the capabilities that the categories of reason lack. With it they say they can open all the doors of the palace.

But what guarantees can this new key give them? Basically, just that it is not the old one. Every irrationalist interpretation of the world that doesn't consist of an explosion of enthusiasm is a polemic against the impotence of reason. A polemic that is often perceptive and correct, but that does not provide a sufficient reason to accept as a definitive criterion everything that reason is not.

Explosions of enthusiasm, on the other hand, are at times more interesting and fruitful. They allow us, albeit in a confused way, to penetrate the internal constitution of these irrational activities, to learn a little more about what their processes are. The thing that has paralyzed such investigations, though, and kept them from yielding anything but feeble results up to now is that descriptions of such activities have always presumed it necessary to ascribe to them an absolute value, far superior to the value of reason. This preconception has of course distorted the description and obstructed any serious inquiry into the use that might be made of these approaches. Here again, the rush to close the circle and the philosophical need to shut oneself up in an edifice that is habitable in all its parts has prevented any real progress from being made. And these irrationalist interpretations of reality have come one after the other without leading us to any stable achievement. This phenomenon has been repeating itself for centuries — the recognition of the shortcomings of rationality and the attempt to resort to irrational behavior does not date from Kant, but is as old, one might say, as our civilization. And the mass of experiences that has accumulated, while unorganized, is also powerful. It gives the impression of a vast unexplored mine where there is precious material mixed up with the slag.

Here we are at a much less developed stage of evolution and utilization than in the field of rationality. The stuff of reason has been explored through and through, inventoried and organized by Greek thinkers and by scholars. It found its field of application in Galileo and Newton, leading to the far-reaching achievements we know. Its limits were finally set out by Kant, who at the same time signaled (perhaps somewhat prematurely) the exhaustion of the mine that had been producing its wealth. The field of the irrational probably includes regions infinitely more vast than that of reason, and contains the most diverse materials, suitable for a wide variety of uses. The simple fact that we are accustomed to classifying it in the negative column "outside the scope of reason" illustrates the disorganized state of our knowledge of the subject. Organizing the world so that it becomes useful to us, analyzing it calmly and without preconceived passions or aversions, freeing it from the continual nightmare of comparison with rationality, and finally trying to see if some of the data obtained in this way can be used as a criterion for problem-solving, as a key that will unlock a door — this is the task that our investigation today must face. It goes without saying that the methods to be used will not be the same as those used for the rational world, and that the resulting structure/order will not even remotely resemble what we know from the logical-mathematical field. The word "order" itself should not be taken here as anything more than an analogy. We will need to tap into the world of the irrational itself to find the points in it around which its content can coalesce and offer us a foothold we can use. To give directives and indications here would be absurd and reckless. The success of this task will depend on the imagination and acumen of whoever carries it out, on their ability to draw freely on experiences from other fields without being overly influenced by them and on the mobility and richness of their combinatory talents. The ideal result would give humanity one or more new keys able to uncover new laws of reality or, if you prefer, able to construct new systems of correlation that would be available for our use and would allow us to satisfy some of our needs.

(b) No scientist prodded by Kantian fine-tuning to move beyond Kant's categories will linger over research into the irrational, which up to now has offered no methodological foothold. Their mentality already revolves completely around the logico-mathematical rationality that in past centuries has yielded the great discoveries our civilization stands on. And the departure they want to make is not a departure in principle, a springboard into a completely different world, but one that is gradual, following experiences one step at a time that cannot be justified by laws known to us up to now. They do not ask about the absolute reality lurking behind the veil of the categories, but rather how it is possible to grasp and organize reality in terms of categories different from those used up to now. In this they are much less realistic than either idealist or mystical philosophers or positivist scientists. And in this sense one can almost say that they bring experimental confirmation, if not to the a priori necessity of Kantian categories, at least to the Kantian doctrine of categories. The scientist as a rule has not read Kant. But the pervasiveness of Kantism and the very notion of categorizing reality suggests that in the face of a new and inexplicable experience they should adopt a position that this inexplicability is due to the violence traditional categories do to research by forcibly organizing the data into their own molds. This position directly gives rise to an attempt to modify the categories and test them again, in their new form, using the yardstick of scientific interpretation. Modify, I say, not abolish. This is where the modesty of the scientist shows itself, the willingness to try the keys, one after the other, the voluntary limiting of horizons. Once having noticed the use of categories in the formulation of laws, the scientist is continually tempted to test what would have happened if the categories had been differently made. How would phenomena play out in a non-Euclidean space? Matter, energy, substance, causality. How would a world look in which these categories presented characteristics different from those they have had up to now? The a priori element of reality, having entered human consciousness, begins to perform a game of displacements, setbacks and modifications such as to completely transform the image of reality people work with — like a lens that has learned to open and close, to focus according to the needs of the object to be portrayed. And if on one hand it can be said that this adaptation of the categories is imposed by the procedures of scientific research — that is, by experiences and observations that cannot be fit into the categories used until now (those of the Newtonian universe), on the other hand, what may have happened is that scientists, drawn by the vague feeling of being on the verge of creating new instruments for the apprehension of reality, were attracted precisely to those experiences that the new instruments might need. Experience is obviously never something entirely passive, and there is always a reason why the experimenter's attention is drawn to one fact rather than another. Nevertheless, if the conformations of the individual categories have been severely modified by modern science, the consciousness of the categorical nature of reality has not been changed — on the contrary, it has been strengthened. A philosopher could rightly conclude that the new theories in physics have not affected the Kantian conception of the world. We would say that they have taken from that conception the sole consequences that open new and undefined research perspectives to the human mind. These do not consist of a vague and problematic avoidance of categories, but in a calm acceptance of the fact that it is not possible to disregard "categorizing." An acceptance, however, that allows the continual revision of the existing categories — that is, those categories that the human mind, in its present state, cannot do without.

It is not perhaps out of place to point out that such a revision has nothing to do with the debates over the classification of categories that philosophers so often indulge in. It is in no way a discussion of whether there are twelve categories or ten, or four or one. Whether "finalism" is a category in itself or fits into different one. Whether "economics" or "aesthetics" are independent ways of looking at things. It is not a question of organizing the known forms of thought and coming to an agreement about which should be considered original and which derivative. The task is much more profound and creative. The point is to give the human mind the possibility of seeing things in a way that is completely different from the way they have been up to now, to supply the mind with a new sense by which it can discover things hitherto unknown, solve problems hitherto insoluble.

The "critical" position, in the Kantian sense, thus presents itself as the last phase of an entire epoch and way of making contact with reality. Given the opportunity to become fully aware not only of their own methods, but also of the necessary premises underlying each of their constructs, the sciences are stimulated to overcome this necessity and to create new premises for themselves. The task of the mind here is not restricted to intellectual research. It also includes attitudes that may be brought together under the general term "moral." These require violent resistance to a way of seeing things that we are all bound to, a striving for liberation, a leap out of the world we are part of. The goal is to create a "new mindset" for ourselves, to see things with different eyes, to simplify, to reject prefabricated constructs. We must rely on imagination, invention, and intuition to conjure worlds that are different from the one we are used to seeing. Such conversions of the mind, alterations we usually attribute to mysticism or to a desire for purification or for visions, were not necessarily foreign to the people who first tried to imagine an earth that was round rather than flat, or the sun fixed at the hub of the planetary system rather than the earth, or four- rather than three-dimensional space. But while the mystic usually describes the conversion process very accurately, but stops there and gives us no guarantees about what lies "on the other side," the scientist undergoes the conversion silently, often almost unconsciously. But having once passed to "the other side," the new point of view, the scientist's concern is to focus only on what is — I won't say true in an absolute sense — but usable, in other words subject to organization as a structure or law. And getting to this point requires experiments and controls that afford guarantees that there is firm ground that the scientists tools can get hold of. "The other side" is not in fact a negation of "this side"; it is not an absolute, devoid of categories. It is a world of new categories that lay claim to encompassing the old ones as well. Round rather than flat, mechanism instead of finalism, statistical probability in the place of deterministic causality. The validity of the new keys is established in their use — that is, by the greater or lesser possibility they offer in explaining phenomena, in resolving problems, in formulating laws. The greater difficulty is getting used to the new way of seeing. There isn't even a vocabulary for expressing things in terms of the new categories, and it is common to resort to metaphors drawn from the old world. A large part of the task, in the initial stages, is devising "transformation formulas" that will ease the transition from the terms of the old categories to those of the new ones. Just as the laws of perspective allow me to represent things on a flat surface that have volume in space, the "Lorentz transformation" allows me to use the tools I have at my disposal (calculation, measurement, etc.) in normal space for the new Einsteinian space, the way the psychoanalyst, by analogy, attempts to transform what is unconscious into the terms of consciousness. By means of such transformations others can be helped to move to the new level — they can be provided, you might say, with glasses that will allow them to see the new light until they are comfortable enough to do without them and use direct language. But the language itself always preserves traces of this, and etymologies often document such changes of register.

This is, more or less, the current state of affairs.

4. The Philosophical Illness

> *Allmählich hat sich mir herausgestellt, was jede grosse*
> *Philosophie war: nämlich das Selbstbekenntnis ihres Urhebers*
> *und eine Art ungewollter und unvermerkter "mémoires."*

> *It has gradually become clear to me what every great philosophy*
> *up to now has consisted of — namely, the personal confession of its*
> *originator and a kind of involuntary and unconscious memoir.*
> — Nietzsche

[Ventotene, April-May 1939]

"Is there such a thing as a philosophical illness? And if there is, why is it called an illness?"

"There is," we reply. "And it's called an illness because it's possible to recover from it."

"What does it mean to recover from it?"

"It means finding yourself in a new state in which you have the feeling that you can see things you couldn't see before, that you've digested the previous state and moved beyond it. In this condition the problems of philosophy have all been solved at once, because the position the problems were posed from has been neutralized — it has actually fallen apart. And solving a problem means, as everyone knows, being in a condition of not having it anymore."

"But this new state — isn't it also, in essence, philosophy?"

"The same old refrain! Call it philosophy if you like. What matters to me is that it is a later state, beyond the one that included people who were called philosophers, one that makes the philosophers' state look like an illness you've got over and whose pettiness and childishness you now see."

Picture a boy at the beginning of adolescence. He is intelligent, but weak. He is a bit fat — his body weighs on him. If he is sitting down and he has to pick up a distant object, he would rather lean over and reach for it, even at the risk of knocking everything on the floor, rather than choose the more determined but laborious option of getting up. His indolence when it comes to deliberate movements characterizes him, even morally. Sometimes he is so lazy that he actually wets his pants a bit. He would be in trouble if the grownups were to notice, or even the other kids. He lives in constant fear of being exposed. And there are other things as well that it would be terrible for anyone to find out about. For example, he can't tell left from right.

He is not the least bit interested in mechanics, something that ought to be the duty of any respectable boy — for this he is continually reproached by the adults. And he is told that he should have been born a girl, and his sister a boy.

He is not aware of suffering much from these appraisals. They are right, he feels, but he is only a little bit ashamed. The atmosphere he lives in is warm and a bit unclean. What he fears most are sudden explosions, like when his mother notices he hasn't washed, and drags him into the bathroom and attacks him with soap, brushes and towels. If he has been naughty and is ordered to apologize, he prefers to give in immediately rather than suffer the martyrdom of prolonged resistance.

At school he is one of the best students, but the teachers say that if he wanted to he could do a lot better. In classroom discussions he is convoluted and fussy — they call him Mr. Quibble. Even here, there is a certain sluggishness that leads him to go round and round absurd and awkward positions rather than make the quick and violent effort to abandon them. He has little sexual curiosity and no vices. Indeed, he stays away from the lubricious conversations of his classmates. Why? On principle? For moral reasons? No — probably so as not to have too many things he has to hide.

He suffers a little from being different from the other children — having shoes and trousers that are out of the ordinary, for example, bought at a shop specializing in sensible and hygienic items for youngsters; not having permission to buy sweets or licorice after school; not being allowed to play with everyone in the street, but only in certain areas and with companions approved by his parents. He wishes no one noticed these peculiarities that make him an outsider and a bit ridiculous to his peers. But he never thinks of transgressing, or protesting or rebelling. He feels in a confused way that he is part of a higher, cleaner and more moral world that his classmates have no idea about — the world of home, where Tuscan is spoken, where you do exercises every morning on mother's orders. And he would like to live in peace, un-observed, in both these worlds. For this reason he tries to keep them as separate as possible — at school he speaks with the accent of the local dialect, which would not be permitted at home, and he trembles whenever his parents invite his classmates to the house or go to speak with his teachers.

He derives a certain amount of satisfaction from his own per-son, and has a particular need to look at himself in the mirror, to be elegant. He satisfies this need furtively to avoid derision. This he knows is one of the reasons he should have been born a girl.

He spends the summers with certain cousins, all older than himself. They are at once the scandal and the pride of the family. They do not — and would not ever — apologize, even under torture. They say some things that make him shudder, but which after all, on reflection, are not entirely wrong — for example that to follow their ideals they would be ready to trample on any duty to the family. They are full of ideals, of things that excite them. Every summer there is something new. They read many books, many newspapers. It is impossible to beat them in a debate. They crush you with their limpid, linear, unassailable arguments. Pierino (as we shall call him) sees that they are right, even from the first verbal exchange. But there is something that prevents him from taking their side openly and completely. How he wishes they were wrong just once! They live in an enchanted castle, and there they bravely turn back every assault. Within the family they are challenged, criticized, opposed. Conflicts with their parents do not resemble normal teenage pranks or esca-pades in the slightest. They are battles fought to defend a principle. Punishment is unjust oppression, summary martyrdom in the name of an ideal.

Ah, to be like them! Pierino lacks the strength even to imagine it. To abandon the position of a "normal" boy and live perpetually with your lance at the ready!

Yet he does not draw back from their charm; he would like to escape the state of perennial inferiority that their mere presence relegates him to. He senses that his mother secretly takes their side and is disappointed that he is so different. His mother, strict and fair, loyal and pure, who never wastes her time, who always gets more done in a day than she had planned — the favorite of his cousins, the counselor and arbiter in family quarrels.

For his entry into middle school, he receives the gift of a watch, along with numerous sermons on the seriousness of the gift, the responsibility that it entails, the implicit recognition of his maturity that it represents. But right from the first evening, he can't restrain himself from poking around inside it with a pen, and the result is that he destroys everything. Desperation, panic. Confessing his misdeed would mean having the object taken away from him and his being held up to the contempt of all as unworthy to have it. At the same time, the fact cannot be hidden. Pierino conscientiously eliminates every trace of his tampering and presents the malfunction as if the mechanism had spontaneously stopped working.

They believe him — what a relief! With joy and impatience he takes the watch to be repaired. But the jeweler scrutinizes it with suspicion: "This mechanism has been dampened with ink!"

Red-faced, Pierino denies it, but the other persists. That his mother, who is present, does not investigate further and make it her business to get to the bottom of the thing, is a miracle.

He leaves the shop, shaken. He has had a narrow escape. But now something stirs inside him that feels like the Last Judgment. "Your every action will be judged. Even the very hairs of your head are all numbered." It's useless to run away, Pierino, or try to hide. The chickens will come home to roost. Everything you do and you don't do is written somewhere in indelible letters.

He has never been punished for telling a lie, even though he tells them all the time. At home a lie is held to be something so monstrous that no one would be able even to conceive that a good boy could stain himself with one. What he says is believed without question, and this makes the torment even greater. Some punishment would almost make the sin acceptable, exchangeable for a dose of smacks, say, or a certain number of days without fruit. But this way, the weight is all on his shoulders, along with perpetual uncertainty and the terror of the catastrophic day when everything should come to light.

Pierino has a certain need for affection and tenderness that he has difficulty satisfying. His mother, for reasons of hygiene, is against kisses and excessive caresses. And in the family atmosphere there is an air of contempt and gruff reserve concerning any sort of gushy sentimentality. Sometimes he finds himself wondering with terror if he really loves his parents. He has no particular reason to complain about them, quite the contrary. But "love"! He knows what it means — that desire to be close to each other, to hug, to be caressed and pampered. He feels it and often feels a sharp desire for it, but he is unable to associate it with thoughts of his mother and father.

The days of his dad's death were very painful. He didn't believe he would be able to cry; instead, in the moment, he was overcome with acute anguish. But then! That constant feeling of being observed. Am I grieving enough? The guilty conscience every time he has to play, or laugh and make noise, or argue. His mother doesn't scold anymore. She looks downcast, disconsolate. Pierino has an intense feeling of impatience. There are facts and attitudes that touch something deep and elusive in him. His mother, who cries and makes soft, melancholy gestures. Pierino blushes, he is annoyed and ashamed.

He is secretly in love with a girl at school. One of his classmates confides in Pierino, admitting his love for the same girl. He listens eagerly and with pleasure. He is not jealous. It doesn't even occur to him that he could do the same. He feels he is made of different stuff, that he belongs to a different morality in which confessing his love would bring terrible shame. And his companion's sincerity strikes him as unthinkable, monstrously shameless. But that night, before he falls asleep, he broods over his friend's stories, putting himself in his place and fantasizing about situations in which it is always the girl who opens up first.

Pierino is twelve years old. Emilio, the youngest of his cousins, is fourteen. Emilio's current mania is chemistry — all he talks about is atoms and molecules, acids and salts. Obeying his mother's wishes, Pierino receives instruction from him without enthusiasm.

One day, the two boys have a falling out, for whatever reason. Pierino's style of argument is cautious and circumspect, for fear of being overheard by the adults. His cousin fears no one. He screams and yells, loudly throwing Pierino's misguided behavior in his face.

To bed without dinner for both of them. They sleep in the same room. Emilio is calm, as if nothing had happened. Pierino is filled with shame and resentment. He still feels he owes the other an insult. He gets up surreptitiously and yanks his cousin's covers.

The damage is minimal, almost imperceptible, but the reaction is fierce. In a vindictive fury Emilio flings Pierino's blanket, sheets, pillow and mattress in the air.

There is a renewed scuffle and the parents intervene once again. It is Emilio who is punished, because his fault is more blatant, but both of them know who the main culprit really is. Emilio bears his punishment stoically, heaping his cousin with contempt.

The two boys are in their beds, awake. Pierino is tormented by what has happened. His resentment is subsiding. He lacks the strength to keep up the state of war, while the other would be able to prolong it for weeks. It would be so nice to be at peace, to laugh and play together! But of course, he always has the worst of it, not only materially, but morally as well. He feels that he is constitutionally, organically in the wrong. And with these people, being wrong is torture.

Better to own up. It will be over in a moment. Bite the bullet. One sentence.

"Emilio, you asleep?"

"No."

"Let's make peace."

There, it's said. After the first words, the others don't cost anything. Emilio refuses, but he is calm, diplomatic. Pierino becomes pathetic — he begs, he pretends to cry. The other is thinking about the conditions he should set. He has rules of honor and morality that he cannot ignore. He seems to be consulting his own private code.

At last, the condition arrives. Pierino has to lie on the floor and let Emilio press down on his neck with his foot.

It's too much. The condition is unacceptable. But now the ice has been broken. The two speak calmly, as good friends. Pierino begs that he be spared the shameful penalty. Emilio explains to him the moral advantage he will get by submitting to it. Humbling oneself is for the strong. Only someone who has so mastered himself that he can suffer such ignominy without batting an eye is worthy of his esteem and friendship.

Put in this light, the thing becomes more acceptable. After lengthy discussions and negotiation (considering also the fact that Emilio's feet are rather dirty) the ceremony is performed. Emilio, delighted, embraces his cousin. Then, not to be outdone, he gets Pierino to press his own heel down on the back of Emilio's neck. Many acts of mutual humiliation follow.

Pierino is happy, and ashamed, and astonished. His elder cousin appreciates him. For the first time he has brought him into that world of abstract things — virtue, justice, honor — that he seems to navigate with such agility. Ah, to dwell in that world! How clean, how shiny everything is there! He feels alien, out of place, as if he were wearing clothes not his, in a place he does not know.

But now that other world, the warm, humid world of phony gestures and half-performed acts, of small and tired deceptions, has also become uninhabitable. Pierino feels slimy, sticky.

Bathing — he had never realized what joy it holds. He has a shower every morning, long and meticulous. He washes every time he touches something dirty, or something that has been in contact with something dirty. He decides to change the way he shakes hands. He no longer offers a lifeless, soft hand, but squeezes with all the strength in his body. Some women and girls complain about his violence. He gloats.

And he no longer tells lies. Not even the smallest, not even anything remotely resembling one. He now thinks of lies with the same horror of impurity that leads him to perform exaggerated and unnecessary ablutions. If his sister suggests, as she usually does, that he steal cheese from the kitchen, he has outbursts of rage that lead to interminable quarreling.

He no longer has anything to hide, but he is becoming irritable and suspicious. The stress of his efforts has caused him to lose his erstwhile cheerfulness. He feels cleaner now — but so fragile, so close to a relapse!

One day the talk turns to hypnotism. His cousins are quick to exhibit a disdainful nonchalance at the notion of this dangerous craft. Pierino feels with a shiver that indeed he would be quite easy to hypnotize.

He has a talent for languages, and his pronunciation of English is almost perfect. He would like to show off this ability, but he doesn't dare. He feels that there is something weak and accommodating about it, an excessively easy acquiescence in the attitudes of others, too little of himself.

His cousins know languages as well but they take no care with pronunciation. This annoys him and he would like to correct them, but he is immediately silenced: "This is empty superficiality. Knowing languages is a cultural tool, not a means of making a good impression in drawing rooms."

It's true. These damned people have a foolproof knack for getting past the trifles and going straight for the essentials. But it's hard on people who appreciate trivia and are at ease in the land of imponderables. If you try in an argument to defend nuance against the essentials, you will be wrong every time.

Pierino doesn't try. And hearing them spit out lines of Shakespeare in a loud voice with a Roman accent, he feels that they are strong and he is weak; and he feels that they have conquered the language, while he has let it conquer him.

It's like this with everything, even social relations. His first impulse is to speak the language of his interlocutors, to adapt himself to their mindset, to agree with them. "In church with the saints and in the tavern with the gluttons." The wrong note, the eccentric attitude disturbs him, frightens him. In any situation, he would like to say: "I'm one of you." But then he gets angry and humiliated at how easy this is for him. When he feels comfortable and relaxed among people whose tone, accent and preferences he has assimilated, he is surprised to find himself wondering with terror: "And what if the others saw me here, the people I got along with so well yesterday, speaking in a language that's so different?"

He needs to feel that he is in good company, that he is part of the majority. But something inside warns him that the security he gains in this way is fictitious and that in reality he is on the weaker side. He can delude himself until the reckoning comes. But none of the groups he now and then surrounds himself with would stand up to the first assault. And he wouldn't feel able to fight or suffer for any of them.

Others vaguely sense this as well. They gladly welcome him as a good companion who won't spoil the game. But they feel something foreign in him, and they instinctively exclude him from the really intimate and important things. He sees this and it hurts him, but he blames himself. He has sought security by belonging to everyone. Now he begins to suspect that he would be better protected if he fully belonged, heart and soul and against everyone, to just one thing.

He lays out projects for himself. He will study Italian literature thoroughly, starting from the beginning. He will read a great many pages per day. But then he is always behind in what he's set for himself and never gets further than the pre-Dante authors. He recites poetry out loud in the hope of understanding it and liking it better. He reads the verses of Leopardi in their order of presentation in the book, feeling guilty every time he skips pages. It is not passion, desire or enjoyment that drives him to read. It is so he can say to himself: "This author has enriched my knowledge."

To himself? No, to the invisible and infallible eye of his cousins.

An eye that is pitiless, unforgiving. And impossible to deceive.

That would be like confessing to himself that everything comes down to a question of appearances and prestige. He has had experience with half-measures, with botched actions. It's precisely this that he's fighting against. To be able to say in good faith "I've read this book," you need to have read absolutely all of it, without skipping a line, paying attention to every word. Again and again he stops, with the worry — the nightmare — that he has been distracted, that he has skated over something. He knows no distinction between important and less important books. He is not able to browse. The result is a slow rate of reading that will remain with him for life. Every book abandoned in the middle brings remorse — he will never be able to say honestly that he has read it.

The oldest of his cousins, sent by his mother, came and spoke to him one day about sexual matters. He warned him against vices and dangers and initiated him in his own moral position between Stoic and Quaker, in the need to set moral standards for the sex act — never to perform it as an outlet for instincts, but only *sub specie aeternitatis*, with the woman you will always love, for the procreation of children.

Pierino has no trouble going along with this, and his need for cleanliness is transformed into pride, into a feeling that he is adhering to a superior morality of which his schoolmates know nothing. Here his natural inertia comes to his aid. How much easier it is to abstain than to act! If virtue consists of nothing more than avoiding vice, he feels capable of challenging anyone.

He is now fourteen years old. This summer the whole family is abuzz about the religious mania of Ennio, the second of the cousins. Ennio has just returned from an educational trip, visiting churches and shrines, theologians and mystics. The country house where the large family has gathered echoes with violent arguments.

The uncles, good industrialists with intellectual pretensions, imbued with Spencer and Lombroso, are beside themselves at this offensive against "the most modern achievements of science." Ennio seems to enjoy taking the wind out of their sails. He tenaciously defends the literal sense of every word in the holy books and flaunts his observance of every ritual, attributing to each a profound significance.

There is in him the joy of understanding something the others don't, and of having discovered values that they have misunderstood. And then there is the need, a characteristic of his mindset, to home in immediately on final consequences, a romantic tendency toward sacrifice mixed with an irrepressible passion for scandal. There is no superstitious and obscurantist practice in which he does not recognize a sublime transcendent value, inaccessible to the flat positivist mentality of the uncles. His style of argument, a mixture of formulas from idealist philosophy and mystical phraseology, sounds new, outrageous, and irritating within the solid domestic walls.

Pierino listens with no great interest. This year he feels more presentable, armed as he is with his own intellectual activity, with Leopardi and the Dolce Stil Novo. And he becomes quickly irritated at his cousins' perennially siding against set positions and accepted opinions.

One evening Ennio is worked up and breathless after an argument, and Pierino, who followed it without understanding everything that was said, asks him for clarification. Ennio enthusiastically and abundantly provides it and takes the opportunity to make his case once again: "What I ask is that you be honest with yourself, and brave enough not to retreat in the face of difficulties. The path I offer you is thorny. But the goal is bright. The choice is yours."

The choice is yours! What I ask of you! Pierino is beside himself. This he did not expect. He had never dreamed of being an actual party in the proceedings, of being called upon to take a position, to participate for himself, to serve, like a soldier. It is as if a veil were torn away. Ennio's world there at his fingertips, no longer as an object of interesting discussions and gratifying disputes, but as something that tomorrow he might belong to totally, consumed by that same passion, burned by that same flame!

There is no possible doubt. A few short days of indecision are mostly a psychological formality, and then Pierino is an adept, an enthusiast, a fanatic. And standing behind him are all the boys in the family, half a dozen of them.

But he is number one, the favorite. Ennio flatters him, coddles him, points him out as an example to others. Weeks and months follow of impassioned study and fierce debate. Pierino has become a point man. He attacks, assails and scolds without care. He is no longer afraid of anything — he is now on the side of the strong. He feels shielded, the member of a collective, and this gives him the strength to withstand blows and overcome the opposition.

At school he openly disseminates propaganda for his faith, heedless of the mockery. He is no longer ashamed of being different from the others — on the contrary, he flaunts it. He dresses badly, having given up all thought of being an elegant young man. When a tie is worn out he continues to wear it, only now with the knot in the bottom part. If this slovenliness draws a reproach, his look conveys an attitude between regret and disdain, as if to say: "Yes, I know — it's a defect, but I have more important things to think about."

In arguments he is aggressive and pedantic. His onetime tortuousness is now handy for proving at all costs the correctness of his position. And this polemical fervor helps convince him of his cause. He feels more solid now. Nobody — he thinks with pleasure — can say that I should have been born a girl.

Meetings with his cousins (who live during the winter in another city) always give him a burst of ideas and moral energy. But at the same time, they renew his sense of his own inferiority. By now they have become his closest intimates. They no longer look down on him; they consider him one of them. But there is no getting away from it — they are the masters and he is the pupil. Winning an argument with them is more impossible than ever.

Every time he sees them he soaks up their ideas, and then back at home he strives to master and develop them. When he returns, proud of the work he has done and with some new idea, laboriously worked out, he finds that they are already a thousand miles away, intoxicated by new discoveries.

There is something in them that Pierino cannot quite get hold of, something that makes them walk straight and sure, without a trace of hesitation. Even in life's least important matters he feels like a defenseless soldier in front of an armored squadron.

On the subject of art, for example, Pierino has a certain taste for poetry and painting, and a great passion for music. But how difficult it is for him to justify his judgments and feelings! His cousins' opinions are on the contrary invulnerable, secure in a fortress of coherence that protects them on every side. It is as if there is an invisible device that connects and binds together all their thoughts and actions so that each of them is supported by all the others, and the possibility of embracing new ideas is unlimited.

Pierino wavers, feeling unsettled. He is looking for a guiding thread, a touchstone, a key.

He finds it when he reads Croce's *The Essence of Aesthetics*. From that day he becomes the best in the class in composition. Writing a theme, once a nightmare, is now pleasure. All he has to do is think about it a little, "place" the topic within the system of modules or categories, and develop the analysis in the appropriate direction. Pierino enjoys works of art much more now, and he has the elements he needs to offer sensible judgments and support them. All at once the world has revealed to him his invisible armor.

By now he feels like an initiate. Speaking with "lay people" he has the impression of moving easily in a region filled with arrows and indicators visible only to him. With those who have "done the reading" he feels part of a privileged caste of people who need few words to understand each other.

He is no longer aggressive now in arguments. On the contrary, he is calm and impartial. And he no longer forces himself to walk upright, head held high. Supported by a strong backbone, your muscles can relax.

The Universal! Pierino understands that this is the point, the touchstone. The only true philosopher and member of the caste of initiates is someone who has grasped the Universal. The others are vulgar empiricists. Grasping the Universal is not for everyone, and it isn't something that can be learned. There is something in the way of speaking and almost in the expression and behavior of someone that tells you whether he is capable of grasping the Universal, "the concept of everything and nothing." The Universal is his cousins, the empirical his uncles. The Universal is the invisible eye that sees, it is actions taken under the ever-present weight of totality, books read to the last word, and bathing after every impure contact. The Universal is considering each thing, each act, not for itself, but for something it represents — something you are terribly afraid of forgetting, that you wish were always present, that you would rather chain yourself to than be abandoned by.

Pierino understands the Universal, and the categorical imperative and action for its own sake. He has known these things for some time, since he decided to leave his warm, damp world and take the side of his cousins. But now his world is organized, housed in an edifice where it is no longer possible to get tangled up and lose the thread.

The decision is made — he will study philosophy. He has only read a few books, but his determination is unwavering. He sees philosophy as the most concrete of the sciences, the one he can no longer live without, the one that will come with him and guide his every action. If someone laughs at the abstractness or nebulousness of his ideas, he gets cross. He feels that there are some things that can't be explained without a certain amount of fellow feeling and sympathy from the listener — things that come from inside, that the mechanistic nature of pure reasoning cannot come remotely close to. It is a world you can only enter at a leap, or perhaps you need to be in it already.

The world is mind. Nature is non-being. Liberty is necessity. Pierino is surprised at the scandal these words provoke in ordinary people. They have a precise meaning and it doesn't take much to understand them. The reasoning is almost always brief and fairly simple. All that's required is to untangle it from the often repetitive pages of the book and follow it with a wish to approve. Accept the meaning conveyed by the words and adopt a point of view from which this meaning can easily be approached. And then, having mastered this point of view, hold it tight, clutch it fast, and from that height survey the surrounding world. From there things take on a new light, the main highways are clear, contradictions resolved. Perfect harmony appears where chaos once seemed to reign. A sentence fills up with concrete meaning, receives unforeseen confirmation. Putting it to use, drawing out its developments and corollaries, becomes easy and entertaining, and this before the amazed eyes of the uninitiated.

He now fluidly uses the big words: Self, Spirit, Thought. Whose thought? Man's of course. And yet if you say "human thought," instead of "Thought," it seems to lose everything. Anyone who speaks of the "faculties of the human psyche," and can't talk about the "extrinsecation of the Self" — well, this person is not and will never be a philosopher. Philosophy is feeling, communing and living with a capital letter at the start of a word.

There is definitely a tacit agreement among those who "speak in capital letters" to look down on anyone who uses collective plurals. But it is not something that can be explained in words. Simply posing the problem is a sign of an anti-philosophical mindset. This speaking in small letters without giving or requesting explanations is the sign of recognition.

Pierino doesn't entirely understand the thing, and he is a bit unsettled by it. All around him he seems to find members of his own family speaking the same allusive language he does, containing so much intimate and personal experience, family feuding, shame in front of others. Sometimes it makes him feel uncomfortable and embarrassed. He feels liberated from certain nightmares he thought were his alone but he suffers to see them somehow devalued, trivialized. He is often inclined to think that the other person talking like this doesn't really "get it."

Now he has to create some cover for himself. There is this

blessed inertia to be overcome. Resolutions, programs, schedules follow, one after the other. And books, always read with that suspicious irritability towards himself, his actions ruthlessly analyzed down to their most obscure motives. He is now unable to move without carrying a book with him. Actually, several books, to allow for his various possible frames of mind. He questions the morality of his every action.

He has become miserly with his time. But there are things no one knows. For example, that many — very many — of the hours at his desk are wasted in empty daydreams. His sister, who suspects, has no qualms about disturbing him. He gets annoyed with her, but also with himself. You have to be clean, clean, clean.

He is at the theater with a university classmate. The piece is modern, one that Pierino knows well, having heard it repeatedly two years earlier with his sister and her friends and an entire musical *clan*. He had openly participated in a sort of morbid, female enthusiasm that had developed around this opera. They had played it, sung it and commented on it at home for weeks. They had written to the composer. They listened to it religiously, boys and girls alike, leaning over each other in a corner of the gallery, their lights trained on the open score.

Pierino is now ashamed by all this and is anxious about today's verdict on the piece. The passions and uncontrolled feelings of his adolescence are now to be examined before this most respected and feared tribunal, the promising young philosopher, darling of the professors and hope of the faculty. He feels like someone honoring a respected guest in his home.

End of the first act. Pierino has once again felt the utter thrill of the first time. His soul boils with music. He would like to share with his companion the poignant words spoken before, interspersed with motifs sung in a low voice. But he cannot, he dares not. He tries to translate his confused feelings into the language of orthodox criticism.

His classmate is indifferent. The opera has made no great impression on him. He liked a certain tonal sensuality and the oratorical and moralistic intensity of the choruses.

Sensuality? Moralism? Hasn't he read Croce? If anyone in Pierino's family had delivered a judgment of this type he would have rebuked and annihilated them with four tight logical arguments. But now he shyly hedges his answers. His classmate lets him win too easily and smiles with superiority.

A flash. Could Croce be passé? He has noted in his companion a certain satisfaction in using the forbidden terms, as if this freedom were reacquired. Pierino feels petty, like a neophyte. So philosophy isn't something that's just there and has to be learned. You need *to do it*. Discipline, toil, patience — these are all very well. But then there's that ironic smile. You struggle and fight to acquire these things, to move easily in that world, to adapt the armor to your body. And just when you've learned to walk safely, and you feel you can go on the offensive, the ground collapses beneath your feet and your armor falls to pieces. Pierino now feels a sort of resentment mixed with triumph toward his masterly cousins, these heroes of the family table, able to pontificate in front of an audience of self-taught uncles and sentimental aunts in the name of stale philosophy. For the first time he feels superior to them.

At the university the battle against Croce continues. Every week a student takes the podium to debate his classmates and the professor.

Pierino listens eagerly but understands nothing. He sees that each of them defends a thesis representing a side, but he wouldn't begin to know how to explain which side, or to take a position himself. He would love to get up there himself, but to say what?

In any case, he will try. He has always had a need to pit himself against others which irresistibly draws him into any sort of competition.

With the assigned subject in hand and faced with the blank sheet of paper, he has no idea what to write. The thoughts in his head would cover half a page. And then what? He has to talk for three quarters of an hour and it is considered elegant and admirable to be surprised to hear that the time is up, with many remaining pages still in your hand.

So, at least let's put down these four ideas.

In writing, the ideas get longer. The connections, developments and digressions multiply. The pages fill up easily, one after another — the 45-minute time limit is far exceeded. The writing gets progressively smaller. Pierino takes extreme care not to lead himself astray. If he has written twenty pages, he wants them to be proper pages, full, dense, without margins or paragraph breaks. The invisible eye is watching. When twenty pages become twenty-five, thirty when typed, it's a joy, a triumph.

How easy difficult writing is! The words with capital letters are sweeter than the others. Their own weight allows them to be moved with greater conviction. Pierino no longer doubts that he has truly understood them, seeing how smoothly they flow in his hands. He reads over what he has written, imagining that he is sitting at his desk as a listener — he wouldn't understand a word. He has passed the test.

Now don't be mean. Pierino is not a cheater. He is deeply convinced of everything he writes, and what he writes makes sense. There is nothing further from his intentions than to deceive anyone. If he were to have the least self-doubt, he is the type who would find no peace until he had freed himself of it completely. Difficult writing guarantees that his ideas are important and worth writing down. It absolves him of the offense of not having understood the others and confirms his rightful place in their world. It is already something to have mastered the terminology. But here the terminology is not just a tool, it is a safeguard.

Pierino reads *The Critique of Pure Reason* with a commitment, scrupulously maintained, not to move forward without fully absorbing every single paragraph. But there are authors he is absolutely unable to digest — Nietzsche, for example. He has picked him up several times, but has always had to leave off after the first few pages. Nietzsche has no beginning and no end; there are no 'transitions'. So disconnected and inconsistent! An uninhabitable world. The beginning of each fragment reads as if you were starting a new book — you see no connection with what came before. You have to pay constant close attention; you can never surrender to mechanical reasoning or predict a conclusion; you never feel that you are being helped along or supported by the harmony of the structure. You can't give an opinion on the book — you have to give a hundred thousand, it contains so many ideas. Pierino hates aphorisms. Kant is so much easier.

(If I think of everything that separates me today from my friend Pierino, the most symptomatic is this — the only philosopher I am now able to read is Nietzsche).

Pierino doesn't have, and doesn't miss, the imaginative and creative gifts of his fellow students. Happy to admire them in the arts, he views them with a certain disdain when they turn to philosophy. He feels that there is something in their seductive theories, in their hotly formulated "needs," that is not genuine. Too easily he sees the human being behind their efforts — complete with personality, nerves and grievances. And he is annoyed by the tawdry way all this is cloaked in philosophy. He is by now strong enough to absorb a shock or two, and he shrugs his shoulders at the accusations hurled at him of rationalism and moralism. What he looks for in every problem is not so much the solution (any solution) as the neatness, the cleanness, the honesty of how the problem is set. There should be no misunderstandings. What is intended should be clear, and the meaning of the words known. He has a certain trick of taking a deep breath when he gets mixed up and begins to get excited: "Let's see then. You say 'reality.' What exactly do you mean by 'reality'?" This pose of implacable calm drives the others wild.

Taking Croce apart with this method becomes a game of patience. Just test the whole system step by step, connection by connection. And the result is that the system falls to pieces. The circle of forms of the mind proves to be full of cracks and gimmicks. The parallel between art and logic, economics and ethics comes down to an extrinsic need for symmetry. All that's left are individual discoveries and observations, with prejudices removed and appropriate distinctions made. Pierino could never go so far as to abandon all this valuable material just because the structure had been shown to be inconsistent. He has no iconoclastic urges; he is no triumphant destroyer. He feels instead a certain melancholy, a loss at having to give up a dear and certain guide, a serene and calming father.

His companions continue to accuse him of being a Crocean. He defends himself but feels that they are not entirely wrong. It is the Crocean spirit that he brings into play against its own creator, the order and patience, the untangling of the threads, the "disjointing."

The problem for him is always the placement, the collocation of the faculties in the world of the mind — the relationship between art and knowledge, between knowledge and will, and between economics and morals. He tries out new constructions and develops new connections. But he doesn't suffer any crisis or feel in any way unsettled. He feels that he is working from within a world for its own rearrangement. The main guidelines he already has.

At a certain point the possibility flashes on him that these elements whose order and placement he has been so tenaciously looking for do not admit of any order — that they can live as they are, separate, parallel, independent, without necessarily developing one within the other, without any hierarchy or precedence. The idea excites him. He feels that he has taken a step forward, free of a superfluous need, a prejudice. And he no longer thinks as much about defining and organizing as about describing. But this process needs its own theoretical justification, it must also be framed in a vision of the world and have its own name that ends in -ism. He throws himself into the pluralists, the individualists, the empirical critics: he studies Mach and Avenarius, he enters the labyrinth of Leibniz.

He has become a strong man. His solid and sincere appearance alone is made to inspire trust. Friends ask him advice about personal matters and younger cousins consult him about what career to follow. Mothers eye him with interest for their daughters.

He himself is so sure now of his own solidity that he doesn't even feel the need to boast about it. He likes to be a confessor — to speak the authoritative, persuasive words that unselfishly, without anger, show someone where their responsibilities lie. He is content that someone, thanks to him, is able to recognize calmly that they are wrong. He has a naïve trust in his qualities as a psychologist. He willingly lets people have the satisfaction of talking about themselves, as long as they accept him as their guide. He feels he is a liberator, a benefactor, the eye of the world. In a situation that calls for reprimand with sympathy, the gift to others of revealing to them their own misery, he feels at home.

Those who know him thoroughly do not allow themselves to be caught in his web. They evade, they struggle, they hate him. "That may be," says his sister, "but I don't care. You are a psychologist by profession." He is not pleased. He knows he is upright and correct even with himself. He sees these rebellions as a sign of his own deficiency, which he seeks to dissect and rectify.

His honesty sometimes borders on impudence. "My private life," he is pleased to repeat, "is public. It is open for anyone to judge." Confession for him has become the surrogate for abstention. He eludes the vigilance of the implacable eye by disclosing the secret things it would have had to discover. By this stratagem he can endure its gaze undaunted. It is stripped it of its function — by preempting it he has devalued it.

Pierino's ideas about sexual morality are now broader and more liberal, and he no longer considers as sinful certain acts and contacts that in the past would have made him cringe. But he wouldn't be able to bear their nagging weight if he kept them secret. There is a haste in him to expose himself, as if for fear of being anticipated by others. He could not bear it if others were to guess before his confession the things he says about himself, or if they were to talk about him behind his back. He opens up to all his friends, but begs each of them to keep his revelations to themselves. If he happens to criticize someone, he is agitated that his words might be reported to the person concerned, and he eagerly looks for an opportunity to say them himself to the person's face.

And he boasts to himself of this fainthearted candor as if it were a virtue, a strength.

One day something happened to me and I attempted to describe it in the following story:

A Poet

Near my house there is a shop that sells antique books, and the shopowner is a poet. A real poet, not a versifier. A man whom I believe will leave his mark on Italian literature.

A bookseller-poet — it's easy to imagine him with a large pipe, a beard, a skullcap and a long coat, good natured and refined. The reality matched this only in part. The pipe was small. The skullcap was a normal hat that he never took off. Refined, yes, but not good natured.

Sullen — that would be the dominant note. The eyes look you

over with annoyance and suspicion. The gaze is turned inward, and not calmly but with fear. You imagine a man who is completely self-absorbed, lost in his nervous tics and idiosyncrasies and "complexes."

I was a regular at the shop but I avoided the owner. I couldn't stand his hectoring manner. If I ask for a book he lets me know he's a poet. If I speak to him of poetry he looks at me as if to say: "Come, come sir! I sell books."

Yesterday I found him more welcoming. He recommended books to me and spoke about his own reading. I confess that the pleasure of conversing with a celebrated man of letters outweighed my antipathy, and I hazarded a question:

"Is it true that a definitive edition of your poetry is coming out?"

"Possibly," he replied angrily. "But to what end? The papers won't cover it and the public won't buy it."

My bitterness rose up. "So you're not a poet, you're just ambitious. All you want is to be successful." And I came out with a couple of conventional phrases to the effect that success is no measure of the value of a work of art, etc.

He interrupted me.

"Not true. The poet writes only for success. Don't come talking to me about art as expression, as an end in itself. The ability to express yourself is clearly a requirement in poetry, but it is not poetry. Poets speak because they have something to say — something different from ordinary people, something exceptional. Who would write poetry about fatherhood, something everyone knows about? I only know one poet who writes about fatherhood, and he turns it into motherhood — the desire of males to give birth. The things the poet expresses are forbidden instincts. He writes about his faults. And he does it to free himself of them, confess them, purify himself. If the public turns its back on him, these faults come back to torment him even worse than before."

Please don't think my poet is crazy. He's just using jargon, the jargon of psychoanalysis, a science that sees everything in terms of repressed instincts that re-emerge in the form of neuroses and idiosyncrasies that you can escape only by getting to the root of the problem — that is, by unraveling the knots in the unconscious, digging around in the labyrinth of memory until the initial impulse and the repression have been found.

When I hear strange talk like this, I have a strong desire to understand it. I am a healthy man. But I always suspect that the nervous energy of sick people contains some richness that I lack. At times my good health threatens to become too easy for me, and to turn into something burdensome and banal.

"I understand," I replied, "I grant what you say. I accept that writing poetry is a liberation from forbidden instincts, to calm the nerves. But I don't see how this purification can only happen through the approval of the public. Isn't it enough to have said these things, to have brought them out in the open? Isn't it enough to look at yourself, to objectify and contemplate yourself? Isn't this the supreme enjoyment of art, the catharsis?"

But the words died on my lips. This is the celebrated theory, the real truth, what more or less everyone has said from Aristotle to Croce. My poet wants more. He wants poetry to yield up other forms of liberation that touch the secret and inexpressible depths of the human essence. And I thought of the inevitable sense of modesty that takes hold of every "sane" or "normal" person the moment they reveal to others some hidden — and therefore true — part of themselves; of the tremendous effort of honesty required to tell "everything" to everybody. Of the intolerable sense of nakedness someone feels who sees this intimate personal gift received with careless indifference.

This, then, not "catharsis" or "exposition" — this is poetry for a true poet. I was ashamed of my shallowness.

I could feel his calm, malevolent gaze. By now I was in his power. I struggled to find an acceptable path to my goal, which I did not want at all costs to abandon, and to the conclusion I knew I had to reach — that an artist has to write in any case, with or without public approval.

"Never mind the satisfaction," I replied. "You don't write just for relief, to free yourself. Even if the poet has to suffer for eternity, even if he gets no personal enjoyment from his poetry, isn't it still his duty to write? Anyone who has this expressive ability and has something important to say is morally obliged to let the public share these riches."

"Says who? Why? Who's making him? This is morality, philosophy. I don't understand philosophy. I can only talk about psychology. The categorical imperative means nothing to me. I only see things that exist."

I blushed. I tried to put it right:

"No, I don't do philosophy. I also only do psychology. But it seems to me that a given mental faculty, even beyond any duty, comes with an instinctive, irresistible need to exercise it. The organ creates the function. A writer cannot help but write, regardless of whether he should or shouldn't, or whether it's a pain or a pleasure. The poet is slave to his abilities."

This was more like it. I was getting warmed up. I thought I had hit the mark. That I was being human and fair. This time the poet couldn't say no. A sort of enthusiasm took hold of me. The pleasure of winning the argument was merged with the stirring feeling of fighting selflessly for an artistic value, for guiding a man back onto the path of trust and productivity.

I was speaking. The poet was speechless. His gaze was absent. His features had crumbled. It seemed as if the unity of his face had dissolved and every wrinkle had an existence of its own. I had the sense that I was arguing my case in a vacuum.

I felt no rancor, but rather humiliation. He lives in a prison, suffering torture every day, but he refuses to leave it except through his own efforts. There is something strong and serene in his care-worn face — the calm of unwavering despair. To my restless desire to deal with the problem, he opposes a stubborn attachment to the tangle of delusions and resentments that constitute both his strength and his poetic impotence. He throws in the face of my need for clarity his right to suffer, complain and be unhappy. In no way does he envy my health.

"You are right," he said. "Goodbye."

Since yesterday I've loved that poet. I can't stop thinking about him.

I wanted to publish the story, but I felt that first it was my duty to show it to the interested party. Or rather, I took this opportunity to renew relations with him.

He snatched it out of my hands and rushed into the back of the shop. After a bit, he returned.

"Sir, everything you have written is false. I must beg you not to print this story. I can't stop you, but you would be doing me a great disservice. It would involve my shop, and I'm responsible to other people for it."

He had turned green and was shaking. For the first time he called me by my name, but he mangled it, deliberately it seemed, as if to keep me at a distance and deliver the message: "You are so unimportant, so despicable, that I won't even take the trouble to pronounce your name right."

I had expected all this, but I was stunned all the same. It bothered me that the shop boy was there to witness the embarrassing scene. I had felt that the ice was breaking, that I had been at the point of becoming a close friend. I protested weakly and then agreed.

After that day my house became a sort of refuge for the poet. He would come round on a Sunday afternoon and flop down on the couch, complaining about his troubles, his family, his shop. I listened and played him records by Bach and Ravel. But there was something suspicious and uncertain and reticent in his friendship for me — a fear of being exploited, of having to give, when all he wanted was to receive, to stretch out and rest.

And he wasn't wrong. There are great advantages to taking on a sick person as a teacher and doctor. It completely takes away the sense of passivity and dependence. It leaves you great scope for choosing among his various teachings, and the possibility of compensating for your own inferiority by feeling sorry for him and taking care of him in turn. You can get angry with him without feeling bad about it.

Has it ever happened to you that you had to tell a person something really harsh and then didn't have the courage to look him in the eye? To reveal to him some side of his character that he would never have had the strength to see on his own? You hesitate, you fear the reaction his modesty and susceptibility will unleash. You want to spare him your presence when he is suddenly left to face his own shame. Well, if you choose to take him aside with a humble and fraternal tone, expressing understanding and affection, consoling him and trying in every way to soften the blow — if you do this, you are nothing more than a vulgar show-off, in love with yourself, infatuated with your own role, and incapable of understanding and loving your friend. You would like to deliver the blow that will start him on a painful internal struggle, and at the same time have his gratitude and admiration. At that moment when he feels low and contemptible, you want him to see you as his pure, selfless, immaculate liberating angel. Kicking you across the room would be the least he could do.

Instead, tell him the same things in a towering rage, in a violent quarrel, so that you will be at least as wrong as he is. Spit these truths in his face like poison off your tongue. Give him a foothold to defend himself from, a reason to hate you and look at everything you say as false and evil. Then, what you have to say will penetrate his heart in a way that is human, gentle, and beneficial. He will be free to take it in as something of his own, and will be able to respect himself for not having held a grudge against you. He will not be afraid of you. Could this be the sense of the myth of Nereus, the soothsayer you had to fight to get him to make a prophecy?

Without wanting to, this was how my poet behaved with me. In his bloodless and absent gaze, in his unwillingness to talk about anything other than himself, I had a warranty against the excessive attention of the "saviors of souls." It was clear to me that he saw things more deeply than I did, but the angry and malicious harshness of his interpretations left me entirely free to accept them or not. I listened to him with partial attention the way an affectionate son listens to his elderly maniac father — but with an open, defenseless heart, ready to let myself be struck by the arrow that should find the mark.

One day he asked me point blank:

"Are you so sure, sir, that you are sane? Why do you do philosophy?"

Starting that day, I no longer do philosophy.

I would have trouble explaining why. I was never at a loss in defending my profession against unbelievers. I could demonstrate to anyone how much implicit philosophy there is in their daily decisions, and how impossible it is for anyone to do without an idea, however confused and imprecise, of the Universal. I could refute the accusations of uselessness that philosophy so often attracts, and show how much modern science owes to men like Descartes and Leibniz, just as all of 19th century culture is infused with Kant. I knew how to demonstrate ironically to my interlocutor that in his own attack on philosophy he himself was taking a philosophical position.

I was wonderfully versed in this entire repertoire. But under that green eye I was unable to show it off. I felt uneasy, naked, defenseless. I had remembered someone, now long-buried, with his filth and his fears, and the anxiety of being found out. My mother, recently dead. My cousins, far away, one a suicide . . ., I don't know what to say. Everything seemed so petty and personal now about that empirical me who once was called Pierino.

The question had been direct and precise, not theoretical. Not "What is philosophy good for?" but "Why do you practice it." It had nothing to do with the unity of the real and the transcendental, the relation between theory and practice, or the concept of the concept. What it did have to do with was me, with a small 'm'. All that was left for me was to confess, or keep quiet.

I kept quiet, but I had to change professions. And since that day I have felt more free, and I think I understand more than I did. There is a whole series of things that I am no longer afraid of: speaking imprecisely, saying "human beings" instead of "the Mind." Since that day I feel neither horror nor disdain for the natural sciences, and I no longer feel the need to write in a difficult style. The word "empiricist" is no longer an insult. And since that day, what the Universal might mean no longer enters my head.

I am leafing through a philosophy journal. A gentleman is speaking with great pomposity of the "magic circle of philosophy."

So let him tell me, that gentleman, how he entered that circle. It will emerge that he too had a dad and a mom, and friends, and that now he has nervous tics and behaves in a certain way with women. He will also tell me the less pleasant things that he is a little ashamed of. Nor will he hide behind the transcendental Ego or claim that his personal affairs are not important. He'll tell me them, to please me. And maybe, afterwards, he'll feel different, and his entry into that magic circle won't seem like such a great and glorious thing anymore — and he won't be so afraid of leaving it.

5. Philosophical Criticism and Theoretical Physics

The obvious is difficult to demonstrate — and not always true.

— Eddington

[Ventotene, May-June 1939]

In 1787, Emanuel Kant wrote:[1]

When Galileo rolled his spheres down the incline with a weight which he selected himself, or when Torricelli let the air carry a weight which he had previously imagined to be equal to a known column of water, or yet later when Stahl converted metals into chalk and that in turn into metals by removing something from them and then restoring it, a light came on for all researchers of the science of nature. They comprehended that reason penetrates only what it itself brings forth according to its design, and that it would have to proceed with principles of its judgment according to enduring laws and to require nature to answer its questions, but not to let itself totter, as it were, at the end of a leash of nature. For otherwise accidental observations, made according to no previously conceived plan, do not at all cohere in a single necessary law, which reason still seeks and needs. With its principles in one hand, according to which alone harmonious appearances can hold for laws, and with the experiment in the other, which it conceived with respect to those principles, reason must indeed go to nature to be taught by it, but not in the role of a school boy who allows everything to be dictated as the teacher wishes, but rather as an invested judge who requires the witnesses to answer the questions which he poses to them. And thus even physics has to attribute this exceptionally advantageous revolution of its manner of thinking to the sudden notion of seeking (not fictionalizing) in nature — and commensurate

---

[1] *Kritik der reinenVernunft* [*Critique of Pure Reason*], Preface to the second edition.

to what reason itself puts into it — that which it must learn from nature and of which reason would know nothing of itself. In this way natural science was first brought to the sure path of a science after having been nothing further than a mere toying around for so many centuries.

In 1939, one of the most daring present day scientist-philosophers wrote:

> I believe that the whole system of fundamental hypotheses can be replaced by epistemological principles. Or, to put it equivalently, all the laws of nature that are usually classed as fundamental can be foreseen wholly from epistemological considerations. They correspond to *a priori* knowledge. . . .[2]

The entire development of modern physics falls into the century and a half between these two formulations.[3]

Are we justified in saying that Kant would today be happy with Eddington's words, and would consider his dream realized?

The preface to the second edition of the *Critique of Pure Reason* gives us clear indications of the intentions that motivated Kant in his work. He appears to be spellbound by the appeal of thought revolutions — the sudden reversals and inversions of viewpoint that in a flash reveal the hidden reason for what had seemed to be a miraculous coincidence or the sign of some finalistic organization of the world. The Copernican discovery that the whole universe seems to rotate around the earth only because the earth itself rotates is the most obvious example of such revolutions. But others, deeper and more intimate and achieved in the same way, all at once opened

---

[2]Eddington, *La filosofia della scienza fisica*, Bari 1941, p. 70. Quite deliberately, I have put dots in place of the end of this sentence, which reads: . . . and are therefore *wholly subjective*." Eddington uses the word subjective rather naïvely, as a non-philosopher; and this expression, placed next to the Kantian quotation, would have represented a distortion of his thinking.

[3]It seems to me much more correct to start the new era of physics with the discovery of non-Euclidean geometry, beginning around 1820, rather than, as is common practice, with the theory of relativity and the discovery of Planck's constant around 1900. We shall see better below the reasons that justify this view.

the *royal road* of science to mathematics and physics. It must not be thought, says Kant, that it was so easy for mathematics to find its way. For a long time (and especially in Egypt) it was nothing but pure groping. And the revolution that allowed it to set out on a secure path with inexhaustible potential is due to the lucky intuition of one man. "A new light must have flashed on the mind of the first man (Thales, or whatever his name may have been) who demonstrated the properties of the isosceles triangle. For he found that it was not sufficient to meditate on the figure, as it lay before his eyes, or to look for the pure concept of it, as it existed in his mind, and thus endeavor to get at the knowledge of its properties, but that it was necessary to produce that figure, as it were, by a positive *a priori* construction trough those *a priori* concepts that he himself inserted and represented in it; and that, to be sure *a priori* of anything, he must not attribute to the object any other properties than those which necessarily followed from what he himself, in accordance with his own conception, had placed in the object."

The progress of human thought, or at least of science, thus consists for Kant of sudden revolutions, of "cataract operations" that all at once light up the whole field of research and give access to the road science will safely tread forever. In every case, essentially, it is about overcoming an anthropomorphic illusion — or if you prefer, performing an act of humility. It is only our foolish pride that leads us to place the earth at the center of the universe and rotate the stars around it, to see man as the goal of creation, and to depict God as looking like us. The aspects of nature that appear to conform to our ideas and purposes do so only because without realizing it we continually mix the boundaries of our minds into our consideration of nature. Nothing to marvel at, then — no miracle, and no privilege for us if the resulting image shows remarkable conformity with the concepts and forms of our intellect.

It may at first glance seem strange and paradoxical that the first person with the courage to undertake this reversal and personally overcome this anthropomorphic idol should be repaid by a bountiful harvest of results. Kant insists that it is only one individual, generally, who dares to make a revolution. Humanity is compelled to follow along, almost in spite of itself, thanks to the great success of the new attitude and the extraordinary fertility that rewards such an act of modesty. It might have been expected that anyone who dared to debunk the myth of an orderly and harmonious world almost miraculously adapted to our organs of understanding would find nothing but chaos and disorder once the illusion had collapsed.

If regularity and harmony are not actual features of reality, but rather conditions we impose on it, it might be supposed that recognizing this would bring down the edifice of science and leave nothing in its place but brute causality.

But in actual fact what happens is the opposite. Once the *a priori* origin of laws is known they do of course lose their mysterious appeal, but they also come much more securely under our control. We are no longer compelled to look for their effects in the exterior world, occasionally welcoming its regularity as a gracious gift of the Creator. We instead penetrate the internal mechanism by which such regularity is projected onto the world, and instead of later almost chancing upon pieces of ourselves in the *real world* and marveling that the *laws of nature* are so neatly consonant with our own intellectual patterns, we now hold in our hands the threads of the fabric from which this illusion is created and we control it, panoramically you might say. We have become its masters, able to follow it however it evolves and anticipate its development.

It is as if we had penetrated the trade secrets of a skillful magician. We have entirely lost our belief that a mysterious force directs him, but all of a sudden we can repeat his tricks and vary them endlessly.

Dominion over nature has thus become the payment for our unbelief, or (if we want to remove the Faustian deal with the devil) our humility, the renunciation of our salvation and birthright — the abandonment of the crazy dream of the absolute *"eritis sicut Deus, scientes bonum et malum"* is rewarded with an extraordinary dominion over the world. It is as if grace had been granted to one who had stopped hoping for it. The courage to recognize that we have been abandoned by God, to give up being the center and purpose of the universe, immediately opens our eyes and enriches us with an immense patrimony.

We have expressed these things in mystical language quite deliberately. When Kant speaks of revolutions owing to the daring of a single individual, of sudden illumination, of avenues abruptly opening to someone who has been groping blindly, he is surely aware that a truly great breakthrough in knowledge always comes not so much from a rational effort or a dialectical development as from an emotional and moral reversal, an inversion of values, a victory over ourselves and over what we are most deeply, persistently and unconsciously tied to. Anyone who accomplishes a reversal of the magnitude of a Thales, a Copernicus, or a Bacon must first of all struggle in their innermost self in a way not very different from the person who seeks a state of perfect passivity and humility before their god. Molinos said that we mustn't ask anything of God — not even our own salvation. Scientists must give up on this idealized version of a natural world that speaks their language, a world organized around their needs and their sensory organs. Only this absolute emptiness and purity, this absence of *anticipation* will open their eyes to themselves and the world, letting them see how much of themselves they have projected onto the world so that they can bring such projection under control. One day, a man seeking grace was told:

> "You desire grace and are ready to ask for it. But are you sure you will recognize it when it touches you? What if it were something completely different from what you were expecting? Something that made you lose God instead of finding Him?"
>
> "Well," I would say, "that would no longer be grace. I would have no reason to call it by that name."
>
> "In truth I tell you," came the reply, "you are not worthy of receiving grace."

The scientist is not so different from that man. As long as he expects nature to yield findings favorable to him and conducts his investigations as if nature were his friend and shared his same substance, the answers he gets will be incomplete and inaccurate. He will have to grope for fragments of order and regularity. Only when he abandons the pretense of a law that conforms to his own intellect will the myth of a beautiful and orderly natural world be revealed to him as an illusion due to his own pride and self-love. Only then will the grace of knowledge come to him with open arms. Only then will the intimacy attained with that illusion make it useful to him. He has lost nature but found himself, and just there where he had admired harmonious arrangements and wonderful, simple symmetries, he finds these are nothing more than his own image, projected and multiplied to infinity by an ingenious trick of mirrors. Knowledge of nature is therefore the possession of this hidden game, and science is nothing more than the capacity to make use of it, to use it for one's own ends, altering and shifting the effects, reproducing methodically what *Nature* had offered us in fragments and almost by chance. Anyone who wants to know nature intimately should look inside themselves.

So behind every great discovery, every revolution in science, there is a moral victory — the destruction of a firmly entrenched idol lodged in the recesses of our soul, one that is extremely difficult to notice and extremely painful to get rid of. This idol consists mostly of a blind and infantile love we have for ourselves, a need to feel surrounded by forces that are friendly to us and to see what we feel in our innermost selves repeated in the universe, in objective reality. This idol that we are bound to with every fiber of our being assumes the most diverse form and lurks in the most unlikely disguises. It was called the geocentric system in Ptolemaic astronomy, final cause in scholasticism, absolute time in Newton, and in classical electromagnetism, the ether. In some cases and to some researchers, it appeared in the form of a *universal constant.* What mask is it hiding behind today? This will be one of the objects of our research.

In any case, whoever is the first who manages to destroy this idol in their heart is not generally understood or appreciated by their contemporaries. There is always a personal price to be paid for a moral victory. Not only must one's own resistance be overcome, but that of the surrounding world as well. But the scientist who has mustered the courage to achieve this great reversal in his or her own heart can count on an important ally in passing on the new attitude to others — the success that this liberation brings in the field of science and the great and sudden productivity that rewards the act of honesty and renunciation. The world will first be interested in the new discoveries for what they are in themselves, but then it will want to learn the method that led to them. Scientific curiosity will soon change to human curiosity. There is no better propaganda for a new intellectual and moral attitude than the fact that it has shown itself to be a key that can open many doors in science and knowledge. If, therefore, at the basis and origin of scientific discovery there is an attitude of mind that includes all its tendencies, affections and preferences, the discovery itself will in its turn affect the world of religious and moral affections and sympathies. Backed by the authority of its success, it will impose the moral transformation that stimulated it in the first place on the culture of the time.

Kant proposed to bring to metaphysics the revolution that had already set geometry and physics on a firm footing. Whether or not he succeeded is not something we want to investigate here. What he did do, however, was appreciate the nature and character of this reversal, and put into theoretical form its patterns and psychological phenomenology. He placed in the hands of his contemporaries and of posterity a sort of intellectual and moral method for achieving scientific discoveries. The fact that his contemporaries and posterity were hardly aware of this gift and — at least consciously — made little use of it is due in part to Kant himself and the interpretation he gave of his own doctrine.

He did not fail to note an essential difference between the secure positions reached by mathematics and physics following the revolutions by which these sciences as such were founded. The former became a completely *a priori,* pure science. Its propositions follow necessarily from initial assumptions, and experience can be completely excluded from its development except as a control and confirmation of results reached by calculation. The latter, on the other hand, is only partly *a priori.* Experience still plays a predominant part, and even if the role of reason is not passive but rather like a judge interrogating witnesses, even if it is reason that decides what questions experience will be asked, it is still always experience that gives the answers, answers that reason could not in any way predict or deduce from principle. In adducing the examples of Galileo, Torricelli, and Stahl, Kant seeks to show how progress can consist of the introduction of an *a priori* element in naturalistic research — the element of choice, grouping phenomena according to criteria that respond to our needs, criteria that bring order and regularity where before there was chaos. But the material to be put in order is not a product of reason. There is no logical principle that led Galileo to deduce that objects near the earth must undergo acceleration and that this has to be 981 cm/sec2, or Torricelli that atmospheric pressure should be precisely 76 cm of mercury per cm2.

Kant was undoubtedly aware of this basic difference between the mathematics and physics of his time, but he tried, as it were, to obfuscate it by placing the two sciences on the same plane, in a parallel position, one in Transcendental Aesthetics and the other in Transcendental Analytics. He sets pure mathematics, founded on transcendental intuitions of space and time alone, in corre-spondence with a pure physics founded on transcendental forms of judgment. He is quick to note at the outset that this physics he is talking about is not the commonly known version.

> We actually possess a pure science of nature in which are propounded, *a priori* and with all the necessity requisite to apo-dictic propositions, laws to which nature is subject. I need only call to witness that propaedeutic of natural science which, under the title of the universal Science of Nature, precedes all Phys-ics (which is founded upon empirical principles). In it we have Mathematics applied to phenomena, and also purely discursive principles (derived from concepts), which constitute the phil-osophical part of the pure cognition of nature. But even here there are things that are not quite pure and independent of em-pirical sources: such as the concept of *motion*, that of *impen-etrability* (upon which the empirical concept of matter rests), that of *inertia*, and many others, which prevent its being called a perfectly pure science of nature. Besides, it only refers to objects of the external sense and therefore does not give an example of a universal science of nature, in the strict sense, for such a science must reduce nature in general, whether it concerns the object of the external or that of the internal sense (the object of Physics

as well as Psychology), to universal laws. But among the principles of this universal physics there are a few which actually have the required universality; for instance, the propositions that *substance is permanent,* and that *every event is determined by a cause* according to constant laws, etc. These are actually universal laws of nature, which subsist completely *a priori.* There is then in fact a pure science of nature.[4]

While the pure mathematics Kant describes is thus something very close to the actual mathematics of mathematicians, and a surveyor of his time would easily have recognized his own intellectual attitude and his own procedures in it, pure natural science, as he calls it, is something very different from the physics of the physicists. It is an empty framework, incapable of expressing by itself any of the particular laws that constitute the content of natural science. The transcendental intuitions of space and time contain the entire edifice of mathematics, since the axioms of geometry are nothing but the synthetic *a priori* forms in which these transcendental intuitions are expressed. Kant says it explicitly, when he differentiates mathematics as a *construction of concepts* from philosophy as *rational knowledge derived from concepts.*[5] If pure intuition is expressed in synthetic *a priori* propositions of the type "at a single point no more than three lines can be cut at right angles," or "a straight line can extend to infinity," or "there are always three points in a plane," all the theorems of geometry necessarily derive from them. But without recourse to experiment it is not possible to deduce the laws of physics from the specifications of the concept of cause or substance.

The revolution, in short, that had transformed geometry from an empirical into an *a priori* science, had in the case of physics only been halfway completed in Kant's time, and he could hardly argue that natural science would eventually be able to free itself completely from experience. So we can answer our own question by saying that if Kant could today read the above citation and hear

---

[4]*Prolegomena,* § 15.
[5]*Critique of Pure Reason, Transcendental Methodology* I i. Cf. *Prolegomena,* §§ 7, 12, 13.

that "when the epistemological scrutiny of definitions is systematically applied, and its consequences are followed up mathematically, we are able to determine all the 'fundamental' laws of nature (including the purely numerical constants of nature) without any physical hypothesis,"[6] he would rejoice as if it were an extraordinary success achieved in a field that was dear to him. But he would also be greatly astonished, as if it were something he could scarcely have foreseen or considered possible.

Kant believed that physics in his time had reached a stage that was almost definitive, from an epistemological point of view. And even though he also thought infinite new discoveries were possible, he certainly did not foresee a radical new Copernican style revolution. Even less so for geometry, which had reached a precision beyond which it did not seem possible to go. The task he set himself was to extend this revolution to metaphysics, not to pursue or renew it in the exact and experimental sciences.

And nevertheless, each on its own, physics and even geometry have achieved a reversal of outlook comparable to what Kant theorized. And from it they have drawn the familiar extraordinary harvest of discoveries and applications. To many this reversal appeared to be in open conflict with Kantian doctrine,[7] while to others it seemed to unfold precisely in the spirit of Kantism.[8]

Both points of view can be supported, depending on whether Kantism is intended as a stable and well-defined body of doctrine concerning the *a priori* forms of sentience and intellect, or as a particular attitude of the mind, a way of addressing problems that was initiated by Kant and can be pursued even concerning issues that Kant never envisaged and did not know of. The question is quite important to our purposes. It will allow us to decide whether recent physics has traveled its path, so to speak, by chance — essentially guided by the need to provide theoretical justification for findings

---

[6]Eddington, op. cit., p. 125.

[7]Cf., for example, Helmholtz, *Schriften zur Erkenntnistheorie*, Berlin 1921; Reichenbach, *Relativitätstheorie und Erkenntniss a priori*, Berlin 1920, and "Der gegenwärtige Stand der Relativitätsdiscussion," in *Logos* 10 (1922) p. 341.

[8]Cf., for example, Gonseth, *Qu'est-ce que la logique?*, Paris 1938; Eddington, op. cit., p. VII s., and Cassirer.

that have emerged experimentally — or whether it has been guided, consciously or not, by an epistemological directive that ought to be identified so that scientists can be made aware of it and pushed to apply it systematically. And, more generally, that will allow us to see the relations that exist between philosophy and natural science and the services that the former may offer the latter.

Kant's essential concern was therefore to provide a theory for the revolution that had placed geometry and physics on a scientific basis — to demonstrate, that is, that the principles these sciences are based on are not realities in themselves, passively obtainable from the external world, but mental formulations, structures within which we frame the content of our experience, and which we then, so to speak, impose on it. He then also had to show how the *a priori* recognition of this characteristic, rather than shaking the stability and value of science, puts it on a more secure base, makes us masters of its progress and development, and allows us to systematically and methodically achieve results that would otherwise have arrived only in fragments. Kant therefore had to oppose any subjective or skeptical interpretation of the reversal, as well as any doctrine holding that such forms and principles, precisely because they belong to our minds and not to the objective world, represented nothing more than a subjective illusion, an arbitrary distortion of realty.

To do this he had to on one hand undermine the myth of a reality apart, independent of the subject, and on the other show clearly how these forms and principles, although originating in the human mind, can possess the stability and solidity of *eternal ideas* and can be beyond the power of the mind to disregard or alter, since they constitute its essence. In the place of the stability of the objective world he has to substitute the stability of transcendental forms so that geometry and physics can maintain their own universality and certainty.

This is the aspect of Kantian doctrine that most impressed the philosophers. The conversion of the concept of *reality* into a concept of *objectivity* whose basis is the internal consistency and coherence of its representations, the distinction between phenom-

enon and *noumenon* and a firm agnosticism regarding the latter
— these issues have given rise to endless discussions. Philosophy
did not resign itself to abandoning the concept of *reality* or *existence,* and since it could no longer attribute it to *the thing in itself,* it
attributed it to the Subject, the transcendental Self, or to the unity
of subject with object. It addressed to Kant the eternal challenge to
skeptics: in stating that nothing at all can be said about the thing
in itself we have already stated something about it; the denial of
an absolute truth, insofar as it claims to be valid, constitutes the
affirmation of a truth.

These are insurmountable objections that will lead us in an
eternal vicious circle as long as we explicitly or implicitly use the
terms *reality, truth, existence,* as primary, elementary, irreducible
concepts — as what I would call the raw material reasoning is
made of. The only escape from this circle is to make use of elementary concepts of a completely different nature, explicitly pro-
hibiting any use of the terms *truth, existence,* etc., in a meaning
that is primitive and irreducible to anything else. But this is much
more difficult than it might seem at first, because such concepts
are commonly included in our discourse not only as nouns — they
are hidden, for example, under the copula that unites subject with
predicate in our most common propositions. To be free of the
need for reality or truth or existence it is not enough to proceed
discursively. What is required is the sort of reversal of outlook in
which the moral, sentimental and affective spheres are also invested. We do not need to *solve* the problem of reality, but to *undo* the
psychological attitude that poses it and gives it meaning. And we
need to initiate a discourse in which the question "Is that true?" or
"Does that correspond to an objective reality?" no longer has any
meaning and cannot be answered.

If and how such an attitude might be possible we shall see in
part below. In any case, however, it is not the attitude of the philosophies commonly referred to as post-Kantian. For them, the need
for reality or for the object is still the central need. Conscious of the
impossibility of giving up on solving this problem as long as the
words *true* and *real* are given a meaning — that is, as long as the
mental attitude that produces them is accepted as legitimate — and

incapable, on the other hand, of overcoming this attitude that they consider the philosophical attitude par excellence and which they would never let go of lest they lose their own reason for living, these philosophers dither over *subject-object* dualism, looking for a point of entry into the circle that will allow them to develop its terms coherently. One minute they stop on the absolute Subject, the next on the absolute Object, now on an initial and original unity of subject and object — always giving these starting points a character that allows the satisfaction of our need for objectivity, for reality.

It is undoubtedly right to call these philosophers Kant's heirs. They took up one of his main problems, dissecting it in depth, illuminating it in many of its aspects, and experiencing, so to speak, its intractability. During the course of their explorations they made some remarkable discoveries about some fundamental aspects of the subject-object relationship and the development of one from the other (the concept of *dialectics* is a typical example). But they moved further and further away from the natural and mathematical sciences. Their object of study was no longer the revolution that opened the way to progress in these sciences by identifying their *a priori* elements. It was instead the problem of the *a priori* objectivity or non-objectivity of such elements, and whether or not it was possible to attribute the property of reality to knowledge constituted in such a way. The problem of the *conformation* of scientific knowledge had turned into the question of its *validity*. If this is defined as the essential problem of philosophy, it is clear that philosophy, understood in this way, can be of very little help to science.

But from Kant other paths branch off.[9] He had codified, so to speak the *a priori* forms by which our intuition and intellect organize the content of knowledge. Doubts soon arose about whether the codification was precise and the list of categories exhaustive. It was realized that the formative and organizing activity of the mind goes far beyond space and time and his table of judgments. Other aspects of mind came to light that Kant had ignored whose character was equally universal, essential and necessary. Kant's concern

____

[9]See E. Colorni, "Apologue." [Ch. 6 below. Ed's note].

had been more epistemological than psychological, and the forms, the categories he theorized as synthetic *a priori,* were the usual categories that had served for centuries as the basis for philosophy and science: quantity, quality, substance, cause, time, space, etc. Wanting to investigate their nature and position in the mind, he had simply imported them wholesale from the tradition of his time.

But the newly acquired awareness that these categories had no reality in themselves and were simply the necessary forms of our minds attracted the attention of many to the spirit itself in all its breadth and in all its various manifestations, even those not purely scientific and cognitive. Other forms and categories were found that had every right to be categorized as universal. Other areas of *objective reality* passed within the dominion of transcendental forms: beauty, goodness, the *divine* itself. Other approaches went even further in undermining the traditional image of the world of the mind. These considered to be original, obscure, primitive and essential formations, hidden in the innermost meanderings of consciousness and until then kept out of view by the need in classical thought for order and clarity, responsibility and justification: anguish, terror, the sense of death, pain, or else the *libido* or the sense of guilt, or the inferiority complex, or eros or *sympathy.*[10]

Those who approached these mental forms with a *philosophical* mindset sought to proceed according to the transcendental method. They emphasized, that is, the autonomy and necessity of these concepts, exhibiting them as first and irreducible components of the world of the mind, describing their behavior and development as something essential and original, as the very substance that human reality is made of. The earlier rational-logical terms that had been used to break down the world of knowledge and action were replaced by the new *mental atoms* as a new raw material for composing the mosaic of the human world. But more than to the work of reconstruction, they committed themselves

---

[10]These are things that are so well known that there is no need for citations. I would just like to recall, for the concept of Eros, or of love or sympathy, Klages's book *Vom kosmogonischen Eros,* Scheler's studies, *Wesen und Formen der Sympathie, Liebe und Erkenntnis,* etc.; and finally, Denis de Roughemont's interesting essay *L'amour et l'occident,* Paris 1939.

as philosophers to the *affirmation* of these forms — advocating and describing a method of introspection that would reveal them as original elements and would recognize them as separate and independent data of the soul. As such, they affirmed in them the stability and solidity, the objectivity, and the non-decomposable quality commonly attributed to what is called real. And they spoke of *existence,* arriving by another route — and carrying a different psychological and human cargo — at the same port that the so-called post-Kantian philosophies had reached.

It is precisely in this common point of arrival, in this shared need, this equal concern with finding a stable base that could be taken as objective, that many diverse ways of proceeding might perhaps recognize among themselves the network of kindred premises and aims that allows them to share the name *philosophy.* And perhaps precisely the lack of such a purpose is what leads them to contest the right of various ways of proceeding to call themselves by that name, even though they start out from the same observations and the same body of material. Philosophy, they say, cannot help but have a cognitive end. Striving, that is, to affirm a truth (even if it is that it is not possible to reach any truth). Any activity that does not set itself this purpose, even if it makes use of data and findings taken from philosophy, may be a science or a practical activity or something else, but it certainly is not philosophy.

We will certainly not be the ones to contest the legitimacy of this use of the term *philosophy.* We would only like to observe that with this statement philosophy tied itself to the use of concepts such as truth, reality, and existence as primary and irreducible concepts — and this is the case even when its essence and freshness come with the affirmation that the concepts to be used as primary and irreducible are of another type entirely. With this usage philosophy defined itself, in short, as the science that uses the terms truth, reality, existence, etc. as primitive and irreducible terms.

At the same time, similar and parallel to this one, there are other currents that also take their cue from the discovery of an affective intentionality in the dark depths of human consciousness — of a fluid world of tendencies, sympathies, and errors, which appears as something more profoundly original, more elementary and more primitive than the clearest and most common forms seen by the science of the mind as autonomous in the human soul. Only rather than dealing essentially with the affirmation of these forms, with their justification and recognition as necessary and transcendental data of the mind, these currents are more interested in their use. Rather than emphasizing their universality and existence, they are concerned to see whether, taking them as heuristic criteria, as working tools, it might not be possible to present the whole of mental life, or particular aspects of it, from a different perspective, one possibly more useful for certain purposes. Whether what had always been considered the most typical and essential attitudes of mind — knowledge, will, feeling, memory, rationality, morality, etc. — might not be productively viewed as complex formations, made up of a combination or evolved form of other simpler elements.

The process involves the decomposition and disaggregation of the world of the mind, similar to what in physics led to a view of the atom, initially held to be indivisible, as a complex structure of protons and electrons. The essential forms of the mind show up as the result and almost the exterior crystallizations of this *intentional*, subterranean, fluid world, inaccessible to the tools of common logic, that meanders beneath the stable and manufactured world where people set up their points of reference, the safe havens for their ideas, the common and generic foundations that guarantee that they can communicate, converse, and put up with each other. Nietzsche, with iconoclastic bitterness, pointed the way, and there were those who followed him with the calm detachment of the investigator.

The presence of this subterranean world could not be demonstrated through reasoning, which would have presupposed the validity of the very formations that were to be rooted out. Nor would it do to approach this world directly through a process of intuitive introspection, of anti-rational asceticism. Centuries of irrational and mystical experience had exhausted the domain of what could be obtained through the simple elimination and denial of reason. The best way to show that a substance is not simple but composite is not to reason over its essence, nor look at it from all sides, nor abandon it in search of other substances that might be simpler still — it is to actually take it apart and then rebuild it using the elements thus obtained. Only when we can master its process of formation, so that we can repeat it, influence it, modify it and anticipate it as we like — only then can we say we really know it. Indeed, knowing it does not in this case mean anything else but this *mastery of it.* And the word *knowledge* loses its meaning of ascertaining or affirming the reality or truth of something and takes on that of mastering a process.

Perhaps precisely because of this difference in the meaning of the term *knowledge,* we are already outside the actual field of philosophy. But this is not what interests us here. What we want is to see how modern psychology lets us glimpse the possibility of breaking up the mental formations that seem most stable and elementary and resistant to decomposition.[11]

---

[11]In the cultural world it is rare to hear psychoanalytic methods discussed dispassionately. This is perhaps the primary indication of their power to disintegrate. We do not use violence and aggressiveness except against those who threaten us directly. And this ought to be enough to demonstrate our thesis, which seeks only to state that such methods have shown themselves able to disrupt values and formations that our culture is tied to with its innermost fibers. Whether this is a good thing, this disintegration, or whether it wouldn't be better to put up a defense against it as a threat, we do not want to decide. I just think that we will be much more aware of such values and the opportunity offered to keep and develop them, if we don't reject taking them apart. Their utility to us depends on how well we know how to manage them. This is not to deny that psychoanalytic methods are presently in an absolutely rudimentary stage of development, and that many cures have made patients worse rather than better, and that psychoanalysis is a dangerous instrument that can produce results opposite to those desired. But even this is an argument more for than against its utility, just as it isn't an argument against the explosive power of dynamite to observe that a number of facilities were blown up by its discoverer. A method of treatment that does not touch something living and sensitive could not do any harm either. Here one has the impression of being on extraordinarily rich and fertile terrain whose method of cultivation is not yet well known. Nor do I want to deny that many applications of psychoanalytic methods in the world of culture and art are puerile and superficial. They are often simple transpositions from one field to another, undertaken without attention to the specific nature of each problem. Better cultural preparation on the part of the specialists in psychoanalysis would certainly do no harm. But the discipline is damaged by its ambiguous position between science and philosophy. The philosophers do not want to handle it, assigning it to the competence of the scientists — who in turn reject it as falling under the category of philosophy. And I might be permitted to express hesitantly, from the end of this little note, the suspicion that in this as in many other things, such a lively concern to identify the criteria that distinguish science from *philosophy,* and to cleave so rigidly to the boundaries of one's own area of expertise is owed not so much to theoretical considerations as to a desire to expel from that area arguments that would be too difficult or laborious or perplexing or

This began with pathologies — with neurotic phenomena, phobias, idiosyncrasies, hysteria. A method of decomposition was found that would allow these phenomena, which weigh on the sick person with such force and necessity, to be thought of as bundles, knots, reservoirs of the shadowy life of tendencies and passions that snakes through the unconscious of each of us. Imaginary defenses against imaginary dangers, fantasy atonement for fantasy sins. The rich and unknown world of childhood, with its indecipherable *intentional* language, its rapid and unthinking transpositions of meanings, its sudden storms of passion and jealousy — this world so radically different from ours, populated by omniscient and omnipotent demigods, benevolent and malevolent and simultaneously loved and feared, whose actions are often mysterious and incomprehensible (in fact, this is how adults mostly appear to children). This is a world in which the boundaries between the true and the false, between the possible and the impossible, between reality and dreams are blurred and imprecise — a world that appears to be the hidden culprit behind almost all of our psychic defects and manias. These are relics of our childhood life, which emerge arrogant and disturbing among the orderly and regulated structures of our lives as civilized human beings, residues that are badly digested or buried in shallow graves. Reconnecting them with the complex from which they arose, bringing back to consciousness that suppressed and vanished life that had taken such devious and malign revenge for its own exclusion actually amounts to recovery. The patient witnesses this resurrection with a wonder that approaches enchantment.[12] The pieces again fit together, the knots come loose, the defenses relax, the terror and bitterness subsides.[13] Health is restored by allowing the unconscious to flower in the light of the conscious. And the illness turns out to have been no more than a bottleneck in

---

dangerous to deal with.

[12]See, for example, Umberto Saba's cycle of poems entitled *Il piccolo Berto* [*Little Berto*].

[13]This, if I am not mistaken, is the core of the method on which all the various schools that originated from Freud's discovery agree. The disagreements revolve around what should be considered as the essential element of infantile affect — whether it is the libido with its fundamental expression in the Oedipus complex (Freud), or the inferiority complex (Adler), or both these things and others (Jung). But these discussions have no crucial bearing on the subject at hand.

the process of channeling the turbulent waters of childhood emotion into the tranquil canals of reason, reality, morality, and coexis-
tence with one's neighbor.

But it is here that we see the great interest of these studies even
for the psyche of a healthy person. This channeling process, this
working of raw material into harmonious and coherent forms is
the task that we all carry out, healthy or not, according to a more
or less steady pattern determined by our own condition as human
beings, by our relations with the surrounding environment, and by
some general features of the collective we live in. Healthy people
accomplish it smoothly and without shocks, the sick haltingly and
awkwardly, running continually into snags and setbacks. But the
process is the same, and as a whole it is the same for everybody,
because it is common to everyone to be born, to feel hunger and
thirst, pleasure and pain, and sexual stimulation. It is common to
everyone to have two eyes, two legs, and two hands that are stimulated in the same way. And all of us have a father and a mother, and
are generally educated by them or by someone who replaces them,
and receive in our infancy tokens of affection and reprimand, gifts
and punishments. And we have other children around us with
whom we have to get along, and we learn to our cost that not all
our desires can be satisfied.

No one is likely to contest that if our organs were arranged
in a different way — if procuring food, say, were as easy for us as
breathing, or if we were born already mature and didn't need to be
looked after (not to invent scenarios even further from our present
state) — then our concepts of reality and intention and reason and
morality would also be quite different from what they are. Such
observations are so banal that most of the time philosophers leave
them unsaid. But assuming such things is dangerous. It leads to
forgetting them, to emphasizing only the necessity, universality
and transcendence of these concepts, their *objective* value.

Objectivity itself, on the other hand, might perhaps be considered an anthropomorphic criterion, derived from the need for
security, from the desire to feel surrounded by a stable and permanent universe, and *necessity*, which it is based on, might turn out to
be something not very different from the compulsion with which

certain neurotic symptoms burden a sick person. Would we want to deny, for example that the *voice of conscience* or the *categorical imperative,* which humanity is so proud of and which Kant used as a basis for the single argument that would enable him to refer to a noumenal reality, undergoes a long and difficult formative process? A process interlaced with repeated disappointments and the forced restraint of our own desires, with the child's failed attempts to escape the all-seeing eye of the parent, for example, or the feeling of nakedness that comes from being caught doing something forbidden, or the realization that the most carefully protected secrets are easily found out by *adults*? The categorical imperative is a peace treaty with this invisible eye. It is a voluntary submission to it after vain attempts to escape. There is no denying that it represents the highest form of morality and civility. What is disputed is that it is something primitive, inborn, irreducible. Actually, precisely because it is highly moral and civilized it is extremely complex and highly evolved. It embodies the transition from the particular to the universal — that is, the replacement of the physical and concrete parent or teacher by an impersonal and abstract entity with all the characteristics of omnipotence and infallibility that the child had initially attributed to single protectors, and which must be withdrawn from them little by little as their human limitations are revealed (this is the phenomenon of attachment to an infantile ideal that the child does not want to abandon even when there is no longer a physical person to embody it). And at this point there is an introjection of this representation from the exterior into the interior world corresponding to what in philosophical terms is a transition from the transcendent to the immanent — the recognition, that is, that the safest place to store what we most love and fear, the things we never want to let go of, is ourselves. A way of protecting the *absolute,* in other words, from the danger of being part of the external world, from the uncertainties it faces there, by bringing it into a world we are the masters of, where absoluteness and universality can be more easily protected (this is perhaps, by the way, one of the most intimate meanings of the *Kantian revolution* we spoke about at the beginning of the chapter. What seemed at the time to be an act of humility and modesty, renouncing a congenial *external world,* appears here as almost an act of jealousy — the elimination of the constant fear that the external world will one day betray us and not meet our expectations. By enclosing it within ourselves, we feel like and effectively become its masters; but nonetheless we are dependent on it, on its necessity, on its absoluteness. Our dominion lies in the ability to serve safely, totally).

I have sought only to give an example, and I am not claiming that my example is exhaustive or complete, or even exact. I only wanted to indicate the tone, the mental atmosphere that has in some cases permitted the breakup of some of classical philosophy's eternal categories.

I know that in using this language I am losing the sympathy of people I value and esteem; I am exposing myself to their ridicule and discrediting this work in their eyes. I know that all it will take is to quote this page in certain magazines to convince the majority of the serious public of my superficiality and fatuity, and to deter them from reading the rest.

And yet I do not believe I have said anything that — once we have agreed on the use of words and the emphasis to be placed on the various concepts — might not be taken as an obvious truism. The fact that such palpable truths turn out to be, in a given context, shocking paradoxes, is exactly what impels me to put them on paper and defy the dangers that this may entail. Observing the way this conversion takes place can be instructive for our purposes.

I will probably be accused of having presented two of the fundamental processes of the mind, processes that both theoretically and historically form part of what might be called the constitutive act of philosophy — that is, the passage from the individual to the universal and from transcendence to immanence — as a child's game, of having discredited them, you might say, reducing them to the dimensions of the little struggles and squabbles that occur in the soul of every adolescent, and in the often petty atmosphere of the family. Now what I would like to ask is, do these two processes, meant to be ideal and eternal aspects of the mind and constituting its very essence, refer (as they do, although it seems superfluous to say so) to the *human* mind? In beings with other organs and ways of life (animals, for example) we have grounds to suppose that they do not occur, or that they do so in a completely different way. When we speak of *mind,* or *subject,* or "I," we are still talking about the mind, the subject, the "I" of men and women, of beings that is, who are limited in space and time and endowed with specific features — who are a certain way, but whom it would not be difficult to imagine otherwise. The two processes in question, if they represent (which they do) two essential aspects of the mind, are felt by each individual as a personal experience. And does this experience not take place at a definite point in time and space, at a certain age and in determined circumstances of life? Does specifying these circumstances perhaps diminish the importance of the experience, its gravity or solemnity?

It is perhaps the essential human experience, the transformation of a child into an adult — from a being with partial and limited vision into one capable of expanding his or her vision to the infinite, of overcoming any obstacle, of grasping the universal. But then, do we want to say that an experience from adolescence, in a certain situation that can be pinpointed in memory, is because of this less important, less decisive for the intellectual and moral consciousness of the individual? Is a person for this reason bound to it by less solid ties?

The answer will be that it is not the gravity and solemnity of the experience that is at issue, but the fact that it constitutes the very means by which we judge every experience, that its transcendence is guaranteed to us not so much by introspection and by the sense of compulsion by which we feel bound to it, as it is by the fact that every judgment we formulate, insofar as it has a truth value, presupposes it, and therefore this also includes the judgments through which each of us expresses its emergence in our own personal past with all its particular characteristics. The answer will be that the Mind or the Subject or "I" of which we speak is indeed the mind and the subject of human beings, but at the same time it is something more inasmuch as it knows and judges that same mind, and finds in it its singularity and limitation and the possibility of being made differently. This answer will not deny that it is easy to imagine other beings different from humans that have intellectual categories different from the human ones. But the very activity of imagining such beings may in its turn be imagined as different from what it is only if it is allowed that it is no longer itself — that it is no longer, that is, an act of imagining, but an act that is imagined.

This brief exchange of questions and answers shows how annoying and irritating the previous statements were. They were perceived as yet another edition of the positivism against idealism argument — yet another conflation of the empirical concept with the pure concept. We would now like to try to show that this is not what is going on.

We have already tried to distinguish two uses of the term *knowledge*: as the affirmation of a truth and as the mastery of a process. In general, all the propositions of experimental science have this second character. When I say that kitchen salt is composed of chlorine and sodium, what this means is that I am able to break the salt down into chlorine and sodium. When I say that small material particles passing through a crystalline lattice undergo refraction, it means that I am able to cause an electron beam to undergo a modification that physics interprets in this way. When I say that the mass of the sun is many times that of the earth, it means . . . not that I am able to put the sun and many globes the size of the earth on two plates of a scale to ascertain that the scale stays balanced, but that this assumption, combined with others implicit in the concept of gravitational mass, allows me to calculate the orbit of the earth, and to predict its position at any time in the future.

Every scientific proposition announces the result of an experiment that has been carried out or can be carried out or conceived — an experiment that is applicable to any object, whether from the material world or the world of the mind. And this does not mean, just to be clear, that specific knowledge is always retrospective. There are experiments whose results cannot be other than what was calculated *a priori,* and Eddington, as we have seen, maintains that all the experiments of physics can be reduced to this type. If I posit *by definition* that the speed of light in a vacuum is 300,000 km/sec, this means that in setting up, for example, the well-known experiment of Fizeau, I will have to employ measurements of time and space that get me that result. If I didn't get it, it would not mean that the proposition about the speed of light was false, but that I employed the wrong measurements of time and space. The propositions of physics, which implicitly contain definitions, are all valid *a priori*. And we shall see much better below that there are many more of them than it would at first glance seem. But this is not to deny that even if they are valid *a priori,* they do no more than express the result of a process whose data we possess — that is, they express our *ability* to adopt that particular definition in physics. In physics, *A is B* means, "I (or others in my place) am able to transform *A* into *B*." It is quite right, then, that philosophy attributes a *practical* value to this type of knowledge and excludes it from its field of inquiry.

Examples of the first type of proposition, on the other hand, would include: "reality is rational," "innate ideas exist," "knowledge is a synthesis of the individual and the universal."

In these propositions it is not a matter of passing from the subject to the predicate by a process whose mechanism is within our control. But they are that first glimpse of knowledge that Hegel compared to a person who doesn't know how to swim jumping into the water — they represent *truth* statements, they give themselves universal, absolute validity, independent of any limitation of the sort that inevitably comes with application or practical realization. To clarify the significance of our distinction, we shall take the example of the second of the propositions cited above, "innate ideas exist." This could be interpreted simply as a scientific proposition. In that case it would mean that in the work of analyzing human concepts to find their constituent elements, we come across formations that we are unable to take apart and we are thus forced to consider primitive. Failing to find other structures that these may have derived from, we take them as innate. We suppose, that is, that humans are linked to them by their own human nature, that they carry them as a simple result of having been born.

This affirmation indicates nothing other than our inability to proceed any further with the task of taking apart and reconstructing these extremely simple structures using structures that are even simpler.

If, on the other hand, we want to give our proposition a philosophical meaning, we must put the emphasis on the word *exis-tence*. Innate ideas then appear not as the destination in a process of dismantling, but as the starting point in a process of construction. That it is not possible to go beyond them is shown by the fact that they are the basis of the very procedure by which human concepts are analyzed. Wanting to go further means falling into a vicious circle — it means wanting to move the earth with your lever anchored on the earth itself.

Understood in this sense, the statement that innate ideas exist takes on an undeniably truthful character. It is a truth, however, that essentially depends on the fact that these ideas have been assumed to be the starting point for all reasoning and thought processes. Every philosophical affirmation that states a truth presupposes at least the validity of the conceptual language (so to speak) such a truth is expressed in, and the validity of its statements is conditioned by the validity of this language. Every statement of truth thus implicitly contains a non-cognitive element, an act of will — the will to use that specific conceptual language in which the truth is expressed. If this act of will becomes explicit, the proposition, initially an assertion, becomes hypothetical: "Innate ideas exist when reasoning follows a logic that assumes such innate ideas as a starting point."

When our proposition is formulated in this way it seems to lose its value, to become a tautology. But the value of it lies precisely in the fact that in ordinary consciousness the hypothesis is generally implicit. This means that our willingness to use that particular conceptual language is so strong and so unconscious — so bound up with our nature — that it does not even occur to us to name it. Noticing this implicit willingness, becoming aware of it, this image that might not be there or might be formed differently, is truly a revolution of the kind theorized by Kant — it is truly a cataract operation. But it is something that philosophy, understood as a cognitive activity, will never be able to achieve. I will never be able to demonstrate in the Italian language my ability to speak German. In the same way, when I have attributed a certain meaning and a certain use to the word truth, I will never be able to affirm as true a proposition in which it has assumed a different meaning and a different use. To do so requires a new act of will — I would say almost a new act of creation.

Descartes — though it seems strange in a rationalist like himself — noticed this. He knew that his truths had value only within a *conceptual language* whose affirmation constituted an initial act of will, or rather the creation of a certain logical sphere. This was the thinking behind his concern about God being a *deceiver.* If God had wanted 2 + 2 not to equal 4 and the sum of the angles of a triangle not to be equal to two right angles, then these propositions that for us are necessary truths would be false. The necessity of these principles exists inside a determined logical system that we wouldn't be able to imagine differently from what it is, but God could. It could also be that, in an absolute reality, such principles might not be true, and would need to be replaced by others. Descartes wriggled free of this thought with a shrug. "Well now," he says, "why should this matter to me, since I know nothing about it. What I care about is what is true in *my* world, in the world of ideas that are *necessary for me,* and whose opposite, for a head built like mine, implies a contradiction. For me, a reality more absolute than this doesn't exist."

It is a troublesome thought this, of a world where our *eternal ideas* do not apply — a thought that Descartes eliminates at once, concerned as he is to proceed with his work of logically deducing the principles of physics and metaphysics from his few initial premises. But troublesome thoughts are not that easy to chase away, and this one came back to bother Kant, and obliged him to introduce a noumenon at the limits of consciousness and to insist on the purely phenomenal nature of knowledge.

But Descartes and Kant were philosophers through and through. Their problem was: "Couldn't *material reality* be different from what we see? Might our representation of the world be pure *illusion*? Might not God have deceived us?" Descartes refuses to think about it. Kant thinks about it to stop others thinking about it, to show that thinking about it gets us nowhere. And post-Kantian philosophy has had a pretty easy time showing both of them that we can think about it without fear, because the problem is already solved in the very act of posing it, in the sense that a reality other than that of the mind cannot exist.

What in fact would a reality outside of thought mean if the concept of reality itself is a concept intrinsic to thought? Everything can be known, Hegel said, except knowing.[14] Speaking of a reality external to knowledge would mean knowing knowledge as extraneous to reality.

(Note — parenthetically — the strong analogy between this argument and the ontological demonstration of the existence of God. There the existence of God is deduced from its essence, insofar as it is an attribute of it. Here reality is deduced from the very nature of thought, insofar as it is a form of it. In both, the passage from essence to existence, from thought to being, is based on the logical implication of one concept within the other.)

What Descartes and Kant got wrong, what forced them to give in to the idealist claim, is that this possible world held together by principles different from those we are forced necessarily to rely on by our thinking, this mythical *new conceptual language,* was conceived by them as a *reality* in the face of which our own thinking would be nothing but *appearance.* By referring constantly to these categories of reality and appearance, which belong precisely to the world they wanted — or were afraid — to escape from, they locked themselves, so to speak, into their own prison; they let themselves be pushed back into the ancient circle. To escape the horns of the idealist dilemma — which boils down to the eternal challenge to skeptics — it would have been enough to present their own doubts by giving them a different psychological and affective connotation — that of viewing the eventuality advanced by them not as a danger to be escaped from, but as a new possibility challenging our capacity for conquest, as a new field of inquiry open to our curiosity. The question to be asked was not: "Is the world of our minds the real world, or isn't it?" but rather: "What would a mental world different from ours be like?"

The first question comes out of the need for *security* and *stability* that always comes with thinking about *reality.* The answer it

---

[14]*Phänomenologie des Geistes,* Einleitung; *Enzyklopädie,* sec. 10.

seeks will guarantee this security and stability any way it can — in the *real* or in something that stands in for it; in the *transcendent* or the *transcendental* (and the answer then ends up negating the question itself, when it is realized that the very notion of reality collapses into nothing more than that requirement).

The second question, on the other hand, emerges from a need for *something new,* a concern to escape from ourselves, a desire to get rid of the patterns we usually attribute to the world. This is the second step of the *Copernican revolution.* The first one consisted of realizing that the *laws of reality* are only forms of our intellect. The second consists of questioning whether these forms are in fact necessary and immutable and intractable. Actually, not questioning whether they are intractable (a question that presupposes the use of the forms themselves) but trying in every way to break them up and to live without them, or with other forms. Both these stages emerge as a struggle against the anthropomorphism so firmly entrenched in our minds. The first dispels the legend of an external world made in our image and likeness; the second overcomes the need to hold on to the forms of our intellect as the only ones possible.

But to move beyond these forms requires truly escaping from them, truly thinking in another conceptual language. As long as we keep talking about reality and appearance, about knowledge and truth, the breakthrough will not have been accomplished, and the philosophical case against the skeptics will still remain fully valid. The statement about the possibility of changing our categories must not be a theoretical statement, cognitive in the philosophical sense, an affirmation of *truth.* On the contrary, it must be cognitive in the scientific sense — intended as the mastery of a method, of a psychological process. To the question, "Is it possible to think using categories different from those thinking is based on?" the answer should not be a demonstration of the possibility or impossibility of accomplishing this reversal, but rather actually doing it, putting such new categories to use, living in this new world.

This is the only possible affirmative answer to the question, and it is in any case not a real answer, or it is so only in a translated sense, in that it is given in a different language from the one in which the question was asked. No formally correct answer that echoed the terms of the question could be anything but negative in our case. But what we want here, more than an actual answer, is the satisfaction of the urge, the desire, and the effort implicit in such a question — a payoff for the mental tension that inspired it. It is as if I were to answer the question whether I can speak German not with a yes or no, but just by speaking it — could my act not be considered an answer to the question? But it would be comprehensible only to someone who knew German themselves, or could at least recognize what I was speaking as German.

This is the nature of the answers that science is able to give, sometimes, to questions in which philosophers can only see vicious circles. Answers that, you might say, leap outside the question itself, but which, more than any formally correct reply, satisfy the underlying concern that gave rise to the question. Philosophy's *impossible* questions, even in their rigid theoretical formulations, are in fact always expressions of some yearning, some deep need in the soul.

The demonstration of the impossibility of formulating them within the same system of thought in which they were posed is the only answer to them philosophy is able to give. But this type of answer does not satisfy that deep seated tension, that desire and need, which often resurfaces later in unimagined forms, stronger than ever.

An effective answer that will satisfy this need can only come in two ways — either by transforming the human mind so that it is no longer troubled by it, or by transforming it in such a way that the need, continually reasserting itself, always finds a new form of satisfaction — finds itself pacified by new attitudes, coming back renewed from them and thus becoming a source of progress and new discoveries. The answer therefore comes with achieving mastery of the psychological mechanism through which the question is posed — with being able to reproduce it, follow it in its phases, and vary it infinitely. The answer to the problem of *reality* is manufacturing human minds to whom the word *reality* makes no sense.[15] As to the question whether a world *in itself* exists in

---

[15]"I have difficulty understanding philosophy books, because they speak a lot about existence; and I don't know what they mean" (Eddington, op. cit., p. 185). It is not paradoxical to say that modern science along with (although it is less obvious) modern psychology,

which the sum of the angles of a triangle does not equal two right angles, the answer is to construct a geometry in which such a sum is actually greater or smaller than two right angles, and show that such a geometry is neither more nor less *true* than the other one, but is, compared with the other one, essentially *new.*

We hope that this has made clear what distinguishes the world of ideas we move around in from the empirical one. It is not a question here of claiming as true that the categories of our mind are *a posteriori* and come to us from the external world. This is a typically philosophical proposition and, taken as such, is completely incorrect because it is contradictory. Leibniz's objection to Locke, "Nihil est in intellectu quod prius non fuerit in sensu, *nisi intellects ipse*"[16] is inescapable. It is the usual objection that we have already seen many times and wherein lies (we would be almost tempted to say) the very essence of philosophy. Empiricism is a philosophical doctrine that is expressed in statements (including skeptical statements) about truth. As such, it is obliged to observe the rules of philosophical reasoning — and in doing so it falls into insoluble contradictions. Science, on the other hand, never seeks to affirm anything in terms of truth. It only wants to enable humans to perform certain actions, or to handle certain objects.

Once again the example of innate ideas may be useful. Empiricism states that "innate ideas do not exist." This statement claims to be true, and as such presupposes the ideas of truth and existence. It thus contradicts itself. It is a statement that also claims to be universal. Valid, that is, in all times and places, and for this reason not subject to experimental confirmation.

The answer that the science of psychology offers concerning the question of innate ideas is neither affirmative nor negative. It starts with some of the innate ideas listed by philosophy and observes how they manifest themselves in people. It follows their

---

have effectively produced human minds capable of pronouncing sentences like this with a precise meaning, and basing great intellectual structures on them.

[16]There is nothing in the intellect which was not first in the senses, *except its understanding of itself.* [Ed's note].

origins, developments, connections and associations. It tries to re-construct the process of their first manifestations in the mind and emotions of a healthy person and to follow its distortions in people who are ill. And often, based on such careful and thorough study and on this encounter with new reagents, these "innate" ideas reveal the possibility that they could be considered extremely complex. They melt into the very souls of human beings. Bound to them by the most intimate fibers of their being, people no longer experience them as inescapable, but are able to dominate them, to command their development and use them as they please. Understanding the formative process of these ideas means being able to interrupt it at any moment and direct it towards other ends.[17]

Do psychologists conclude from this that innate ideas do not exist? Not for a moment. They simply say that they have succeeded, in some cases, in transforming people in whom certain ideas presented themselves with all the characteristics of innate ideas, into people who are free of such ideas, and who are able to command the process of their formation in their inner selves. They limit themselves to indicating the tools, methods and psychological elements used to bring about such a dissolution, thus enabling their eventual use in other, similar cases. The new exemplar of humanity will be introduced as something unprecedented and will be interesting to others because of this novelty.

But they will take great care to avoid claiming they have abolished innate ideas. They will be well aware that in their procedures decomposition and other concepts were used as primitive and indivisible terms, and that the dissolution of the old innate ideas came only at the price of bringing in new *innate ideas.* No claim will be made that the new ones are truer, better, or more correct than the old ones. It will only be asserted that they have been used productively to obtain certain results and that others who want the same results should proceed in the same way.

A certain promotional slant is likely to surface in the descrip-

---

[17]See, for example, an effective description of the state of mind of the man who has freed himself from the "categorical imperative," and who feels "beyond good and evil," in C. G. Jung, *Le moi et l'inconcient,* transl, fr., Paris 1938, c. II.

tion of the work that has been done. And it is possible that the scientists themselves, encouraged by their success, will be deceived into thinking they have come into possession of an absolute truth. But such an illusion comes at a high price — the gradual impoverishment of the discovery itself.

The error of perspective that produces the illusion is to see the reversal of viewpoint that led to the discovery as a liberation from error that opens the way to the truth, when it was actually nothing but a liberation from one way of seeing things to get to another way. A person with a new type of glasses who can see things that were invisible with the instruments used before will rarely resist the temptation to call what they now see "true" and what they saw before "false." But doing so would change them from a scientist into a philosopher. As soon as the scientific discovery presents itself as an assertion of truth, it enters a circle it can never leave. Its practical and heuristic value is sacrificed to its *cognitive* value.

Science, in short, has nothing to do with truth. It is the failure to realize this that has caused the scientific process to be confused with the process of empirical concept formation. If the scientific method is defined as consisting essentially of two states, observation and the generalization or formulation of a law — as it is, for example, by Bertrand Russell[18] — then it is made to consist essentially of the formulation of empirical concepts that claim a truth value. If on the other hand we say, for example, that "every element of physical knowledge has to be an assertion of what was or would be the result of following a specific observational procedure,"[19] scientific knowledge is stripped of its value as a statement of truth, in order to emphasize the *process* it consists of.

Scientific knowledge is not knowledge in the philosophical sense, while empirical knowledge is philosophical knowledge — even though, and precisely to the extent that it presents itself as such, it is a contradiction.

It is precisely this non-*cognitive* (in the philosophical sense) definition of scientific knowledge and its differentiation from

---

[18]*Panorama scientifico*, Bari 1934, p. 7 ff.

[19]Eddington, op. cit., p. 15.

empirical knowledge that allows us to avoid attributing to it *a posteriori* character. We have already alluded to the existence of propositions in physical science that have an *a priori* validity and cannot in any way be invalidated by experience. They are propositions that implicitly contain the definition of a physical concept by means of a natural object or phenomenon (defining time by means of periodic phenomena, velocity by means of propagation phenomena, energy by means of its proportionality to a frequency, etc.). In the course of this work we will deal extensively with these propositions, and we shall see in ch. II[20] that their *a priori* character and experimental nature are perfectly reconcilable. Suffice it to note here that it is the observation of their extraordinary importance in the body of physical theory that allows us to attribute to physics that same *a priori* certainty and validity that in Kant's time was only applicable to mathematics. The certainty that comes from a completed operation, by detaching physical from philosophical knowledge — indeed, from that particular and inferior form of philosophical knowledge that is empirical knowledge. But there will be much more to say about this below.

Faced with Kant's warning not to exceed the formal limits of knowledge, then, philosophy obeyed and science disobeyed. The former consoled itself in its inertia by saying that such limits didn't exist in reality but were illusory and only a projection of consciousness in front of itself. The latter begged pardon for its audacity, claiming never to have exceeded the limits but simply to have modified them and made them mobile and elastic, docile and adaptable to human will. Therefore, if we want, we can switch sides and say that science obeyed, and philosophy disobeyed. But I think the other formulation corresponds better to the emotional tone of the two positions, with the first prompted by a concern for security and a need for logical and moral justification, and the second by an eagerness for novelty and a need to *escape*.

Certainly, the essential question for the scientist suggested by the Kantian discovery that eternal ideas are categories of the mind is: "Couldn't they be composed differently?" The journey from

---

[20]Ch. 7 below. [Ed's note.]

heaven to earth has made them, you might say, more familiar and less likely to inspire reverence. The thought of altering them, in spite of their affirmed and demonstrated transcendental nature, seems more tempting and less sacrilegious. The scientist behaves like a child who has been handed a toy and warned over and over not to break it and to use it according to the instructions printed on the box. The child can't resist the urge to take it apart to see how it works, and sometimes it can't be put back together and is lost forever. Before seeing it in the shop window on display with the other toys, the child wouldn't have dreamed that it could be dismantled, contained a mechanism, and was composed of parts. Getting hold of it destroys all the mysterious charm of the toy — it becomes the object of the child's destructive curiosity.

Before Kant, the basic laws of the mind had been made into a kind of safe harbor that served as a refuge in the face of the dazzling and frightening immensity of the world's diversity. The criterion of "as you love yourself" dominates both Christian and Stoic morality, and Enlightenment thought. In the depths of their own soul people believe they can find the basis for judging the souls of others and, after Kant, for judging nature as well. Do you want to know the world? Look inside yourself. This is the credo that encapsulates the great revolution that shifts the method of introspection and self-analysis, so long valid in the field of morality, into the realm of objective knowledge. The essential laws of our own soul are the criteria for judging not only all other individuals similar to us, but the world of nature as well. If the terms *nature* and *reason* are closely linked and often interchangeable in the moral world of the Stoics and Enlightenment philosophers, in the intellectual-scientific world of Kant their convergence is taken, you could say, to its ultimate consequences. The essential law of human nature is reason, and reason is also the essential law of the outside world, because humanity does no more than project outside itself the essence of its own nature.

The enormous progress of the natural sciences is explained by the fact that they have placed their own fundamental laws inside the human soul and have thus been reduced, in the last analysis, to the study of human beings. By means of the *transcendental* method, humans are in a position to find within themselves what is essential and necessary to their own humanity, what allows them to communicate with each other and to dominate nature.

With the humanization of the eternal laws of reason and nature thanks to Kant, the Enlightenment had reached its highest peak. But, as we have said, it had also arrived at the brink of its own dissolution. Everything human beings have under their complete control loses all fascination for them — it needs to be broken up and surmounted. Kant, in giving people this great toy — their own powers of reason — also fatally sparked the need to break it to pieces, to be dissatisfied with it and look for something else. If the Enlightenment was based on what is the same in everyone, Romanticism looks for what is different and unique. And it is no longer reason and law, but sentiment, character, and passion. It is no longer what people have in common, but what distinguishes them — no longer the universal, but the individual.

In the moral sphere, in the realm of relations with others, this attitude appears once again as an act of humility, a renunciation of anthropomorphism. Individuals, who believed they had in themselves the criterion for judging other people and nature, realized that this criterion was insufficient — that it caused them to miss the most interesting and unexpected part of their fellow creatures. They tired of always seeing in others the image of themselves and set out to find what was different, singular, new. No more "do unto others what you would have them do unto you," but "do unto others what others would like done to them," which is in general different from what you would like done to you. Different, and precisely for that reason difficult to understand, to guess, to discover. It requires infinite attention to detail, detachment from personal habit — it requires love.

Love, whose forms and evolution in the development of modern culture are fascinating to study,[21] is perhaps the spiritual form in which this attitude most typically shows up. Love is no longer understood in the medieval manner as total passion and the mutual annihilation of two beings (Tristan), or the projection of an

---

[21]Cf. Denis de Rougemont, op. cit.

ideal image onto the beloved (*dolce stil novo*), or even as the simple satisfaction of an instinct, but rather — as configured in our society — as a complex sentimental relationship involving the interests and customs of two beings who consider themselves spiritual and moral equals. Love perhaps represents for modern individuals the most direct and searing experience of the "existence of another person," someone who is very often different in character, attachments, habits and childhood memories. Allowing that person to exist alongside you, even desiring their existence more than your own precisely because of its peculiarity without trying to absorb them into yourself, penetrating the interior of that soul with the respect due to something so delicate and unknown, whose balance and harmony might be upset by an equivocal or abrupt gesture.

6. Apologue on Four Ways of Philosophizing*

[Ventotene, June 1939]

A father, sensing that his end was approaching, called his four sons to his bedside.

"My sons," he said, "I am dying. In entrusting to you forever the house in which you were born and have lived, I wish to give you a word of warning. This palace, as you know, is rich and great, and contains everything necessary for life. Our elders embellished it, perfected it, and made every part of it comfortable, and I myself, to the best of my feeble ability, have contributed to this work. Now all this is yours, so be sure you use it wisely and in moderation. Continue the work of your forefathers, increase and improve the patrimony you have inherited, and reap its joys and rewards. And please abide by the only limitation that I solemnly place on the use of what I am passing on to you — *You must never leave this house.*

In any case, you can't. The doors are bricked up and the windows, though transparent, are locked and unbreakable. Any attempt to violate my prohibition would result in your injury and disgrace — you would end up. . . .

I don't want to tell you how you would end up. Instead, I want to tell you why my prohibition should be a source of pride to you, rather than a source of humiliation. You are the first of our line to receive it, and this is the mark of your superiority. I knew nothing of it from my father, nor he from his, and yet it never occurred to us to leave the palace. We did not even think it possible, nor did we ever suspect that there was more to the world than what was within its walls. We almost didn't notice them — the walls, nor the glass in the windows that modified and deformed the view of the road. The road stretched as far as the eye could see in front of us and we tried to examine it in its smallest details, using lenses and telescopes. We never imagined that with a single swerve it could completely escape our gaze. We were happy, in short, in our ignorance, and to us the space enclosed within these walls seemed infinite.

Are you now going to reproach me for showing you that this is not so? For having opened your eyes, rescued you from an illusion? Will you complain that infinity has turned out to be cramped, that the world has turned into a prison?

Go ahead, if you like. I don't regret for a moment that I have told you what assiduous meditation and untiring investigation have shown me. Nostalgia for the happiness of simplicity is always vile and hypocritical, and anyway it never gets you anywhere. And what you know you can no longer forget.

It would be unjust of you to accuse me of having restricted your field of action. Indeed, I have broadened it. Isn't the palace at your disposal today, just as it has always been? Aren't its resources still inexhaustible? And doesn't your increased knowledge allow you to use them more fully? I haven't taken anything from you that you had before. I haven't put you in chains. I have only revealed to you how strong the chains are that you are already in. Now you want me to free you from them. Well it's asking too much.

How can I free you? I am not free myself, and the limits of my actions are the same as yours. I was not allowed to go outside our walls to make my discovery. What I am telling you is not the result of a miracle that let me see our dwelling from outside and thus note its limits. On the contrary, it is the result of a careful and unbiased analysis carried out internally that examined the walls, doors and windows, the arrangement of the rooms, and the color and illumination of the walls. There is nothing about my discovery that is supernatural or mysterious. Each of you can repeat it and see for yourselves, only you must follow the path I have indicated, and assume the attitude that I adopted. Indeed, I dare say none of you will now be able to avoid going down that road and coming to the same conclusions as me. But you too will see that it does not lead to the exit door. Indeed, it shows instead that there isn't an exit, and anybody who looks for one will only go round and round in circles and always end up back where they started.

So act like men and give up this absurd quest. If I cannot give you freedom, I can offer you something similar — the conscious, manly acceptance of your position. No better way will come along for you to make yourselves worthy to come of age. There are many things to be done. The house, even though closed, is immensely vast and you will never finish learning about it, putting it in order and working on its interior. Therefore, don't waste your time on futile cravings and empty nostalgia. Look around you and get to work."

So saying, he expired. His sons mourned him greatly and heaped honors on him as the emancipator of knowledge and the pioneer of a new culture. And truly everything stood as witness to the greatness of his discovery. Returning to their own occupations, they went from one wonder to the next. They seemed to have new eyes, and to be able see things that had until then been hidden from them. The palace they had always wandered around in more or less at random, confused by its vastness, was now simple and harmonious in its structure. Knowing its limits allowed them to take it all in with their gaze, to move through its rooms and halls in an orderly fashion. From the new perspective, many objects suddenly acquired a meaning and a use. The brothers had the impression that they had become richer, or rather that they had acquired a sensibility that allowed them to enjoy their wealth for the first time.

But the barred doors and closed windows were still there, plainly visible now, as a constant reminder of their father's warning. And the sight and memory together lent an undeniable tone of melancholy to their every pleasure. They tried constantly to take their minds off it, but the facts themselves led them back to it. They tried repeating their father's arguments and declaring themselves satisfied as a way of proving to themselves the futility of any effort to get out, but there was always the nagging of the world outside, the elusive *reality* that they saw through the window panes and the sounds from outside tormenting them. They began to argue among themselves, they got irritated, they quarreled. One of them would say they should disobey their father, another would mount contrived attempts to refute and destroy his discovery. With time, instead of calming down, the affair became even more heated and threatened to bring permanent discord to the family. In an attempt to settle the question within himself, each of the sons created a style, an attitude, a way of behaving that governed all his actions and the way he used the house. Even today they are still arguing, fiercely contesting various rooms, the arrangement of furniture and decor. So let's describe them one by one and see if we can't get them to agree with each other. We can start with the oldest.

He was already well along in age when the father died and he took over as head of the household. He was the most serious of the sons, and the most positive and down to earth, even though he didn't have much of an imagination. From an early age he had shown himself to be resourceful and clever with his hands. He had always been happiest disassembling the toys he got as gifts, and studying their parts and mechanisms in great detail. He always kept his eyes open and his hands ready. He was the one everyone turned to when they needed to repair some damage or improve some piece of equipment. In the course of time he had worked and tinkered so much that the house had been transformed in his hands; he had installed many practical and useful devices and the variety and intensity of life in the house had greatly increased.

For this his brothers and even his father owed him a debt of gratitude — even though not everyone liked his dry and spare way of doing things, his indifference and ill-concealed disdain for anything that wasn't tangible or couldn't be constructed, the way he rushed around, always busy and dirty and with tools in his hands, unable to sit calmly at the table or have a quiet conversation or listen to music. They accused him under their breath of being narrow-minded and petty, and being unable to see the big picture. Always under their breath, however, because everyone needed him and no one would have wanted to give up the comforts he had provided for the house.

For his part, he cared little about these whispered criticisms, limiting himself to smiling when his refined and pretentious brothers found themselves in trouble for some trivial reason. He saw himself as the head of the family, although he was sometimes treated as everyone's servant.

For him, his father's words on his deathbed were something utterly strange and incomprehensible. Accustomed to living in the house, and knowing it intimately in its smallest details, the idea that it did not contain the whole of reality, that his own work was carried out only at the level of appearance and was unconnected with the real world — all this seemed impossible and monstrous. When it came down to it, he was unable even to properly grasp what it was all about, and his only reaction was to shrug.

"An old man's fantasies," he declared, "castles in the air built by a mind worn out with too much thinking. If it's true that we live in a closed and finite house, why didn't our father show us the world outside? I am used to believing only what my eyes can see and hands can touch. I agree that there is still much to discover and much to work on. But to say that all our working and discovering is in a certain sense in vain, that it is useful only to us and has no value outside these walls — that is something I just cannot believe."

And in fact he didn't believe it and went on working as if his father had never spoken. But as he worked, the old man's words echoed chaotically in his ears and led him, against his will, to places where the boundaries of the palace and its detachment from the outside world could be most easily seen. Immersed in his work in an effort to forget his father's warning, he would come face to face with it in the most unexpected places. This irritated him, paralyzed him and undermined his confidence in his work. He had also become irritable and suspicious of his brothers, who had begun to look down on his work in the light of the new discovery.

"Well," he said, "and what of it? What if it is true that this house we live in is separated from the world by an insurmountable barrier, that the object of my searching and building isn't reality at all but only looks like it filtered through the glass in the windows. If that were true would it take away from the value of my work? What's the difference whether I am investigating and working on reality or on outward appearance, when my instructions are useful and what I make brings comfort and well-being? You are free, if you like, to give it all up for the sole reason that it isn't the actual real thing. As for me, I'm going to go on working the way I always have as if I were working with reality. I see no need to change anything about my methods. Nor does this *as if* — which, to keep you happy, I am ready to put in front of my results — in any way diminish their value."

This was what he said, and it seemed momentarily to relieve his distress. But he said it with secret bitterness. And while that *as if* perhaps did not affect his results, it drained him of his desire to work. He, too, could now see how small the house was, and the thought of the infinite unknown expanse that lay outside made his efforts within the walls seem paltry. It seemed to him that inside there was nothing more to look for, that the material had run out. Sometimes he would be seized by a frenzy to get out, and would hurl himself violently against the window panes, using his heaviest tools to try and break them. Each time this happened he was weaker and more discouraged, and he was deeply ashamed of the ridiculous figure he had made. He felt old now, and longed for the good times of blissful naivety, when he thought with every step that he had stolen a secret from nature, and had almost convinced himself that he was competing with God. For hours he would sit wistfully at the window, imagining the world outside and shaking his head sadly. Once someone saw him crying.

The first and second sons had never been on good terms. Complete opposites in character, they had always competed surreptitiously, secretly vying for supremacy. One was as active and quick in his movements as the other was slow and solemn. The former was sloppy in his dress and manners, the latter clean and tidy. In the morning the second son would linger in bed, daydreaming, while the other was already at work. And to defend himself against his brother's accusations and ironies, he entrenched himself behind a severe contempt for all manual work. He took great care of his hands and nails and loved to touch rare and delicate objects, which he arranged tastefully around him. Extremely touchy and not very adept at irony, he was jealous of his own things, and never allowed profane hands to touch them. He moved around the house very seriously and deliberately, not stopping to observe details, but delighting rather in sweeping panoramas, spacious rooms, comfortable toilets, and long arcaded porticoes. He loved giving orders and making judgments, and he made up for his lack of competence in details by framing everything in general and comprehensive terms. In this way he claimed the right to speak on any subject and there was no one who could shut him up.

But in spite of these unsavory aspects of his character, it could not be denied that he was the only one of them who knew the house thoroughly — in its design, structure and room arrangement. He was the only one, in the end, who immediately understood the magnitude and significance of the paternal warning, and right from the start he took on the task of explaining it to his brothers. Moreover, the warning suited his lack of curiosity and love of enclosed places very well. He had no trouble adapting to it, nor did he ever feel any real urge to go out into the street to see what it was like. What he did feel about his father's prohibition was not the need to taste forbidden fruit, but rather a sense of offended dignity at having to put up with a proscription, a feeling for the *diminutio capitis* that it entailed. He was accustomed to thinking of his house as the whole universe and he himself the center of it. But now he was uncomfortable with the idea that it enclosed a small limited space beyond which there might be inaccessible roads and fields, and even other houses just as beautiful and ornate as his own.

He was sullen and thoughtful for some time. Then, one fine day, he ran to the windows, lowered the shutters and announced triumphantly to his brothers, "The road does not exist. It is simply a visual mirage. Our father, good soul, accomplished a wonderful thing discovering that we live in a house and determining its limits. But it was precisely this endeavor that kept him from taking the final remaining step — recognizing that outside those limits there is nothing. It is useless for you to make those incredulous faces, and push me towards the window to show me the road with its incessant traffic, the fields with their crops, the sky, the sun — who are you to say that all these things are not just painted on the back of the windows? Have you ever opened them? To be able to talk about a road really existing outside our house, you would have to be able to open the windows. But this you will never be able to do any more than our father did. So when he spoke of a real street he went further than he should have, and instead of forbidding us from going outside, he should have warned us that there is no outside."

His brothers looked at him in astonishment and chuckled behind his back. He would get irritated and accuse them of lack of imagination. "Well," someone said, "then our father's discovery was in vain. So does this mean what we believed before is true?

That our home truly is the whole world, and the world is entirely contained within it?"

"Our father's discovery was not in vain," he replied. "Before him we didn't even realize we lived in a house — now we do. The walls and windows, and the essential difference between the house and the street were discovered by him, and they are his imperishable glory. But his error was in believing that the house was the mirage and the street reality. The truth is in fact the opposite. The true reality is the House, which from now on will be written with a capital letter. Outside it there is nothing, while in it there is every last thing — it is infinite. Instead of wasting your time with vain fantasies about the world outside and gazing in adoration at the spectacle you see outside the windows, turn your adoration to the House, which is both yours and also everyone's. You can change it, if you want to — indeed, it is in perpetual evolution thanks to your work and your labor; it is always new in your eyes. There, you see? I have restored your dignity and honor, I have finally freed you from the chains your father warned you about."

But the brothers cared little for this liberation, which changed nothing about their actual state and made their prison even more impenetrable. They let him talk, at times reacting with irritation at his pomposity. He went away annoyed and set about pacing up and down the corridors of the palace. He was very worried about the structure and the harmony of the room arrangement. He planned enlargements and embellishments. He had walls knocked down, widened hallways and decorated ceilings. He gave the great hall of the Arts a definitive renovation. The History portico became one of the most admired and frequently visited areas. He was pleased with his work and loved taking visitors through the successive apartments, showing how the house now had an internal coherence, how the various parts were linked in such a way that each presupposed what came before and led to what came after. He gloried in this *circularity* or *system* as his highest achievement. The house by now seemed to be his own work. In it he felt strong and armored — its master. He felt entitled to aspire to primogeniture.

The third son had always had a troublesome character. Intolerant of any sort of restraint, he had been a worry to his father and older brothers. They didn't know what to do about him. He had always had little desire to study and there was no one he would allow to teach him. Grumpy and conceited, he had great contempt for any sort of regular and organized activity. He acted as if he could accomplish immediately without applying himself what the others achieved only through long efforts. And the most disconcerting thing was that he sometimes succeeded. He had an odd agility in his movements, a keen eye for the quickest routes and unforeseeable simplifications. He was the only one of the brothers who had a knack for sports, music and art, the only one who had creative taste. His room was so disorderly that he himself couldn't find his way around in it. But if a person knew how to look, there were wonders to be found there — strange and ingenious drawings, fantastic projects that brimmed with vitality and insight, ingenious contraptions and an infinity of things that had been started and abandoned half finished. He was handsome in person, tall and dashing, and women were crazy about him. But there was something dark and cloudy in his gaze that left people perplexed.

Not even for a second did he consider obeying the words of his father. The only thing a prohibition represented for him was an incentive to disobey it. In the house he felt like he could no longer breathe, like he didn't have room to move. He ran up and down like a beast in a cage. To anyone who cautioned him with the usual reasoning, preaching moderation and good sense, he responded scornfully, "That stuff's for you. You keep your house if you think it's so beautiful. I'm getting out even if it kills me." And one day he hurled himself against the wall, made a deep breach and disappeared. The effect on the others was great. They rushed to the breach not so much to save their brother as to see if they could see anything of the world outside. But from the twists and turns of the crack, all clogged with stones and rubble, not even a ray of light filtered through.

They wondered if he would return — some with genuine curiosity about what he would say, others with a keen sense of envy and disbelief. He came back at last, tired, battered, and bleeding, his eyes glazed and bewildered. Everyone crowded around him but it took a long time before he could utter a word. At last, when he had recovered a little, he cast a contemptuous glance around him. "It's pointless for me to tell you what I saw," he murmured, "you wouldn't understand it." And since the others were still staring at him disappointed, he continued with increasing excitement: "How could I, anyway? I would need a special language. People who have always lived within these walls can have no idea about what's outside. You don't have the right senses. Even if I had wanted to bring you back something I saw and touched, it would have been transformed when it crossed this threshold — in this atmosphere it would have lost all its original character. You might have been able to grasp it and understand it, maybe, but by then you would have been holding an object that belonged to the house, and no longer to the real world. The real world is not for lazy people and does not reveal itself to those who want to be safe. It is for the strong, for the daring, for those who are ready to put everything on the line. Whoever wants to see it should follow me. There is a big risk, but the stakes are immense, and only those who are willing to lose everything can gain everything."

His brothers were somewhat perplexed and didn't know whether to believe him or not. He went back to pacing from one room to another in his arrogant and detached way. By now he had nothing but words of scorn for anyone who came close to him. He seemed like a country boy who had come back to his native village after being in the big city. Everything was small, poor and pale compared to what he had seen. And meanwhile, little by little, what he had seen began to come out. He spoke of great houses, vastly more beautiful, richer and more complete than his, of people with eyes a thousand times sharper, hands a thousand times stronger and more skillful. He recounted that in the real world, in the world of the street, anything that seemed like a limitation or an impediment here in the house did not exist. You could walk in a straight line indefinitely, without ever meeting a wall. There was no death, no time, and you could be in many places at once. Sometimes he even amused himself by telling how everything in the real world was inverted, the houses with their roofs on the ground and their foundations in the air, people with their heads at the bottom.

Among his brothers there were those who listened to him eagerly, but they almost always were disappointed. They never found anything really new in what he said. It seemed to them that even someone who had never left the palace could have imagined all these things. They were always made of the same ingredients as the things they were familiar with — the difference was only in size, or in taking a feature to an extreme degree of refinement and purity, or in the application of a process that went on forever, or simply that things could be combined differently from what they were used to. There were those who began to suspect that he was an impostor, and that he had not seen any of the things he told them about. But since they knew him well, they could not doubt his good faith — at least that exterior good faith that consists of not explicitly setting out to lie and deceive one's neighbor. Certainly he was totally convinced that he had left the house and traveled widely in the external world. Whether he had taken precautions to be sure he was not fooling himself, whether he hadn't confused the outside world with some little-explored part of the palace that he was seeing for the first time, whether the desire to see something new and unusual hadn't perhaps excessively stimulated his eyesight, painting in vivid and bright colors a reality that was not very different from what he was used to at home — these things his critics could not and will not ever be able to verify.

In any case, this outside world made in the image of the house thrilled some, but left others disappointed and incredulous. And no one ever found out if the third brother had actually left the house.

The last of the sons had not participated in the disputes of the first three. Born when the others were already adults, he was in diapers when his father died. He had not heard his father's revelations in the last moments of his life, but he had grown up amid the debates they had provoked, and his childhood had been so full of the memory of them, that for him they represented something evident and natural, a simple fact of life it never even occurred to him to doubt.

Not that it troubled him in the least, however. His quiet and positive temperament easily took it in. For him it did not represent a limitation of any kind, and listening to the agitated arguments of his brothers he sometimes wondered with a certain irony if it was really necessary to spill blood over so little. Most of his sympathy went to his oldest brother, who was something of a father figure to him. He loved his down-to-earth way of doing things, his reserved character and few words. He went with him on his rounds of the house and enthusiastically learned his trade, getting to know the palace with all its details and secrets. He began to take his brother's place doing some of his easier jobs, and rapidly became quite skillful, surpassing his teacher. He brought a youthful and daring spirit to the job, along with a broader perspective and a certain unscrupulous boldness.

The eldest brother looked at him with wistful complacency. He no longer felt able to follow him in his daring adventures and his bold and somewhat strange projects. But he knew that this young man of quiet and modest appearance, with his attentive and thoughtful manner, had taken in the best of his teaching. He knew that these projects were only odd in appearance, and that since they were based on serious and rigorous studies, they could take him very far indeed. And he was quietly delighted to have been able, in his later years, to set in motion such a genuine force.

The other two brothers cared little for the younger son. They were too busy with their personal problems. But he did not lose sight of them, and was influenced by them almost without realizing it. From the second brother he had learned to know the palace in its great design, in its comprehensive and yet harmonious structure. But for the third he had a secret and unconfessed fondness. He shared with him an intolerance for the quiet life within the walls and a disbelief in the opinion that the world ended there. This seemed to him a presumptuous and philistine theory contrived to satisfy a sense of vanity without running any risks. And he did not at all share the reverential respect that the two older brothers showed for the main load-bearing walls of the house. He realized that living there was a fundamental limitation and he too felt a certain impulse to disobey the paternal precept. But what he could not share was the disquiet of the third brother, that subverting rage that made him hit his head against the walls and fantasize total destruction. For him it was not a question of dignity — he couldn't have cared less about whether the world he lived in was real or not. He just had the feeling that out there beyond the walls there was something that if approached in the right way might be grasped and made use of. And he was very curious to see how it was made. He never took part in his brothers' debates. He didn't concern himself much with deciding who was right, but he studied the arguments of each very closely, ready to imitate them should it prove useful to his purposes.

This was why the third brother's attempts to get out interested him. He examined the breach in the wall with close attention, but while the others only put their eye up to the crack in the hope of seeing out, he took advantage of it to examine the composition of the wall. He took the bricks in his hands, he studied their shape and how they were arranged; he measured them. He determined the composition of the cement, and tested its consistency and stability. He examined everything with meticulous care and then went back to his room, calm and quiet. He did not for the moment put what he had seen to any use. He let it mature in his mind. He wasn't in a hurry.

7. Philosophy and Science*

[Ventotene and Melfi, 1939–42]

1. The Problem

The Kantian revolution, on a level with the Copernican, consists of the realization that the supposedly *objective* laws of reality are seen as such only because people introduce the forms of their own intellect into them. An anthropomorphic idol that Kant pulled down. Can this revolution continue?

Kant warned of the impossibility of departing from the forms of the intellect in order to get at the thing in itself. Post-Kantian philosophy has eliminated the distinction between phenomenon and noumenon, between knowledge and reality, and has shown that the very concept of reality itself falls within the forms of the intellect, and that therefore there is no reality outside of knowledge.

But science recognizes another type of knowledge that is different from philosophy's — knowledge understood as *the mastery of a process.*

We know a thing when we are able to construct it — that is, take it apart and put it back together. Faced with the Kantian problem, science did not question whether or not it was possible to escape from the world of categories, but whether that world could be modified — whether it might not be possible to think using categories different from the ones commonly noted. And science did not seek the answer in a demonstration that it was in fact possible — a demonstration that would necessarily have presupposed the validity of the very categories it sought to undermine — but by trying to actually modify human heads, as it were, to render them capable of thinking based on fundamental concepts different from those currently in use.

In this way psychology radically altered all the moral categories beginning with the categorical imperative and the phenomenon of will itself, no longer considering them to be prime and non-decomposable elements, but as extremely evolved and complex formations. Primitive minds were no longer studied, as in the time of the Enlightenment, to find the basis of our own reason and morality in a pure and elementary form, but rather to see what there is in them that is radically different from our own. The point was to gather intellectual and moral information about our civilization in its original form, and to pause at the crossroads where human development took one route but could have taken another, one that would have led to forms different from the ones around which our lives currently revolve. Thus the study of *conditioned reflexes* (Pavlov) seeks to grasp the phenomenon of the will at its earliest origin, attempting to modify it, to divert it from the paths by which it is usually routed.

Philosophy responds to the question of whether the human mind could be made differently from the way we know it by saying that the categories the question itself is based on are unavoidable, since any answer you give can only be based on them. Science, on the other hand, strives to build human minds and human souls shaped differently from those we know. And in doing so it maintains that, while not directly answering the question, it nevertheless more effectively satisfies the need from which it arose. In this sense the methods of science can be in a certain way compared to those of a mystic.

Now, what psychology and anthropology are trying to do for moral and affective categories, mathematics and physics have already done very comprehensively for the more typically cognitive categories.

The axioms of geometry are considered by Kant to be synthetic *a priori* forms of intuition. It is no accident that just a few years after Kant's death a solution arrived for the age-old problem of the axiom of parallels. And the solution is developed precisely in the sense mentioned above — not by deducing this axiom from the other axioms of Euclid, nor by demonstrating *a priori* that it is not deducible, but by actually constructing a type of geometry in which this axiom does not apply.

The perfect admissibility of such geometry, and its correspondence with Euclidean geometry, has raised the question of what all the axioms of geometry and, more generally, synthetic *a priori* forms even are.

Today the problem has been solved and we know the answer. The axioms of geometry are implicit definitions of the objects (points, lines, planes, equality of segments, angles, etc.) that geometry itself deals with. Hilbert proved this irrefutably, by the method of constructing geometries in which the axioms are different from those of Euclid. The *a priori* synthetic forms are not, therefore, transcendental principles, or inescapable necessities of the human mind. They are instead conventions so deeply rooted in our most intimate habits, so tied to the very structure of our being and our way of experiencing, that they seem to us to be at one with ourselves. But the recognition that they are unconscious conventions allows us to manipulate them as we like. We are no longer tied to them, and in mastering them we increasingly become the masters of our minds.

This process of breaking down the forms that make up the essence itself of the human mind has been extended from the axioms of geometry to axioms in general, as well as to the principles of logic. The principles of identity, non-contradiction, and excluded middle have undergone the same test. Non-Aristotelian logics are put together the same way non-Euclidean or non-Archimedean geometries were constructed. The axioms of logic are set out in such a way that they too are regarded as conventions unconsciously determined by the very structure of our way of knowing. Logic is seen as *the physics of any object whatsoever* (Gonseth). It is understood that logic amounts to nothing else but a *language* or even a *grammar* (Carnap) — that is, a set of rules constructed for the purpose of regulating the use of concepts and their relationships, and that it is possible to determine these rules differently, in accordance with different needs.

This *unblocking of categories* has on occasion given rise to great advances in science. Around a century after the construction of non-Euclidean geometry, physics needed to make use it. It was noted, that is, that such geometries are not simply the ruminations of imaginative mathematical brains, but have a concrete use in the process whereby humans try to gain mastery over the world around them. One gets the impression that every time humanity knocks down an anthropomorphic idol in the mind and stops seeing the world — in some specific aspect — as made in it's own image and likeness, the resulting benefit is an increase in our knowledge of the world and mastery of its processes. The outcome is a new way of looking at the laws of nature — no longer as a regularity graciously bestowed on us or as a marvelous correspondence between ourselves and the things around us produced by a God doing geometry, but rather as the effect of a more or less unconscious choice based on what we usually consider the primary data of our minds, a choice whose results are all the more vast and varied and rich the greater the variety and richness of the fundamental data.

Now, the discovery that such data are not something fixed and immutable about our minds, but are in our possession, you might say, in that we are able to vary and modify them — this discovery is immediately reflected in the makeup of natural laws.

Modern science was led to these findings, often inadvertently, by the great discovery of Kant. But more often it has been pulled along by the very difficulties and inconsistencies it has encountered on its multifaceted journey.

What we have to do now is bring together these scattered elements and identify their common thread, proceeding systematically where until now we have proceeded almost at random. All the *idols* of physical science have not yet been toppled. Many still lurk beneath the most innocuous outward appearances, in the fundamental concepts this science is based on.

There is reason to suspect that they are in fact responsible for some of the most serious difficulties being debated in contemporary theoretical physics. The task is to identify them, using all the tools that psychological, logical, scientific research now possesses and, once they are identified, to take them apart and derive from this process all the possible consequences for the concrete discipline of science.

2. The Concept of the Experiment (Geometry and Physics)

It is often said that geometry, which arose as an experimental science (measurement of the earth) and proceeded by successive abstractions, has now become a science that is completely *a priori*. Let us examine how experimental, and in what way, geometric formulations still are.

It is correct that the statement of geometric axioms is arbitrary inasmuch as they constitute implicit definitions, or rather limitations placed on the freedom to define determined objects. But the objects to be defined — what are they suggested by? By a set of needs that are determined by the way our mind is configured and the way our most basic sensations (visual, tactile, etc.) are constructed. If we want to call this set of data *experimental,* before which we are *passive* — which we will find in front of us, that is, regardless of what we do — then we can still say today that geometry is an experimental science.

But the knowledge we have acquired about the possibility of our modifying such elementary data (cf. previous chapter[1]) gives us a certain power to modify the axioms of geometry themselves as we wish. In this sense, geometry is no longer an experimental or an *a posteriori* science.

From the above, however, it appears that the concepts of *a priori* and *a posteriori,* of *rational* and *experimental,* no longer have the value that was traditionally attributed to them. *A priori* no longer means *from reason. A posteriori* no longer means *from the senses.* Both the data of reason and the data of the senses appear as elements in which subjective and objective factors are mixed, but whose structure we can modify by means of a logical and psychological procedure.

A priori then becomes this power of ours to modify, which applies both to the objects of our reason and to those of our senses. One could say, for example, roughly that the notion of a *straight line,* from geometry, comes to us from the senses (in particular from the sense of sight, which is a function of the trajectory of light rays), and that the concept of *equality between two quantities* comes to us from reason. But we can modify both the notion of a straight line and that of equality between two quantities. That is, we can adopt axioms that differ from the usual ones, which implicitly define such concepts in a way other than the usual one. A straight line may, for example, be defined in such a way that it no longer constitutes the shortest path between two points. Equality

---

[1]Ch. 5 above. [Ed.'s note].

may be defined in such a way that it no longer has a transitive property. And so on.

Experiment therefore plays a part in geometry in that it suggests the adoption of certain axioms in order to reach certain ends. From the time it was realized that axioms are not synthetic *a priori* principles, but arbitrary conventions or implicit definitions — since, that is, the formulation of the axioms of geometry no longer derived from *transcendental introspection* and became a matter of free choice, the experiment was reintroduced onto geometry. This was no longer to ascertain regularities experimentally and then formulate laws by means of abstraction, but to recommend, on the basis expediency, the formation of certain axioms rather than others. Experimentation in this new sense, however, has very little to do anymore with the experiment as it is commonly understood.

It has been said (by Reichenbach, for example) that while the axioms of geometry are arbitrary because they represent implicit definitions that we can in the abstract adopt as we please, the axioms of physics are not arbitrary, since they represent actual experimental data in the common meaning given to the expression "*laws of nature.*" Let us see whether this is true and in what sense.

The objects physics deals with are the same as those of geometry: lines, points, planes, distances between points, equality of segments, etc. When physics introduces elements that do not belong to the common geometry of space (time, mass) it is easy to geometrize them, introducing new dimensions, and this in such a way that every physical law can be expressed as a geometric theorem, in a geometry with the appropriate number of dimensions. Now while geometry implicitly defines the objects it deals with using axioms, physics defines them directly, using *real definitions* (*Zuordnungsdefinitionen*). It says explicitly, for example, that a straight line is the trajectory of a beam of light in a vacuum or the axis of rotation of a rigid body. The distance between two points is measured using a rigid bar, a time interval is measured with a clock, and so on. When geometric entities are defined in this way using concrete objects that represent them, it is clear that only experimental observation can decide what kind of geometry will result from each system of definitions.

What the difference between geometry and physics comes

down to is that while geometry defines the objects it deals with by means of its axioms, physics defines those same objects by means of *real definitions* — that is, by letting them correspond to certain natural phenomena. So while the former enjoys complete freedom in the choice of axioms, the latter is bound to the consequences implicit in the choice of these specific definitions — but still free to change the definitions if outcomes do not fit them.

But even here the *a priori* and the a posteriori — that is, the arbitrary, conventional element and the experimental element — are mixed in a very intricate way. The real definitions adopted, the natural phenomena chosen to represent the geometric entities, that is, were chosen in a certain way rather than another precisely for the purpose of actualizing a determined geometry. Natural law will therefore never have an apodictic form such as *Space is Euclidean,* but rather the hypothetical form *Space is Euclidean when measuring instruments are adopted that make it so.* There is nothing, *a priori,* that would keep us from adopting different instruments of measurement if we wanted a space that was not Euclidean. Here again, therefore, experimentation does not permit us to state a *natural law,* and does no more than suggest the adoption of certain measuring instruments if we want to realize a certain geometry.

What becomes then of the experiment as commonly understood, as something that gives rise to *natural laws*? Experimenting in this traditional sense usually refers to the observation of regular relations between quantities previously defined and measured. At this point the operation of defining and measuring is only considered preliminary, and it is advisable to take certain precautions in this regard. Once these are in place we may proceed freely to what is considered the real scientific work, which consists of carefully combining the various quantities with a view of observing the possible regularities that this combining might produce.

But we now know that the operations of defining and measuring are vastly more complicated and decisive for the entire structure of physical science than was held to be the case half a century ago. There is a well-founded presumption that most so-called physical laws can be traced to this newer and more general kind of *experiment* which, rather than revealing natural laws, suggests certain forms of definition and measurement. This has been the case with the most celebrated landmark experiments of recent physics. The Michelson-Morley experiments initially gave rise to the Lorentz contraction *law*, but shortly thereafter it was used to suggest the reform of definitions and measurements that goes by the name theory of relativity. The experiments that led to the discovery of Planck's constant have also been very beneficially interpreted in this way.

If this process were to be completed organically, physics would be utterly transformed, not only in its internal structure but also in its epistemology. It would indeed be an experimental science, but not an empirical one. An experiment would only have the function of directing free human choice towards certain initial conventions, adopted to meet certain needs. Everything else would follow automatically by way of pure logical deduction.

How this can actually happen will be shown in the next sections, in which the two main obstacles in the way will be identified as the two idols of *reality* and *causality*.

3. *The Concept of Reality*

Interesting research may be conducted on the psychological construction of the notion of *objectivity* in the field of physics. Some of this has been initiated by Bachelard. In any case, many examples could be cited of the pitfalls the realist idol has introduced into physical science. The most famous came from considering space and time as entities in themselves, as *existing* structures. Geometry was chained by this for millennia to the Euclidean form, and physics for centuries to the Galilean. Another incarnation of the realist idol is the concept of the *ether*, which all of classical electromagnetism hinges on, yet another is the particulate theory of matter.

What is the nature of this stumbling block that the notion of *reality* represents for the free progress of physical research? It essentially consists of the introduction of an anthropomorphic element — the tendency, that is, to represent physical phenomena in the form most responsive to our need for stability and security. A typical example of this tendency is *modeling theory*, which seeks to represent all physical phenomena in the form of a mechanical model composed of particles that move, collide, attract and repel each other.

Today modeling theory is in crisis. But is it safe to say that the realist idol has been completely defanged by recent directions in theoretical physics? Are there not realist idols that remain to be eradicated, still lurking in some corner of scientific reasoning?

We believe there are. One of these idols is the concept of the *field*. It is said that an electrical or magnetic charge or a gravitational mass creates a field — that is, confers determined characteristics on the space surrounding it. This expression has been very useful in describing electromagnetic and gravitational phenomena, but the electromagnetic or gravitational field has as a result become an "entity" which we act on as if it were an actually existing object. This way of looking at things has perhaps kept us from looking at the problem of electromagnetism from a perspective that would have proven useful. There will be more on this in the second part.

What further favors the development of the realist idol in physics is a misunderstanding hiding in the way the concept of *identity* is commonly used. It seems that for a given object, the notion of *the same object* in different conditions of time and space is intuitively determined. But this assumption is arbitrary, and can give rise to a number of serious difficulties. What does it mean to say that something is equal to itself? What does *itself* mean? Does it mean a thing equal to the given thing? Apparently not, because otherwise our proposition would result in a useless repetition. There is no possibility of a direct comparison between a given thing and what is usually called *the same thing,* in another place and at another time. In short, the principle of identity makes sense only if it is supposed that, given a certain thing, the expression *the same thing* has a definite and uniquely determined sense. Now since this does not happen in most cases that involve physics, the principle of identity affirms nothing more than the necessity of establishing a convention that allows us to say *when* something has remained equal to itself. The logical investigations surrounding the identity principle (cf. mainly Frege) can therefore be very useful in clarifying some of the serious and intricate problems in modern theoretical physics.

But the central concept in which physics pays its maximum

tribute to the realist idol is the concept of the *universal constant.* Planck said of constants that they *are messages that Nature sends us from its depths* — that is, he considers them to be the ultimate objective element, that the whole construction of science is based on. Now, the concept of the universal constant is as contradictory as the concept of absolute motion. Physics has freed itself of the latter only in recent decades, but it still bases all its constructions on the former.

What does it mean to say that a certain quantity (for example, the speed of light in a vacuum) is constant? That it is constant for the instruments it was measured with? And the constancy of these instruments — how was that established? By comparison with quantities assumed to be constant. And so on.

The experimental observation of the constancy of a given quantity is therefore expressed in the observation of the covariance of that quantity with respect to a given set of measuring instruments, which makes us suspect that there is a hidden affinity of structure between that quantity and the instruments that measured it. The task of physics, in this case, is to discover this affinity of structure, so as to reduce the observation of the constancy of that quantity to a tautology.

Eddington's studies on the unification of universal constants are extremely interesting in this connection. What needs to be done is precisely to reduce the number of independent universal constants to as few as possible, and then see if they cannot be traced back to the use of certain measuring instruments for the fundamental quantities of physics.

4. The Concept of Cause

What does it mean to say that a phenomenon is the cause of another phenomenon? This is more difficult to answer than it seems. The concept of cause is itself linked with a whole series of psychological notions. It is constructed by analogy with the phenomena of *wanting, producing,* and *acting.* A relation of succession is not sufficient to determine a relation of causality. Centrifugal forces arise on a rotating body. It does not correspond to our elementary sense of causality, however, to say that rotation is the *cause* of these forces. A more accurate examination shows that the centrifugal movement is not due to rotation, but to inertia. It is therefore not the centrifugal movement whose cause is to be sought, but the rotation's.

For some facts it is deemed necessary to search for their cause and for others it is not. For example, no cause is sought for the fact that a body is standing still. Aristotle believed he had to search for the cause of uniform motion. We, however, do not think this necessary, and we search only for the causes of variations in motion.

The concept of cause is expressed in physics essentially by the notion of force. Each time a body experiences acceleration, it is said to be subjected to the action of a force. So the principle of inertia is nothing but a camouflaged definition of force. Now there are some cases (impact, traction, etc.) where it is clearly apparent how force acts as the cause of the acceleration. In other cases only the acceleration can be observed and the force is assumed to be there, precisely because it is among our most rooted convictions not to conceive of an acceleration with no cause.

Now modern physics has managed to remove a number of phenomena from the search for cause. The Michelson-Morley experiments had initially suggested to Lorentz and Fitzgerald the hypothesis that linear and uniform movement was the *cause* of the contraction of rigid bodies. A more accurate examination of initial definitions revealed that there was in fact no causal relation between movement and contraction, but that the definition itself of the rigid body in motion entailed that its dimensions when viewed by a stationary observer change in the direction of a contraction. What difference is there between this way of presenting things and saying that the movement caused the contraction? The difference is that in the second case we are introducing an element that is metaphysical and anthropomorphic.

It is in the spirit of post-Galilean physics that linear and uniform movement is never viewed as the cause of anything whatever. Yet there is a case where such movement is considered a cause, the case of electromagnetism. An electrical charge in linear and uniform motion *creates* a magnetic field — it is the cause of it. But here again the apparent causal connection can be eliminated and presented as a kind of optical illusion due to the fact that the measurements of a moving charge are different from those of a stationary charge. But what is even more important is that this can be extended to the case of any moving charge, which frees all of electromagnetism from any causal relation. Such an extension would also shed light on the problem of the geometry of a system in accelerated motion, and of the gravitational field it gives rise to.

If every causal relation in physics (that is, in effect, every law of nature) could be dismissed as shown above, we could reduce all of physics to a purely *a priori* science and relegate its experimental side to the simple function of recommending certain initial assumptions. The entire experimental apparatus of present-day physics — what gives it its mechanistic character — would be left in the role of simply confirming the accuracy of certain calculated relations. We can explain with an example. Take the equations of two curves. By solving the system with respect to the variables, we can easily determine the coordinates of the points where the curves meet. Having done the calculation, we draw the two curves on a sheet of paper and observe that they meet exactly at the points previously determined by calculation. Can we now say that the second procedure constitutes the experimental confirmation of the first, and that it demonstrates the correspondence between the Laws of Nature and our mental calculations? No. This is nothing other than a repetition of the first procedure — but making use of a different means of expression. The drawing on paper constitutes a kind of *calculating device* that immediately reveals the values of the variables that will satisfy both equations at once.

Exactly the same thing would apply to physics experiments if the program mentioned above were fully implemented. A physics experiment would constitute nothing more than a device that automatically performs a calculation when the data are inserted. The result cannot be different from what was theoretically predicted — if it were we would have to say that the data put into the device did not correspond to what was used in the theoretical calculation.

Thus the element of contingency, one of the essential characteristics of causal relations, would disappear. It would no longer be based on *trust in the constancy of the laws of nature*. What seemed to be *production* following fixed and immutable rules, an admirable display of fidelity to a "custom" of nature, turns out to be nothing more than the consequence of the fact that humans have used certain instruments to establish their points of reference in space, time and the measurement of energy.

8. PROJECT FOR A
JOURNAL OF SCIENTIFIC METHODOLOGY

[Melfi, May 1942]

General Character

The journal need not be of an informative nature since two excellent examples of this already exist—*Scientia* and *Il Saggiatore.* Its character should be critical and philosophical. Whether there is theoretical justification for the expression "scientific philosophy" as opposed to "philosophy of science," and whether or not this represents an independent attitude of the mind is of little concern to us. For us it is sufficient that the field of study corresponding to the name be quite clearly delimited. Generally speaking, it ought to include all questions in principle related to sciences that make use of experimental methods and scientific tools. It follows that in addition to physics and mathematics, which should provide most of the topics covered, the biological and psychological sciences should also be represented, along with economics and statistics insofar as they seek to build for themselves a logical tool based on axiomatic fundamentals.

There are two points of view from which the topics may be approached:

(1) Studying the extent to which the development of scientific theories and discoveries influences philosophical concepts and problems (for example: space, time, causality, equality, object, the individual, etc., for the physical sciences; life, the will, the self, guilt, for the psychological and biological sciences).

(2) Showing how a thorough analysis of the basic principles of the various sciences, in which all the achievements of philosophical thought are brought into play, can be useful to the sciences themselves and contribute to their progress.

Part I: Articles and Essays

The cooperation of leading Italian and foreign scientists could be sought, as long as they contributed articles of a critical nature and not expositions of scientific discoveries and theories. Much space should instead be given to presenting leading interpretive and methodological trends. The articles could be separated into the following groups; for each I will give some topics, as examples.

(a) Basic articles:
> On the concept of the experiment.
> Universal constants and units of measurement.
> The finalist illusion in physics.
> The finalist illusion in biology.
> The realist illusion in physics.
> Geometry and experience.
> On the axiomatics of the principles of mechanics.
> On the axiomatics of the theory of relativity.
> On the axiomatics of quantum mechanics.
> Precision physics and field physics.
> On the concept of instinct.
> On the present state of the argument between mechanical determinism and vitalism.
> Is it possible to build an economics independent of psychological assumptions?

(b) Profile of leading contemporary thinkers, both scientists who have been guided in their work by methodological considerations and philosophical interpreters of scientific doctrine:

Heisenberg	Bachelard	Jung
Bohr	Gonseth	Adler
De Broglie	Reichenbach	Durkheim
Eddington	Cassirer	Lévy-Bruhl
Dirac	Destouches	Frazer
Hilbert	The Vienna School	Von Mises
Weyl	Hayek	Robbins

(c) What is living and what is dead in:

Mach	Lamarck
Poincaré	Darwin
Helmholtz	Haeckel
Hertz	Driesch
Riemann	De Vries
Duhem	Freud
Meyerson	Walras
Enriques	Pareto

(d) Essays on the classical philosophers and scientists, for example Galileo, Descartes, Leibniz, Newton, Maupertuis, Hamilton, Laplace, etc., always from the point of view of scientific methodology.

Part II: Variety

The journal will also include lighter articles, polemics, etc. For example:

On reading philosophy (dialogue).

Dialogue on finalism.

Apologue on four ways of doing philosophy.

An error by Bergson.

Debate on Geremicca's[1] book, and on those favorable to it.

Part III: Review

Thorough critical examination of important, recently published works.

Part IV: Criticism

Critical assessments of books should be predominantly informative, with a brief evaluation. An attempt should be made to provide a certain level of completeness of information, so that the reader is made aware of everything published in Italy and abroad on the issues covered and has a clear view of the contents of each work and its place in current scholarship.

Below are drafts of some of the articles in parts one and two.

---

[1] *Spiritualità della natura* [*The Spirituality of Nature*].

9. On the Concept of the Experiment*

[Melfi, 1942]

By experiment we can mean two things: (1) observations of regular relationships between quantities previously defined and measured, and (2) observations concerning the structure of some of our complexes of feelings, which lead us to adopt certain definitions rather than others.

For example, the proposition "A beam of light in a vacuum moves in a straight line" can be an experimental proposition in both the above senses. It is in the first sense if the distance between two points has already been defined using a procedure that does not involve the propagation of light (for example using rigid bodies), and if the straight line has already been defined as the shortest distance between two points. And it is so in the second sense if we use this statement to physically define a straight line as the trajectory of a beam of light in a vacuum. It could be argued that in this second meaning the proposition has no experimental character. On the contrary, it has. It in fact presupposes that it has been observed that the propagation of a beam of light possesses the feature that geometry (or rather, a certain geometry) attributes to a straight line (for example that one and only one can pass through two points, etc.).

Physics has always considered its essential job to be establishing experimental propositions in the first sense. Those of the second type are generally relegated to early introductory chapters where primary concepts and units of measurement are established and are not taken up again in the course of the discussion. But to be based in this way on propositions of the first type implies a whole series of implicit metaphysical premises of a realist-finalist character — such as, for example, a belief in the constancy of the laws of nature, the harmony of the cosmos, nature's preference for simplicity, a geometrizing God, etc.

Present developments in physics now allow us to wonder whether it might not be possible to reduce the large number of ex-

185

perimental propositions to propositions of the second type — that is, whether or not it is possible to transform the so-called "laws of nature" into a series of observations on the conformation of our basic sensations (visual, tactile, etc.), which advise us, *without imposing it on us,* to adopt a certain kind of axiomatics which, once established, the propositions of physics would descend from by simple logical deduction. Such an assumption would contribute to liberating physics from the realist-finalist premises mentioned above, but it would also (and this is much more important) open the way to a much greater clarity in the actual formulation of physical laws.

Implementing this program should be one of the essential purposes of the journal.

10. Fragments

Philosophers in Conference

A philosophy conference is designed so that everyone can participate in a discussion. It is divided into sections, by topic: immanence and transcendence, logic and mathematics, causality and determinism, values and being, etc. The philosophers introduce themselves in turn and expound their theses. As soon as each has finished, the others take part. One accepts the first part of the communication, but rejects the second. The other differs in the emphasis on one aspect. The third feels that the thesis needs completion. The speaker listens courteously, attentively, and then responds.

You would say they were extremely interested in each other, ready to benefit from each others' contributions and listen to their objections, willing to work together to build a harmonious and systematic vision of the universe. But when you get to know them better you realize that what they are about is not a discussion, but a confrontation. They listen to their colleagues but think of themselves. The words that resonate in their ears come up against a set of formulas that each carries around, built up over years of work and experience, and which none of them would be willing to surrender under any circumstances. No one takes the trouble to try and understand what he hears, nor enter into the motives, needs and points of view that led to its formulation. Each takes it as neatly done, and compares it with his own world. Is there some point of agreement? If so he rejoices in being able to concur with its illustrious proponent. Do their positions diverge? Here he finds himself compelled to express a reservation. And the discussion proceeds in this way — logically, coherently, but perfectly pointlessly. Each one speaks about himself, and tries to translate what the others say into his own language. What he says cannot be the slightest help to anyone else. Even when there is some agreement, the feeling you get is almost always that it is external, simply a formal coincidence — that the point of departure and the point of arrival differ as in the case of two distinct roads that happen to follow the same path for a stretch.

No real philosopher is able to penetrate the thinking of another philosopher. He can only understand himself. Try and bring into contact, today, Bergson, Husserl, Croce. They know each other, they value each other — they may even be able to come to an agreement. But rest assured that each will remain locked in a world that is completely unknown to the others.

Do not delude yourselves — that Plato continues and completes the thinking of Socrates, and that Aristotle does the same for Plato. Don't believe in philosophical genealogies, traditions or schools.

Such links are only found in schoolbooks, where systems are laid out in a language that has only 25 words. Study any of these thinkers a little more deeply, trying to enter into their psychology and surroundings, the society they lived in; attribute meanings to the words they used or perhaps borrowed from the philosophies in vogue when they were young — and you will see that you meet in a world of its own, with its own laws and its own needs, self-sufficient and incapable of being different. Some formulations from the philosopher who came before may perhaps be used and exploited, and some problems he left open may perhaps be solved, but in a way he would never have accepted, or would have found absolutely contradictory. And to the later philosopher it will seem incomprehensible that the earlier one didn't see the shortcomings and contradictions of his own doctrine. Descartes, who was not stupid — how could he defend the famous vicious circle his demonstration of the existence of God is based on? And Kant surely had enough intelligence to realize the insoluble difficulties the doctrine of the noumenon runs into. Could Locke himself not have seen the consequences that Berkeley and Hume drew from his psychology? And was Plato really so blind that he couldn't see the problems that Aristotle then set out to solve?

In order to proceed, to correct the doctrine of a philosopher and solve his problems, you would in any case have to acknowledge that he was to a certain extent lacking in intelligence. But to admit this you would have to be on a completely different level from him — that is, you would have to fail to understand him. Such and such a philosopher had the great virtue of affirming that. . . . But his limitation lies in not having seen that. . . . His great virtue is that he said things that resemble those that we say, and his great limitation is that he left out one that we say. This is how the history of philosophy is commonly constructed, a history that prides itself on surpassing mere philologism and rising to the "contemporary" vision of the real thinkers.

The fact is that the greatness of a philosopher never lies in "resolving" a problem, but in "posing" it. And that how much of a philosopher one is depends on how true and at the same time new, unimagined and hard to discover the problem is that he has posed. Anyone limited to solving a problem set by others is not a philosopher but something like the assistant of the philosopher the problem came from. In a certain sense he is part of the other's personality — he is an executor, an applicator, a tool. He breathes the atmosphere and cooperates with it. But he did not create it. The faculties he employs are primarily logical and combinatory. I would not accept the name philosopher for someone who "takes a doctrine to its logical conclusion" or applies it in different fields. He is a logician perhaps, not a philosopher.

But then what is a philosopher?

*The Need for Unity**

I have in front of me a litigious page written by a great contemporary thinker, which says: "It seems to me that it doesn't take much to understand that to think is always to think about unity, and that unless you resolve the object before you into one, you have not come to the end of the problem." This citation is only a pretext. In the context in which he used the sentence — that is, in an argument against the dualists, I am in complete agreement, even thought I would have used different arguments.

If I weren't afraid of looking foolish I would like to ingenuously ask the philosopher, "Why is thinking always thinking about unity?" Let's imagine his answer. "Thinking," he would probably say, "is always necessarily thinking about the universal. The universal is one, by definition. Otherwise it would not be universal." I would ask again: "Why is thinking always thinking about the universal?" "Simply because it is thinking," he would reply. "If it were not universal it would be empirical intuition, sensation, perception, etc., but not thinking. The term stands precisely for that activity whereby one considers reality in the light of the universal." Basically, his answer would resolve itself into the following system of equalities: Thought = Universal – Universal = Unity – Thought = Unity, and would mean nothing more. There is a tendency in humans to see things in a universal and unitary way. This we call thought or philosophy. Wanting to claim that philosophy is not unitary is like claiming that philosophy is not philosophy. I agree with him on this. And I would leave you with one last question: "Why does such a tendency exist in humans?" Here the philosopher would definitively label me a fool and send me back to the Kant I studied in high school and at university. The Kant who taught that a transcendent use of the categories of thought is not permissible; that the thing I am asking about is that very tendency to unity that my question would cast into doubt; that at this point it is not the *why,* but the *what* that takes the stage. And finally, that the observation and experience that each of us has of what is necessary and permanent in ourselves — of what constitutes our deepest and most universal self — presents us with this need for unity as the condition for all thinking. "One can also think of multiplicity," he would continue, "and see the whole world as overlapping data and inconsistent facts, irreducible to one another. One can believe in an initial pluralism, and that the connections in things are emergent, due to our own arbitrary organization. But what is multiplicity, after all, if not an instance of unity? Is it possible to think of the multiple without thinking simultaneously of the one? And don't the overarching terms themselves — 'pluralism,' 'atomism,' etc., point to a need to embrace with a single gaze the immense variety that unfolds beneath them?" I would agree with him here as well. There is no escape from unity. It is a reality that doesn't need to be deduced because it conditions all our deductions. As long as our thoughts exist, so will the need for unity, which is the same thing as thought itself. But I can't help mentioning something extremely banal. The unity my philosopher speaks of is not a reality of nature. He does not believe, as Scholasticism and the Renaissance and even rationalism did, in a world that is in itself harmonious and unified under a dominating providence. He does not believe in God as organizer of the universe, who reveals unity to us as a law he has imposed on nature. For my philosopher unity is something very different from an established reality or an ideal indicated from outside. It is something that comes to us from within and therefore is not entrusted to the fallacious scrutiny of our experiments or our synthesizing abilities. It is intrinsic to reality itself in that it is a form of reality as we can conceive it. It is one of the categories, indeed the paramount category of the real — when real is meant not as a fact external to us, but as our own reality. The Kantian revolution, the transfer into the mind of the external laws and ideas hitherto regarded as a given fact outside us, while it did limit the use of these forms of reality, gave them an a priori security that they did not have when they had to be taken on faith or shown to be something that existed outside. Now for the first time the unity of nature is indisputable because there is no longer any question of observing it in nature, but rather it is by definition the very essence of our thinking about nature.

All this is evident, and I apologize for having repeated something so well known. What surprises me at this point is that my philosopher, in possession of this certainty, seems almost to turn to others, and to himself, saying: "Now you know with absolute certainty, a priori, that thought is unity. What are you waiting for?"

Our task from now on is only to look for unity in physics as in biology, in psychology as in politics and morality. Thought is unity. Whoever thinks must therefore achieve unity. At this point I am no longer able to agree with him. I would be tempted rather to say that from the moment we realize that it is the fundamental characteristic of thought itself, unity is devalued.

Just as a child who consciously says "I am a child!" at that moment no longer is one and cannot claim to be one, so I would allow anyone to claim the construction of unity as the task of philosophy except someone who has recognized unity as the essential law of thought. This is not a paradox.

Our Image
Dear Silvia,[1]

I write to give you good news about our little one. In the first month of her life, she has already grown by a pound. She sucks well, sleeps well, does not cry too much. She has begun to follow persons and things with her eyes and to have a special expression when she sees her mother. [. . .] During the first days I felt I was touching Providence with my own hands. Birth is an extraordinary phenomenon. The most complicated events happen with the regularity of a watch: frontal presentation, dilating pains, release of the water. Everything happens rapidly, logically, with precision. The baby is born. And everything is predisposed in such a manner that as soon as one mechanism of breathing ceases, another immediately takes over. The baby right away uses the new mechanism with utmost competence. Taken to the breast it sucks with a seriousness and commitment as though it had been years in training. During the first days the milk of the mother is not milk. It is a slightly laxative liquid, exactly the fluid the infant needs to rid the body of what is left over from the months of growth in the uterus.

[…] I said to myself, God Almighty must have thought a lot about us when he arranged all this. He combines everything just right. Everything is so harmonious, coherent, economical. Everything has a purpose; nothing gets lost. There really must exist some "finalism" in nature that organizes matters along the simplest and best organized lines. No man-made machine can equal these natural mechanisms.

But I have had second thoughts when I have seen my wife tired out by the nursing and the nurses of the hospital busying themselves around my baby even though she was bursting with health. A little creature like that is capable of occupying a woman all day long. I thought: "OK — I praised Providence for the things through which it has made my life easier. But why doesn't it occur to me to blame Providence for those things it has forgotten to arrange well for me?" For what arcane end does nature oblige me to carry the baby in my arms for a whole year? To provide it with everything it needs, to keep it warm, to supply it with food, to change it seven

---

[1]Silvia Colorni Schwartz. Translated by Sarah and Albert Hirschman. [Ed's note].

times a day? If Providence has built such a beautiful machine to feed the child couldn't it also invent one to dry it? Nature is courteous and attentive insofar as the taking of the food is concerned. But how unhelpful it is with respect to the opposite function!

You may object that man himself with his civilization is responsible for these discomforts. Yet primitive people and animals experience similar difficulties. They too must take care of their children, feed them, protect them, clean them, teach them many things. They too receive some gifts from nature, but must work hard to supply themselves with those that they do not receive.

True enough, we find a certain order in some things. But we also note an enormous disorder in an immense number of others. All our labor consists in nothing but the attempt to remedy this disorder. In spite of that we call nature perfect and regular. As soon as, at some point, we see a bit of work already done for us, we fall to our knees and are ready to adore [. . .]. As far as I am concerned, I would be much more grateful to Providence if it had saved me not the initial laxative for my baby, but the continuous worry for her catching cold or getting too hot or becoming ill [. . .].

Do not fear that I am embarking upon a dissertation on optimism and pessimism; that I want to decide whether the world is beautiful or ugly, or to side with Candide or Pangloss.

I am asking a different question. Has nature arranged its laws to feed the needs of man or is it rather man who has taken advantage of a certain number of things in accordance with his needs and has arranged them to his convenience? And then [. . .] has said: "Here are the most perfect laws of nature as they have been arranged by Providence for my use." With these laws of his own making, man has built up his own concept of nature.

Man is unfazed when he meets with the irregular, the disorderly, the useless and noxious, and with all kind of phenomena whose purpose he is unable to decipher. Here too there is a law, he says, a most beautiful and perfect law. "It is so perfect that I am not yet strong enough to understand it [. . .]." He has created words like 'contingency', 'chance', 'accident', and others like 'mystery', 'unknown', 'inexplicable', 'unexplored' [. . .] that precisely indicate that there is something there that he hopes one day to put to use for his own purposes. "It is a question of time," he says.

There is always a law, according to man. [. . .] I am sure that a scientist or a doctor would not be at all embarrassed by [. . .] these disappointments of a novice father. Every one of the drawbacks about which I have complained is part of a marvelous order, once one knows how to look. It isn't the danger of my child being dropped and getting hurt the consequence of gravity, a universal law if there ever was one? And when the human body overheats or becomes too cold, does that also obey some quite precise rules? In so far as the whooping cough is concerned, the doctor assures me that science is hopeful of understanding the nature of this disease and of rendering it harmless. In short, man attempts to incorporate every disorder into some order, close or remote, present or future.

But what if there were an absolute, definitive, hopeless disorder? An area of experience that would now and always escape any kind of net, that would be impervious to every system and to every harmony? How would man behave in that eventuality? I cannot demonstrate to you that this kind of disorder exists in nature. What I can tell you is that if it existed man would not notice it; he would pass next to it and would perhaps even touch it, but would not receive any impression from it.

Man does not have any organs suited for conceiving disorder. And if he had, it would no longer be disorder; it would precisely enter into the system of his organs. Man has this specialty: to take notice only of what can be useful to him [. . .]. The irregular runs through his fingers — and that is the reason for which he says it does not exist.

Imagine that among many dots scattered about by chance, we isolate six that are symmetrically arranged and then we exclaim: "How marvelously nature has built the hexagon! How perfect is this figure! If one joins the vertexes with the center six equilateral triangles appear and they all are equal and the sum of all the angles is always equal to eight right angles! If one draws a circle around the hexagon, we can see that the side of the hexagon is equal to the radius of the circle! How clever we have been to uncover, in this chaos of dots, the monster of regularity! Surely, all the other dots will turn out to be similarly regular and all we need is to continue our efforts and we will find ever new harmonies!"

This is more the less the way we operate in the sciences. We choose among the immensity of the world some little tune that has about it a certain regularity (just as from a huge amount of noise we isolate sometimes a new sound that constitute a new melody). And we are incapable of hearing the rest. And it is that little tune that we call 'nature'. From birth, man is bound by a certain number of conditions that are simply there and are never questioned: two legs, two hands, two eyes, ten fingers, one heart. From that moment on he makes use of everything that corresponds to his mode of being and denies the existence of all that is unsuited to it. With what that turns out to be suited he builds his concepts and his values — beautiful and ugly, useful and noxious, good and evil. I assure you that if he had seventeen hands instead of two, symmetry, equilibrium, and proportion would be based on the number seventeen.

We see only what we look for, and we look only for what suits us. Little wonder then, that the world, as we are finding it, suits us. In this manner the myth arises that nature is beautiful and regular, or logical and mathematical. A myth which, as you know, is believed by both the materialistic scientist and the mystic.

Another example: you know that the animals after having given birth eat the placenta. We throw it away. [. . .] Because we think we know the function of this membrane, in our view it has had the purpose of enveloping the fetus. [. . .] But when the animal first saw this blood-stained thing he probably asked himself: "What is this thing good for? Let us try to eat it." [. . .] Suppose now there were a scientist among the dogs or the horses: he would be convinced that the natural function of the placenta is to satiate the mother after giving birth. And he would exclaim: "How excellent a provider is nature; it provides our dogs and our horses with exactly the food they need and for which they crave."

Nature, believe me, is like a mirror that reflects the image of him who scrutinizes it. And man, the most intelligent of the animals, substitutes his own image for the mirror.

The Return to Nature

A well-known physician recommended a sun cure for my month-old baby, describing it as very much "in accordance with nature." The next day a different doctor expressed great surprise that his colleague would dare expose such tender limbs to such powerful radiation. I asked him to explain and his only answer was, "But it goes against nature!" Neither of them had evidently ever bothered to find out what the word nature really meant. I despised the doctors. I decided, on my own account, in favor of the sun — but when I think about it, I find my decision was based on nothing more than a confused sense that it was easier this way, more *natural.*

I normally read the descriptions that come with the medicines I sometimes have to take very carefully. A liver and spleen preparation against anemia commends itself to my benevolence by explaining to me that animals and savages devour the viscera of their victims first. A garlic compound to aid digestion explains that primitive peoples attributed miraculous virtues to that plant. O hallowed wisdom of beasts and savages! I would like to see some statistics on deaths from disease among walruses and Zulus before relying so confidently on their health practices. And still it is undeniable that the return to nature is more than just the myth of an epoch or the fashion of the moment. It is an inclination that humans seem unable to get free of. They overcome it in one field, and here it is popping up, unexpected and unimagined, in another — and even in the very discipline on whose behalf it was supposed to be eliminated. The fact is that human beings, having reached a highly developed (I don't want to say advanced) stage of progress, feel a desire to go back — to throw off the burdens they have voluntarily weighed themselves down with, which they had thought would benefit them so much. Why? Disappointment, distrust of the path chosen, and a need to start over? Exhaustion from the effort? A sense of the futility of all efforts and the impossibility of reaching any goal?

A first observation is that when it comes to this return to a primitive state — people don't really mean it. Their theoreticians have been forced to transform it and deform it in such a way that it is almost unrecognizable. And no one is seriously offering to walk on four legs. The myth of nature has not slowed so-called progress in the slightest. Indeed, it has sped it up. Every discovery, every theory that aims to give people new and useful tools is presented as a return to the simple, the elementary, the primitive — like the elimination of prejudices and superstructures to achieve more direct and immediate contact with reality.

When the myth of nature took the form of a political ideology, a clearly defined program, it gave rise to one of the greatest social upheavals in recorded history. It was an impulse, in other words, only apparently aimed at destroying, when in fact its purpose was to build. When it set itself up as a moral ideal, it identified itself with reason and with the struggle against the passions — taking the side, that is, of what is most complicated, artificial, and unnatural in the human psyche. When people believed that reason had failed in its task, and sought a faculty of intuition, desire, and love that they could rely on, it was this that presented itself as the simplest and most immediate — like humility and poverty against the pride and artificiality of the intellect. And if reason wanted its revenge one day, it would set out to demonstrate that it was itself something original in the human psyche, something *innate*. Any program, any ideal, in other words, can be presented as a return to nature. And the word nature can be given the most contradictory contents. But it always serves as an excellent testimonial for whatever it happens to contain at any given time. When people are convinced that such and such an ideal, or program, or method, is really the simplest, the most primitive and most natural, they accept it without resistance, they abandon themselves to it with enthusiasm. In fact, among humans, one of the most frequently used recipes for success is to present oneself as the restorer of a lost simplicity. So are we dealing with a farce, an insincere pose? A demagogic disguise intended only to gain favor with a gullible and sentimental public? Even if this is so, it remains to be explained why people give so much credit to this myth that turns out to be an accessory of every formula or tool they use to understand or take possession of reality. There must be some profound reason for this — some consistent and fundamental mechanism of the human psyche that leads it irresistibly to conceive every conquest, every step forward, as a return. How is it, in short, that humans love the simple and primitive so much that everything that seems desirable or useful gets transformed into it and given its name?

*On the Concept of "Love"**

Love represents for us an example, or perhaps the only example, of a faculty that is entirely positive, and that cannot be converted into the opposite of its opposite. The whole of rationalist civilization is based on the identity A = not not A, which is also the principle of non-contradiction. Love cannot be conceived as the negation of hate, precisely because in the atmosphere we move in when we speak of these things, negation is exactly equivalent to hate. See in Scheler (*The Crisis of Values*) the distinction between Christian love (positive) and resentful love, considered as the attempt to get rid of a feeling of inferiority with respect to values contrary to those one loves.

Now does such a love really exist as a deep and original feature of the human mind or is it itself a simple intellectual construction, originating in the need to find the new by denying the old? Which is probably an essentially positive feeling in the human soul. Indeed, the concept of negation is probably something emergent, and the affection that we can consider as primitive and free is an entirely positive feeling, consisting of free expansion in the direction of an object of which no moral qualities are asked, and whose evaluation depends on love rather than love on its evaluation. One could characterize the feeling by saying that it is aimed straight towards its object, while others are aimed indirectly — that is, they are directed towards a false object hiding the true object which is something else. When we talk about "freeing ourselves," about eliminating the [. . .] in us and becoming once again spontaneous and sincere, our aim is precisely to achieve a positive feeling of this kind. If this is the case, we should say that the principle of non-contradiction and the entire civilization that derives from it (rational, mathematical-logical, therefore mechanical) is a deviation, a construction based on an original disease — the disease of "setting one against the other." This may be the case. In any event, it is perhaps better, instead of talking about health and disease, to talk about two attitudes — one "all positive," the other "positive negative." The latter has been exploited to the fullest extent possible. The former has not been exploited at all.

What I do not concede to Scheler is that this way of being, this *love,* is an entirely mental fact, independent of sexuality. On the contrary, it is closely tied to it. Freud is instructive here. Indeed, sexuality is the first essential example of an affection that attributes value to the object where it is applied, an affection of pure "expansion" and not of "evaluation." And following this along with what I said in the preceding lines, the whole construction of reason could be interpreted as a kind of prideful dualistic disease that arose out of the original disinterested and positive "libido."

These considerations also make me question whether early Christian love should be interpreted as positive love (Scheler) or resentful love (Nietzsche). There is certainly in Christianity a strong desire for the "liberation" of pure love. But it seems to me that in its search for objects there is still a strong dose of resentment. In the transition from Judaism to Christianity there is something analogous to what happens in a son with respect to his father. The father (i.e. God) is initially fair and strict. We admire and fear him. We are under him because he guarantees order. This order, conscience, morality, is his all-seeing eye (see Freud). At a certain age, we realize that the father can also be loved, and we feel that he is closer to us, more "human." We are now able to maintain order on our own, without constraint. Constraint and fear seem childish to us; we despise them. We are capable of a freer order, without such rigid rules. We no longer fear the father — now we can love him. If we manage to love him without being afraid of him we finally feel like free adults. Christianity is basically a reconciliation with the father — that is, the discovery of a love. The father is replaced by a sense of guilt and self-punishment (original sin, poverty, chastity, etc.). This applies to Christianity as a religious concept due to a [. . .]. As a mass movement it is another thing altogether.

Scheler draws political consequences from all this. Specifically, he condemns all humanitarianism, bourgeois ideology, and ideology of equality as deriving from resentment. I would agree with him that they derive from resentment. But what he proposes as a way of restoring the ideal of love — essentially a return to the medieval concepts of chastity, chivalry, etc. (the vilest form of reactionary thinking) do not seem at all suited to the purpose. It is undeniable that modern education tends to distribute goods to the masses (mental as well as material) that in the past were the prerogative of the few. And this is not resentment. What to do? Preach — be good, love each other, etc? This would go nowhere. I agree that leveling mechanisms are not a solution, but at least frame the issue so that it can be resolved. The question is similar in the case of a single individual. If he does not have nervous imbalances detrimental to his personality, there are two methods available: either deal with him at once as a sick person, a lunatic, and treat him accordingly at enormous expense and with little certainty of success, or let him organize his own defense, let him create his own *modus vivendi,* in which he is not of course cured, but which allows him a passably productive life. If at this point we introduce an attempt at a radical cure on the basis of this provisionally achieved balance, we have a much greater chance of success. The individual will already be stronger, more able to tolerate the treatment, and will already have learned certain organizational processes that will prevent his giving up and suffering a relapse. This is the way it is in the social sphere. Humanitarianism, leveling, is indeed, at its core, negation of negation — that is, resentment. But it is precisely this that can create the temporary balance, the artificial *modus vivendi,* that can give someone the strength to be free. If the meaning of "economic deprivation" is presented honestly, it will be understood not as a moral lesson, a *Weltanschauung,* but as recognition that the economic element (or resentment) is the only point of purchase that can be grasped to produce concrete advancement. The concept of the "leap from necessity to liberty" has this meaning. Only once this economic balance has been reached is it possible to speak of freedom. The error of economic ideology is to set itself up as definitive, as a true *Weltanschauung* — which obscures its instrumental character, prevents individuals from moving towards a personal moral approach and, worse still, by turning the economic element (or resentment) into a kind of moral absolute, makes it more difficult to maneuver it with the kind of agility that would enable one to reach the goal more quickly. Resentment, first used as a very practical tool, at some point made slaves of those who used it, and became a myth, an end in itself — they wanted to base a kind of morality on it. It is the usual defect of hypostatizing, of making everything into a philosophy. The resentment (or the economic) should instead be put to use as the most powerful weapon for achieving a balance that will allow access to the "kingdom of freedom." But quietly, without *Weltanschauung*, without philosophy. A tool — nothing more.

And what on the other hand is "love"? Scheler's mania is the constant attribution of objective values, the constant distinguishing of high and low, etc. Love would be the "objective value," the "high," the absolute. For us of course it is nothing of the kind. If anything, we could call it a stage in our liberation from complications that impede us, a "stage" of health. Looking at it with unprejudiced eyes, one sees that Scheler's description of pure, evangelical love is not very different from the love any lover has for their beloved. Here again, the value of the object is determined by the strength of the feeling invested in it, and not vice versa; here too, selfishness and altruism are identical; here too, the elevation of the self is realized in doing good for the other, etc. (Does this make it necessary to situate this feeling in metaphysical, inaccessible spheres?) Could the precept of evangelical love not be reduced to this: "Love everyone with the same dedication, with the same selflessness, with the same joy with which you love your beloved"? It is plain that to achieve this requires the elimination of resentment, but even before resentment, the causes of resentment. We know this feeling and for now we can achieve it only in the individual and subjective domain. Can it be transported to a collective field? Or made so that each individual can truly achieve it for all their fellow human beings? We are still a long way from this. But the way to approach it is to create in the meantime a tentative equilibrium, and to do this we so far know of no other means than to gratify resentment — that is, to put it in a condition where it can be more easily eliminated.

Another observation: I said that this love would represent direct and "sincere" — and therefore free — contact between the feeling (*Trieb*) and its subject. Its opposite would be love for something that is not itself truly the love-object — that is, love that exchanges objects, swaps the means for the end. Are we not here close to the Kantian distinction between the categorical and the hypothetical? The parallel is very useful. Kant would also like to reach the immediate, the direct, the "motiveless," the positive. But what is his method? The negation of the mediated, the indirect — indeed, the progressive elimination of it. And what is the characteristic that this positive then assumes? Universality. And where is it located? At the end of an indefinite process. It is like this: when the positive, the direct, is reached by eliminating its opposite (and this is the route followed by our entire rationalistic civilization), it is affirmed, in *all fields,* as a *universality placed at an infinite distance, which can be approached indefinitely.* These are the concept-limits of our understanding based on the negation of negation: the concept of totality, of infinity, of approximation. That is, idealist and transcendental philosophy, and mathematical calculation. The other way, alternatively, would be not so much eliminating negation as going backwards along the path that led to it. *Returning to simplicity, that is.* This second method, which has often been mentioned as an imperative (return to nature, etc.) has never actually been applied. And therefore it is not entirely clear what its points of arrival are. We can perhaps already sense that it would allow us to attain a direct, positive moral attitude, integrally experienced and not arrived at only by approximation. On the other hand it would constrain us to do without some of the most important tools we have for mastering reality (calculation, organization, society, etc.). Now we should study whether this new point of arrival could provide us with other tools, and if so, what they might be. Or better still, we should see what help our awareness of the possibility of following this other path could provide in resolving the paradoxes of our current organization of reality.

Notes for an Article on "Primitive People and the Categories of the Mind"

Bibliography: Bachelard, *The Formation of the Scientific Mind*; Jung, *The Problem of the Unconscious in Modern Psychology*; Cantoni, *Primitives*;

De Martino, *Naturalism and Historicism*; Freud, *Totem and Taboo and Other Essays*; Cantoni, *Philosophy between Science and Myth*.

I) The central thesis is expressed by Bachelard, on p. 9.

In Bachelard, the thesis that the scientific mind is trained *against* nature (p. 22).

Supporting this argument against the thesis of the presence of mythical-mystical elements in the modern mind means that these elements are a category of the mind. No: they are errors or rather a difficult past to be eradicated.

Bachelard says (p. 38) that science has to fight constantly against metaphors. Okay, but what should be considered a *metaphor*? In our thinking (and in scientific thinking) we always make transpositions of meaning. What is the principle of identity if not a rule to establish when to attribute to two different things the same. . . . Indeed, thinking consists substantially of this. Some are considered legitimate, others aren't. Which are legitimate? Is there a pre-drawn line up to which it is permissible to metaphorize (forces, inertia, energy, cause, etc.) and beyond which this is no longer permissible? We say that history, mankind's development, has imposed a line of this kind, and that what we find in us of the primitive mentality is a remnant, a residue from this line, and that the advancement of this line — that is, the improvement of science — must consist of eliminating more and more of these residues, to better pursue this essentialization. But would a line of development in an entirely different direction be possible, admitting other systems of metaphor and excluding still others? Perhaps it would. And the primitive mind stands as a virgin starting point from which all directions are possible.

Bachelard says (p. 53) that every element of value in the sciences needs to be psychoanalyzed.

Grace, in scientific terms, is called empiricism of a particular type. Not so much "to make things speak" as "to silence ourselves." In this sense the ego, the *Geist,* as Klages puts it, is also the enemy of science. But it is an impersonal, logical, rational ego. It is the imposition on reality of our abstract thinking. It is assumed that by making it abstract, we have made it purer, more consistent with reality. On the contrary, it has only been made more generic, therefore more likely to give the illusion of reality. The struggle against Ego and Reason is also carried out in the empirical sciences, with the question — how else could we think? And the answer that experience gives us, which actually cannot be accommodated in our normal frameworks, is essentially a lesson in modesty, which teaches us not to always anticipate what will happen to us.

To say, "there is the one and the other" is idealist mischief. There is finalism and causality. No. We must decide between finalism and causality — we must decide between *Geist* and *Seele*. But this decision need not entail radically eliminating one of them — e.g., abandoning millennia of civilization for some undifferentiated ecstasy. It can be done in the sense of the previous note.

On the relationship between fear, and death, and culture, see Klages, p. 69 my note. What is fear for the primitives? How does one go from it to wanting to eliminate death?

Finalism is the desire to consider the whole world in our image. It is a trait of the primitive mind that the development of the *Geist* has gradually eliminated.

Shall we then say that a mystical return to primitive communion means a return to finalism? Perhaps not. Perhaps finalism is the coarsest form of dominance of the *Geist* — a form that has since been progressively refined into causalism, which is itself but a more refined form of anthropomorphism, the attribution of our reason to nature, rather than to our feelings and will.

*On the Oedipus Complex**

In psychoanalysis, the Oedipus complex is usually considered something original, autonomous, primitive. The male is attached to the mother, the female to the father. Sometimes it happens inversely, insofar as the male has feminine tendencies, and the female masculine, or insofar as the father is feminine, and the mother masculine. But in short this inclination of one sex toward the other is regarded as a primal instinct in children, impossible to break down further. I don't know if there has been sufficient observation in these hates and loves of the initiative taken by the parents. They are almost always the originators of such situations. The love of parents for their children is almost never pure — on the contrary, it is almost always contaminated by identifications, by substitutions. Let us take a simple and normal case. As a rule the mother's love for her son is initially mystical. The same goes for the daughter. Up to this point there is no distinction of sexes. She loves in the creature a piece of herself, coming from her own insides and still kept long bound to her own body by suckling. What happens when this being begins to speak and move, to have a personality? It is a tragic moment for the mother. He is no longer the piece of herself; he is detaching, escaping. He is no longer that piece of her own flesh, responding with smiles to smiles, reaching out with pleasure for her breast. A deep resentment begins to form in the mother for the new being that is developing. With terror she notices facial features and attitudes that are not her own, that make her son or daughter different from herself — her husband's features. Little girls, they say, most often resemble their father. These features must be unbearable to the mother when they appear. She sees them as signs of betrayal, of irrevocable loss. She begins to hate these traits. Sometimes, she already hated them before. Sometimes the moment of the child's initial development coincides with the moment when the mother's first infatuation for the husband has passed, when she no longer loves him, and is transferring all her resentments and personal grudges to him. Sometimes, finally, it is precisely the jealousy for the child that makes her hate even in her husband these traits that are like a tangible sign of the child's mutilation. The tragedy between mother and daughter is complicated by a tragedy between wife and husband. And the husband? In the first year he was uninterested in his son, in this piece of flesh tied to the mother. But in the second and third years, things change. His rights are now at least equal to those of the mother. Indeed, his less frequent appearance gives him a halo of distinction and privilege. When he's home, his right to have his child all to himself is recognized. The new, firm flesh somehow excites him. He finds and cultivates a new source of tenderness which sometimes compensates him for his dwindling tenderness for his wife. It is his revenge for the year of pregnancy and lactation in which he was relegated to the sidelines. He uses it in any way he can to vent grudges, revenge, resentments against his wife.

Let's take the other case. The first year passes as in the previous case (I do not believe that there are forms of maternal love that are not narcissistic, and it seems to me that the first year, except in cases where the mother hates the child, should pass more or less identically for males and females). It may happen that the mother, at the moment when the child's ego begins to develop, manages to prolong the situation of the first year. As a rule, I would say she will always try to do so. Whether she succeeds or not will depend on many external factors: the relationship with her husband, her natural characteristics, the appearance of the child, etc. Let us suppose that she succeeds; she will have perpetuated the initial narcissistic state in her relations with the child. The child will remain the flesh of her flesh, the being whose health she will be anxious about all her life. Her love for him will have the character of a triumph over her husband. The husband will remain a stranger in the family, the stranger who is feared and deceived.

And the child? In both cases, the child is the weak and insecure object of these forces that are foreign to him. His decisions usually follow the direction of the conflict between the parents. This is not to deny that some of his initial tendencies are a constituent element of the conflict. But they are *one* element, and almost never the most decisive. The child's loves and jealousies are primarily a reflection of the parents' loves and jealousies. Hatred of the father is an example of this. I cannot exclude the fact that sometimes it is largely because the child sees him as a rival for the mother (especially if the child has been shocked by the observation of sexual relations between the parents). But it is very often (I dare say much more often) the precise reflection of the mother's hatred of the father, her fear of him, her sense of guilt towards him, her sense of cold or resentful respect towards him. This is how the children come to be defenders, protectors of the mother. Out of this feeling, if they then happen to observe the parents' sexual relations, deep disappointment may result, due to the mother's betrayal, to her "going over to the enemy," a hatred for both of them, a sense of abandonment whose solution is a return to narcissism, or the search for a new object (grandmother, wet nurse, or other), but accompanied by pity — that is, love for oneself.

The other conclusion to be drawn from all this is that the mixture of male and female elements in each character is not a *prius* that determines the choice of the object of concentration of the *libido,* but a consequence of having been "chosen" by one or the other parent. On the contrary, I would say that the type of sentiments of each, not to speak of the type of perversions requiring real processes of substitution, identification, and fixation are necessary, is irrevocably determined by this experience — by the choice, that is, of the parents. And first of all I would deny that the union of son-mother and daughter-father is a rule that can be taken as fundamental. It is a rule that has so many exceptions that it loses much of its value. That this relationship occurs with somewhat greater frequency is probably determined by the physiological fact that the male more often resembles the mother, and by the fact that in the affections of the parents the consciousness of sex is of decisive importance — rather than by inherent tendencies in children.

But for children, at a time when the satisfaction of *libido* occurs as a rule in ways other than through the sexual organs, when in fact these organs in the female have not yet been discovered and in the male have a function other than sexual, at a time when the secondary differentiation between the sexes has not yet appeared, it seems to me difficult to think of an instinctive and regular attraction of the male for adult female beings and vice versa. In any case, it seems to me that this attraction, even if it exists in a germinal state, can only be assigned a secondary role in the choice of the object.

It should be noted that the mother's choices, in the cases of both male and female, have qualitative characteristics that are very different from the father's. So far, we have chosen to describe the Oedipus complex in its classical form (mother-son), and the inverse form (father-daughter) has been set against it as equivalent. But we must not forget that throughout the first year, the position of the mother is of absolute preeminence, both for the male and the female. It follows that the mother's choices, for both sexes, have a character of preservation, fear of the outside world (narcissism?), while the choices of the father have more of a character of triumph, of offense. The first is a defensive love, the latter an aggressive love. It is the father, not the mother, that the child is "afraid of being eaten by."

I will attempt to characterize some of these situations, taking into account the feelings that start with the parents and determine those of the children.

Mother and son. It is the typical defensive love, narcissistic par excellence. It is dominated by the vivid terror of protest against the outside world which one day, fatally, inevitably, will detach the two, swallowing the son. The sense of being devoured is suggested to the son by his mother. For the son (and sometimes for the mother as well) the father symbolizes the external world.

And the monster lurking in ambush that cannot be avoided. The two of them have their world to themselves, the only one where the monster cannot penetrate, the mother's lap. They are fortified there. Not only the son, but also the mother. In the son she has finally found her refuge. This being she will tremble for all her life will also be her protector, her defender. Defending the mother will later be the only virile attitude assumed by the son — and it will essentially be a struggle against virility. He will detach himself from his mother only to defend her, to defend his mother's body and the closed and secure world of his child self. The tone of his entire emotional life will be determined by this original sentiment. Or he will not have the strength to detach himself from this world and will abandon its active defense. He will remain in his mother's arms all his life and will identify with her. This is homosexuality (Freud: *Narcissism, Massenpsychologie*).

The one he loves in his life will always be himself as the son of his own mother. Either the possible, the hoped for, the loving defender who has grown to tower over her and whose strength she alone admires without fear because she knows every intimacy of him, or the weak, the helpless, the tender one, hiding from the world under the veil of her caresses. The somewhat bigger boy, that is, or the somewhat smaller.

The daughter and the mother. The fear is not so distressing. The mother knows her daughter's fate more intimately from her own experience. The outside world will be gentler with her, it will not swallow her up. The mother has no reason here to be jealous, as she was with her son, of those mysterious relationships between male and male that she knows nothing about, but from which she has everything to fear.

*On the Axiomatics of the Theory of Relativity**
Special Relativity

Special relativity is generally based on two principles: The invariant speed of light. The principle of relativity. Of these two postulates, the first is taken as an experimental observation, and the second as a hypothesis suggested by our need for harmony and simplicity, and not contradicted by experience.

Now the edifice of special relativity could also be constructed in a different way. It could be conceived as a reform of the system of space-time measurement. Instead of taking as a basic unit of measurement a length (rigid body) or a time interval (clock) and then deducing the other quantities (velocity, acceleration), we might adopt as a primitive unit the distance between two given points and the propagation speed of a given phenomenon (light in a vacuum, for example). From this, we would automatically derive the measures of space and time at any point of an inertial system, and, for the passage from one inertial system to another, the Corentin transformations. These results can be reached without introducing the principle of relativity as an independent postulate.

This method, essentially that already been followed by Reichenbach in his *Axiomatik der Raum-Zeit-Lehre*, has the advantage of replacing postulates *imposed* by experience with the adoption of units of measurement *recommended* by experience — that is, of substituting experiences of the second kind for experiences of the first kind (see Art. I).

General Relativity

If we wish to extend what was said about special relativity to the case of any system in motion, the problem of general relativity will become one of determining space-time measurements for any observer in motion with respect to an inertial system in which Euclidean geometry applies. These measurements will be taken again assuming the distance between two points as fixed and the speed of light as constant. In general it will result that the three-dimensional geometry of the system in question will not be Euclidean. Vice versa it should be demonstrable that if the measurements taken by an observer with the above method give rise to a non-Euclidean geometry, we can always find a system whose points are shifted with respect to the observer in question so that its geometry is Euclidean. In such a system there will be no gravitational field.

This formulation of the problem differs somewhat from the classic formulation of general relativity. Here it is not a question of finding a formulation of the laws of nature that is invariant with respect to any transformations, and then to attribute to each system the geometry required by the gravitational field in it, but rather to find the transformations that allow passage from one system to any other, having assumed for all systems certain conventions about space-time measurements — and this without making any assumption about the form of the natural laws.

Formulating the problem in this way, we would probably reach the same conclusions as general relativity about gravitation, but the new approach would perhaps allow us to attack other problems (in particular that of electromagnetism) in a way different from the usual one.

In this case it would no longer be a matter of formulating the laws of an electromagnetic field in a way that is invariant for any transformation, but to account for their structure by systematically studying the behavior of moving charges by means of "Transformation auf Ruhe."[2]

*On the Axiomatics of the Laws of Mechanics**

The principle of inertia is notoriously a disguised definition. It defines a body in uniform motion as "not subject to any force," and therefore a body in non-uniform motion as subject to a force. Is it possible to consider the principles of the conservation of momentum and of energy as extensions of the principle of inertia — that is, also as implicit definitions of force? We believe so.

Let's consider in fact a system of two bodies. We will say that the system has not been subjected to the action of any force not only when the two bodies continue in their linear and uniform motion, but also when they have modified their motion after having collided. What will have to remain unchanged in the system will

---

[2]This essay refers to studies still in progress and far from completion.

not be the motion of the two bodies, but a function of this motion — a function to be determined by setting conditions derived from plausible requirements. First of all we can require that the change caused by the impact in the state of motion of one of the two bodies is measured by the change caused by the same impact in the other body — that is, what remains constant in the system is the *sum* of the functions in question for each body. Once each body is identified through a constant characteristic (its "mass"), we can require that the change in a body brought about successively by two other bodies of equal mass and equal velocity should be identical to the change produced by one body of double mass and equal velocity — which is the same as saying that our function will have to take the form mf(v). We will then be able to observe that the function in question must be able to express both a change in the absolute value of the velocity of each body and a change in the direction alone — that is, the functions in question must be two, one vectorial, and the other scalar. Finally, it will be observed that since two bodies in uniform motion with respect to an inertial system are also in uniform motion with respect to any other inertial system, the constancy of our functions must be invariant with respect to Lorentz transformations. All these conditions limit the choice of our functions so as to determine them unequivocally, and the result is the relativistic expression of the quantity of motion and energy.

This was demonstrated by Langevin, although starting out from somewhat different premises.

The preceding developments may be of importance for the following reason. The theory of relativity arrives at its expressions of energy and quantity of motion from Maxwell's equations, which it assumes are guaranteed experimentally. But the experimental control of such equations supposes that a definition of energy and momentum is available. In addition, when the fundamental principles of mechanics have been defined independently of electromagnetism, it remains possible to deduce the laws of electromagnetism themselves using certain results of relativity, and thus achieving a deeper understanding of those laws.[3]

---

[3]This article also refers to ongoing studies. The first part of these, concerning special rela-

Geometry and Experience*

The axioms of geometry are implicit definitions — or rather, they represent the limitations imposed on our freedom to define the objects they refer to. But these objects can be of two types. The first of these is such that to obtain a concrete representation of the objects it is necessary to imagine them realized by a physical phenomenon (e.g. the straight line produced by the trajectory of a light ray in a vacuum), in which case the definition implicit in the axioms is a "real" definition (*Zuordnungsdefinition*), and the axioms limit the number of *objects or phenomena* that can be assumed to physically embody this particular geometric entity. Or, the geometric entity in question is such that it can be defined through an opportune combination of other, previously defined entities (for example, the angle equal to a given angle can be defined without recourse to superposition when the distance between two points has been previously defined) — in which case the axioms limit the number of *expedients* that we can use to define that particular geometric entity.

For the purposes of physically constructing a Galilean system, it makes sense to distinguish between these two types of definition; and it may be useful to study Hilbert's *Grundlagen* from this point of view.

It is by no means certain that a set of physical phenomena can always be found that can simultaneously express all the axioms of a certain geometry. For example, if you want to realize this geometry through light rays taken to be straight and of uniform propagation speed, there is no guarantee that Euclid's axiom will be verified. And this axiom, if it is verified for the system built by a certain observer, is necessarily not verified for the system built by another observer whose movement with respect to the first is not uniform.

On the Idols of Physical Science*

In a meticulous and insightful investigation, which he called the *psychoanalysis of objective knowledge,* Gaston Bachelard enumerated a series of "epistemological obstacles" that damaged science in the 17th and 18th centuries by providing fallacious and pic-

---

tivity and electromagnetism, is finished; but it would be too technical for the journal.

turesque explanations of phenomena, harmonious panoramas of the universe that satisfied systematic and finalistic needs, and thus diverted science from the terrain of objective and unprejudiced research. Standing before this heap of fallen idols and lost illusions, one feels a strange sense of contentment and regret, like someone who finds the toys and puppets of their childhood in an old chest.

But I wish Bachelard or someone else would tell us the story of how these idols fell, and would investigate the process of how they came to melt into the fabric of scientific knowledge, or collapse noisily in the face of a discovery, or manage to survive still — leading a hidden life and struggling insidiously on the fringes of science. It would be an interesting research project, and I believe that in this story of human emancipation from scientific prejudice philosophy would cut a pretty poor figure. It would turn out that the vast majority of the victories gained were achieved by science alone, using its own resources.

BIBLIOGRAPHY

AA.VV. (2004) *Eugenio Colorni 1944–2004. Dalla guerra alla Costituzione europea*. Ed. Maria Pia Bumbaca. Roma: Municipio III.

AA.VV. (2009) "I documenti su Eugenio Colorni conservati nell'Archivio Centrale dello Stato." Ed. Giulia Vassallo. *Eurostudium3w* (April-June).

AA.VV. (2010) *Eugenio Colorni dall'antifascismo all'europeismo socialista e federalista*. Ed. Maurizio degl'Innocenti. Roma: Lacaita.

AA.VV. (2011) *Eugenio Colorni e la cultura italiana tra le due guerre*. Ed. Geri Cerchiai and Giovanni Rota. Roma: Lacaita.

AA.VV. (2011a) *Eugenio Colorni federalista*. Ed. Fabio Zucca. Roma: Lacaita.

A Colorni-Hirschman International Institute. (2018) *For a Better World. First Conference on Albert Hirschman's Legacy*. Ed. Luca Meldolesi and Nicoletta Stame. Pardee School of Global Studies, Boston Univ., Boston, Oct. 6–7.

____. (2019) *A Bias for Hope. Second Conference on Albert Hirschman's Legacy*. Ed. Luca Meldolesi and Nicoletta Stame. IEG, World Bank Group, Washington DC, Oct. 25–26.

____. (2020) *A Passion for the Possible. Third Conference on Albert Hirschman Legacy*. Ed. Luca Meldolesi and Nicoletta Stame. Berlin School of Economics and Law, Berlin, Oct. 24–25.

Adelman, J. (2013) *Worldly Philosopher. The Odyssey of Albert O. Hirschman*. Princeton (NJ): Princeton UP.

Bachelard, G. (1938) *La formation de l'ésprit scientifique*. Paris: Vrin, Paris.

Barié, G.E. (1933) *La spiritualità dell'essere e Leibniz*. Padova: Cedam.

Bavink, B. (1944) *La scienza naturale sulla via della religione*. Torino: Einaudi.

____. (1947) *Risultati e problemi delle scienze naturali. Introduzione alla filosofia naturale dei nostri giorni*. Vol. 1. Trans. Eugenio Colorni. Firenze: Sansoni.

Bobbio, N. (1975) "Introduzione," "Note," and ed., Colorni 1975.

Borgese, G.A. (1928) *Corso di Estetica. Dal Neo-classico al Romantico 1927–28* (year 6). Ed. G. Tagliabue. Milano: Lithography P. Capra.

____. (1930) *Lezioni di estetica. Posizioni verso il Croce. Posizioni verso il Manzoni 1929–30* (year 8). Ed. M. Gorra. Milano: Typog. Mariani.

____. (1931) *Lezioni di estetica. Lineamenti di storia della critica* (year 9). Ed. S. Spellanzon. Pavia: S.A. Bruni Marelli Arti Grafiche.

____. (1934) *Poetiche dell'unità. Cinque Saggi. Precursioni estetiche* (complete reproduction Milano: Arnoldo Mondadori, 1952).

Cantoni, R. (1941) *Il pensiero dei primitivi*. Milano: Garzanti.

____. (1941) "La filosofia tra scepsi e mito." *Studi filosofici* 1.

Cavaglion, A. (2011) "'Il mio poeta'. Eugenio Colorni, Umberto Saba, e la psicanalisi," in AA.VV. 2011.

Cerchiai, G. (2009) "Nota del curatore," "Introduzione," "Note ai testi," "Note a piè di pagina," and ed., Colorni 2009.

____. (2016) "Cinque scritti metodologici di Eugenio Colorni nelle carte di Vittorio Somenzi." *Laboratorio Ispf. Rivista elettronica di testi, saggi e strumenti*, XIII.

____. (2018) *La filosofia di Eugenio Colorni*. Milano: Franco Angeli.

___, and G. Rota. (2011) "Introduzione," AA.VV. 2011.

Colorni, E. (1928) "Roberto Ardigò." *Pietre* 2 (under the pseudonym 'Rosemberg').

___. (1930) "Recensione a *La giustizia* di Max Ascoli." *Civiltà moderna* 6.

___. (1930a) "Recensione a *Saggi critici* di Giacomo Debenedetti." *Leonardo* (February).

___. (1930b) "Sviluppo e significato dell'individualismo leibnziano." B.A. thesis.

___. (1931) "Recensione a *Estetica* di Adriano Tilgher." *Il convegno* 1–2.

___. (1931a) "Recensione a *Parole all'orecchio e Parliamo dell' Italia.*" Ed. V. Cardarelli. *Il convegno* 1–2.

___. (1931b) "In memoria di Enrico Sereni." *Israel* (13–20 marzo).

___. (1931c) "Recensione a *La carne, la morte e il diavolo nella letteratura romantica* di M. Praz." *Il convegno* 5.

___. (1931d) "Utilità e moralità nella filosofia di Tommaso Campanella." *Rivista di filosofia* (July-September).

___. (1931e) "Recensione a *Studi crociani* di Guido Calogero e Domenico Petrini." *Il convegno* 11–12.

___. (1932) *L'estetica di Benedetto Croce. Studio critico,* Milano: Società Editrice "La cultura."

___. (1932a) "Recensione alla ristampa dell'*Introduzione alla metafisica* di Piero Martinetti." *La cultura* 3.

___. (1932b) "Recensione a *La scuola di ballo* di Arturo Loria." *Il convegno* 7–8.

___. (1932c) "Di alcune relazioni tra conoscenza e volontà." *Rivista di filosofia* XXIII; now in Colorni 2009.

___. (1933) "La filosofia giovanile di Leibniz." M.A. thesis

___. (1935) "Prefazione," "Nota bio-bibliografica," and "Esposizione antologica del sistema leibniziano." Leibniz 1935.

___. (1935a) "I problemi della guerra." *Politica socialista* (August) (under the pseudonym 'Agostini'); now in Colorni 2019.

___. (1936) "La lotta all'interno del fascismo." *Nuovo Avanti!* (31 October); now in Colorni 2019a.

___. (1937) "La spontaneità è una forma di organizzazione." *Nuovo Avanti!* (12 June) (under the pseudonym 'Anselmi'); now in Colorni 2019.

___. (1937a) "La funzione del maestro nella scuola fascista." 3 articles. *Nuovo Avanti!* (July) (under the pseudonym 'Agostini'); now in Colorni 2019.

___. (1937b) "Direttive per la costituzione di posti di frontiera e per il lavoro all'interno." September; now in Colorni 2019a.

___. (1943) *Ultime volontà* (2 May); now in Colorni 2019a.

___. (1944) "Introduzione." Rossi Spinelli 1944; now in 2019.

___. (1975) *Scritti.* Ed. N. Bobbio. Firenze: La Nuova Italia.

___. (1980) "Pagine di Eugenio Colorni." Solari 1980.

___. (1998) *Il coraggio dell'innocenza.* Ed. L. Meldolesi. Napoli: La Città del Sole.

___. (2009) *La malattia della metafisica. Scritti filosofici e autobiografici.* Ed. Geri Cerchiai. Torino: Einaudi.

___. (2009a) "Libero arbitrio e grazia nel pensiero di Leibniz." Colorni 2009.

___. (2016) *Micorfondamenta.* Ed. Luca Meldolesi. Soveria Mannelli: Rubbettino.

___. (2017) *La scoperta del possibile. Scritti politici.* Ed. Luca Meldolesi. Soveria Mannelli: Rubbettino.

___. (2018) *L'ultimo anno, 1943–44. Genesi di una prospettiva.* Ed. Luca Meldolesi. Soveria Mannelli: Rubbettino.

___. (2019) *Critical Thinking in Action. Excerpts from Political Writings and Correspondence I.* Ed. Luca Meldolesi and Nicoletta Stame. New York: Bordighera P.

___. (2019a) *The Discovery of the Possible. Excerpts from Political Writings and Correspondence II.* Ed. Luca Meldolesi and Nicoletta Stame. New York: Bordighera P.

___. (2020) *"La malattia filosofica" e altri saggi.* Ed. Luca Meldolesi. Soveria Mannelli: Rubbettino.

___. (2021) *The Last Year, 1943–44. Genesis of a Perspective.* Ed. Luca Meldolesi and Nicoletta Stame. New York: Bordighera P.

___, and A. Spinelli. (2018) *I dialoghi di Ventotene.* Ed. Luca Meldolesi. Soveria Mannelli: Rubbettino.

___. (2020) *Dialogues.* Ed. Luca Meldolesi. New York: Bordighera P.

Coppa, C. (2012) *La ricerca socio-economica come scoperta: Albert Hirschman e Eugenio Colorni.* Ed. Mita Marra. Napoli: Giannini.

Croce, B. (1913) *Il breviario di estetica.* Bari: Laterza. English trans: *The Essence of Aestetics.* London: Heineman, 1921.

___. (1955) *Terze pagine sparse.* Bari: Laterza.

Deleuze, G. (1991) *Qu'est-ce que la philosophie?* Paris. Italian trans. Torino: Einaudi, 1996.

De Martino, E. (1941) *Naturalismo e storicismo nell'etnologia.* Nuova ed. Lecce: Argo, 1966.

De Rosa, D. (2004) *Spose, madri e maestre. Il liceo femminile e l'Istituto magistrale "Giosué Carducci" di Trieste 1874–1954.* Udine: Del Buono.

Eddington, A.S. (1941) *La filosofia della scienza fisica.* Bari: Laterza.

Esposito, R. (2010) *Pensiero vivente. Origine e attualità della filosofia italiana.* Torino: Einaudi.

Freud, S. (1921) *Massenpsycologie und Ich-Analyse.* Wien: I.P. Verlag.

___. (1930) *Totem e tabù ed altri saggi.* Bari: Laterza.

Gadda, C.E. (2007) *I quaderni dell'ingegnere. Testi e studi gaddiani 5.* Ed. G. Lucchini. Torino: Einaudi.

Gerbi, S. (1999) *Tempi di malafede. Una storia italiana tra fascismo e dopoguerra. Guido Piovene ed Eugenio Colorni.* Torino: Einaudi.

Geremicca, A.V. (1939) *Spiritualità della natura.* Bari: Laterza.

Gonseth, F. (1928) *Qu'est-ce que la logique?* Paris.

Hegel, G.W.F. (1807) *Phänomenologie des Geistes.* Einleitung. English trans. *Phenomenology of the Spirit.* Oxford: Clarendon, 1977.

Hegel, G.W.F. (1817) *Enzyklopädie der philosophischen Wissenschaften*; Werke, Band 8, Frankfurt a. M. 1979.

Helmholtz, H. von (1921) *Schriften zur Erkentnistheorie.* Berlin.

Hirschman, A.O. (1945) *National Power and the Structure of Foreign Trade.* Berkeley: U of California P, ; third ed., with new introduction, 1980.

___. (1958) *The Strategy of Economic Development.* New Haven: Yale UP, 8th printing, 1964.

___. (1961) "Preface to the paperbound edition." Hirschman 1958, 1964.

___. (1970) *Exit, Voice, and Loyalty: Responses to Decline in Firms, Organiza-*

tions and States. Cambridge (MA): Harvard UP, Cambridge. German trans. *Abwanderung und Widerspruch.* Tubingen: Mohar, 1974.

___. (1977) *The Passions and the Interests. Political Arguments for Capitalism before Its Triumph.* Princeton (NJ): Princeton UP.

___. (1978) "Beyond Asymmetry: Critical Notes on Myself as a Young Man and Some Other Old Friends." *International Organization* (Winter); now in Hirschman 1945, 1980, and 1981.

___. (1981) *Essays in Trespassing: Economics to Politics and Beyond.* Cambridge (UK): Cambridge UP.

___. (1982) *Shifting Involvements. Private Interest and Public Action.* Princeton (NJ): Princeton UP.

___. (1984) "A Dissenter's Confession: Revisiting 'The Strategy of Economic Development.'" *Pioneers in Economic Development.* Ed. G. M. Meier and D. Seers. Oxford: Oxford UP; now in Hirschman 1986.

___. (1984a) "Against Parsimony: Three Easy Ways of Complicating Some Categories of Economic Discourse." *American Economic Review* (May); now in Hirschman 1986.

___. (1986) *Rival Views of Market Societies and Other Recent Essays.* New York: Viking.

___. (1987) "Io, detective dell'economia fascista." *Laurea Honoris Causa to Prof. Albert O. Hirschman* (12 November) now in Hirschman 1990, *Tre continenti. Economia politica e sviluppo della democrazia in Europa, Stati Uniti e America Latina.* Ed. L. Meldolesi. Torino: Einaudi; English trans. in Hirschman 1995.

___. (1994) *Passaggi di frontiera.* Roma: Donzelli; English trans. in Hirschman 1998, Ch. 3.

___. (1995) *A Propensity to Self-Subversion.* Cambridge (MA): Harvard UP.

___. (1998) *Crossing Boundaries. Selected Writings.* New York: Zone.

Hirschmann, U. (1963) *Rievocazione incompiuta,* 1974, typescript.

___. (1993) *Noi senzapatria.* Bologna: il Mulino.

Höffding, H. (1926) *Storia della filosofia moderna. Esposizione della storia della filosofia dalla fine del Rinascimento fino ai giorni nostri.* Trans. from the German by Prof. P. Martinetti; reprint Milano: F.lli Bocca, 1943.

Jung, C.G. (1938) *Le moi et l'inconscient.* Paris: Gallimard.

___. (1942) *Il problema dell'inconscio nella psicologia moderna.* Torino: Einaudi.

Kant, I. (1797) *Kritik der reinen Vernunft.* Second Edition. Italian trans. Bari: Laterza, 1966.

Klages, L. (1922) *Vom Kosmogonischen Eros.* Munchen: Muller.

Leibniz, G.G. (1935) *La Monadologia.* Ed. Eugenio Colorni. Firenze: Sansoni.

Lenti, L. (1983) *Le radici del tempo. Passato al presente e futuro.* Milano: F. Angeli.

Lepenies, W. (2006) *The Seduction of Culture in German History.* Princeton, NJ: Princeton UP.

Levi, C. (1933) "In morte di Claudio Treves." *Quaderni di "Giustizia e Libertà,"* 7.

Martinetti, P. (1903) *Introduzione alla metafisica.* 2 vols.; reprint Milano: Libreria Editrice Lombarda, 1929.

___. (1928) *La libertà.* Milano: Libreria Editrice Lombarda.

___. (1942) *Ragione e fede. Saggi religiosi.* Torino: Einaudi.

Meldolesi, L. (1994) *Alla scoperta del possibile. Il mondo sorprendente di Albert O.*

Hirschman. Bologna: il Mulino; English trans. Notre Dame: U of Notre Dame P, 1995; Spanish trans. Mexico City: Fondo de Cultura Econòmica, 1997.

____. (1994a) "Sulla nozione di squilibrio ottimo." *Equilibrio e teoria economica.* Ed. G. Caravale. Bologna: il Mulino.

____. (1998) "Introduzione. Colorni per tutti." Colorni 1998.

____. (2004) "Intervento." AA.VV. 2004.

____. (2010) "Eugenio Colorni e Albert Hirschman a Trieste 1937–38." AA.VV. 2010.

____. (2017) "Introduzione. Attualità politica di Eugenio Colorni." Colorni 2017; English trans. Colorni 2019a.

____. (2018) "Introduzione." Colorni, Spinelli 2018; English trans. Colorni, Spinelli 2020.

____. (2018a) "Introduzione." Colorni 2018; English trans. Colorni 2021.

____. (2020) *Eppur si può! Saggi ed istruzioni possibiliste.* Soveria Mannelli: Rubbettino.

Morpurgo-Tagliabue, G. (1945) "Ricordo di Colorni." *Arethusa* (July-August).

Piovene, G. (1944) "Ritratto di Eugenio Colorni." *Il Tempo* 7 giugno.

____. (1945) "Non furon tetri." *Mercurio* (December).

____. (1963) "L'università di Milano fra il 1925 e il 1929. G.A. Borgese era per i giovani il più 'stimolante' dei maestri." *La Stampa* 8 March.

____. (1975) *Le furie.* Milano: Mondadori.

Quaranta, M. (2011) "La 'scoperta' di Eugenio Colorni nelle riviste del secondo dopoguerra. Gli scritti sulla relatività." AA.VV. 2011.

Quarta, A. (1977) "Filosofia e metodologia delle scienze negli scritti di Eugenio Colorni." *Bollettino di storia della filosofia dell'Università degli Studi di Lecce* 5.

Rebeschini, M. (2004) *Bruno Pincherle. Interventi e scritti politici.* Trieste: Piazzetta Stendhal.

Reichenbach, H. (1920) *Relativitätstheorie und Erkenntniss a priori.* Berlin.

____. (1922) "Der gegenwärtige Stand der Relativitätsdiscussion." *Logos* 10.

____. (1924) *Axiomatik der Raum-Zeit-Lehere.* Braunschweig: Vieweg.

Riosa, A. (2011) "Giuseppe Antonio Borgese ed Eugenio Colorni tra letteratura e politica." AA.VV. 2011.

Rossi, E. (1975) "Eugenio Colorni." *Un democratico ribelle.* Ed. G. Armani. Parma: Guanda.

Rossi-Landi, F. (1952) "Sugli scritti di Eugenio Colorni." *Rivista critica di storia della filosofia* 2.

Rougemont, D. de (1939) *L'amour de l'occident.* Paris: Plon.

Russell, B. (1934) *Panorama scientifico.* Bari: Laterza.

Saba, U. (1926) *Il piccolo Berto.* Milano: Mondadori, 1961.

Santacroce, A. (1975) "L'opera filosofica di Colorni." *Mondoperaio* 1.

Scheler, M. (1915) "Liebe und Erkenntnis." *Die Weißen Blätter*; now Aischines Verlag, 2015.

____. (1923) *Wesen und Formen der Sympathie. Der Phänamenologie der Sympathiegefühle.* Bonn: Cohen.

____. (1936) *La crisi dei valori.* Milano: Bompiani.

Senise, C. (1945) *Quando ero Capo della polizia 1940–1943.* Roma: Ruffolo. New ed., Milano: Mursia, 2012.

Solari, L. (1980) *Eugenio Colorni. Ieri e sempre.* Venezia: Marsilio.

____. (2004) "La lezione di Angelo." AA.VV. 2004.

Somenzi, V. (1986) "Eugenio Colorni filosofo della scienza." *Filosofia e società* 1.

Spinelli, A. (1984) *Come ho tentato di diventare saggio. I. Io, Ulisse.* Bologna: il Mulino.

____. (1985) *Il progetto europeo.* Bologna: il Mulino.

____, and E. Colorni. (2018) *I dialoghi di Ventotene.* Ed. Luca Meldolesi. Soveria Mannelli: Rubbettino.

____. (2020) *Dialogues.* Ed. Luca Meldolesi. New York: Bordighera P.

Spinelli A., and E. Rossi. (1944) *Problemi della Federazione europea.* Ed. E. Colorni. Roma: Edizioni del Movimento italiano per la Federazione europea.

Tagliacozzo, E. (1980) "L'uomo Colorni." *Tempo presente* (December).

Tedesco, A. (2014) *Il partigiano Colorni e il grande sogno europeo,* Roma: Editori Riuniti.

Vassalli, G. (2004) "Intervento." AA.VV. 2004.

____. (2010) "Ricordo di Angelo (Eugenio Colorni e la Resistenza romana)." AA.VV. 2010.

Vassallo, G. (2009) "'Il Prof. Eugenio Colorni' nelle carte dell'Archivio Centrale dello Stato." *Eurostudium3w* (January-March).

Vigorelli, A. (2011) "Antifascismo tra i giovani. Il caso di Pietre." AA.VV. 2011.

Villani, L. (1944) "Eugenio Colorni." *La Rivoluzione Socialista* 1 (14 June).

Index of Names

Index of Subjects